International Development Studies

Theories and Methods in Research and Practice

International Development Studies

Theories and Methods in Research and Practice

Andy Sumner and Michael Tribe

Los Angeles | London | New Delhi
Singapore | Washington DC

SAGE Publications Ltd
1 Oliver's Yard
55 City Road
London EC1Y 1SP

SAGE Publications Inc.
2455 Teller Road
Thousand Oaks, California 91320

SAGE Publications India Pvt Ltd
B 1/I 1 Mohan Cooperative Industrial Area
Mathura Road
New Delhi 110 044

SAGE Publications Asia-Pacific Pte Ltd
3 Church Street
#10-04 Samsung Hub
Singapore 049483

Library of Congress Control Number: 2007934280

British Library Cataloguing in Publication data

A catalogue record for this book is available from the British Library

ISBN 978-1-4129-2944-8
ISBN 978-1-4129-2945-5 (pbk)

Typeset by Cepha Imaging Pvt. Ltd.
Printed and bound by CPI Group (UK) Ltd, Croydon, CR0 4YY
Printed on paper from sustainable resources

FSC
www.fsc.org
MIX
Paper from
responsible sources
FSC® C013604

Contents

Acknowledgements

I would like to thank friends, family and colleagues, past and present, for their support.

Andy Sumner

Fellow, Institute of Development Studies, Sussex, UK.

I would particularly like to acknowledge the support and understanding of my wife, Kathryn, over the years. For my initial introduction to opportunities in the field of development, and to rigour in analysis, I would like to thank the late Ian Livingstone, latterly Emeritus Professor in the School of Development Studies, University of East Anglia.

Michael Tribe

Honorary Visiting Senior Research Fellow, Bradford Centre for International Development, University of Bradford, and Teaching Assistant, Department of Economics, University of Strathclyde, Glasgow

List of boxes, tables and figures

Tables

Figures

List of acronyms

BCE	Before the Common Era (equivalent to BC – Before Christ)
BRICET	Brazil, Russia, India, China, Eastern Europe and Turkey
CDF	Comprehensive Development Framework
CIDA	Canadian International Development Agency
CPIA	Country Policy and Institutional Assessment
DANIDA	Danish International Development Agency
DARG	Developing Areas Research Group (of the UK Royal Geographical Society)
DFID (or DfID)	Department for International Development (UK)
DS	Development Studies
DSA	Development Studies Association (UK and Ireland)
EADI	European Association of Development Research and Training Institutes
EU	European Union
FAO	Food and Agriculture Organization
G77	Group of 77
GDI	Gender Development Index
GDP	Gross Domestic Product
GEM	Gender Empowerment Measure
GIC	Ghana Investments Centre
GTZ	German Technical Assistance (Deutsche Gesellschaft für Technische Zusammenarbeit (GTZ) GmbH)
HDI	Human Development Index
HDR	Human Development Report
HPI	Human Poverty Index (HPI-1 for developing/low income countries and HPI-2 for industrialized countries)
HIPC	Heavily Indebted Poor Country
HIV/AIDS	Human Immunodeficiency Virus / Acquired ImmunoDeficiency Syndrome
IBRD	International Bank for Reconstruction and Development (the World Bank)
IDTs	International Development Targets (see MDGs)

IFI	International Financial Institutions (mainly the World Bank and the International Monetary Fund)
ILO	International Labour Office (or Organization)
IMF	International Monetary Fund
IRDP	Integrated Rural Development Project
LDC	Less Developed Country
LIC	Low Income Country
LICUS	Low Income Country Under Stress
LLDC	Land-Locked Developing Country
LMC	Lower Middle Income Country
MDGs	Millennium Development Goals
MIC	Middle Income Country
NGOs	Non-Governmental Organizations
NIC	Newly Industrializing Country
NIEO	New International Economic Order
NORAD	Norwegian Agency for Development Cooperation
ODI	Overseas Development Institute (London)
OECD	Organization for Economic Cooperation and Development
OED	Operations Evaluation Department (of the World Bank)
OXFAM	Oxford Committee for Famine Relief
PPA	Participatory Poverty Assessment
PRA	Participatory Rural Appraisal
PRSPs	Poverty Reduction Strategy Papers
PSA	Public Service Agreement (UK HM Government)
PSIA	Policy and Social Impact Analysis
RAB	Resource Accounts Budgeting (UK HM Government)
RBM	Results Based Management
RCPLAN	Resource Centres for Participatory Learning and Action Network
ROAMEF	Rationale, Objectives, Appraisal, Monitoring, Evaluation, Feedback (UK HM Treasury Green Book)
RRA	Rapid Rural Appraisal
SAPs	Structural Adjustment Programmes
SIGMA	Support for Improvement in Governance and Management (Joint programme of the OECD and EU)
SWAP	Sector Wide Approach
TNCs	Transnational Corporations
UK	United Kingdom of Great Britain and Northern Ireland
UMC	Upper Middle Income Country
UNCTAD	United Nations Conference on Trade and Development
UNDP	United Nations Development Programme
UNICEF	United Nations Children's Fund
UNRISD	United Nations Research Institute for Social Development
UNU – WIDER	United Nations University – World Institute for Development Economics Research

USA   United States of America
USAID   United States Agency for International Development
USSR   Union of Soviet Socialist Republics
WDR   World Development Report
WTO   World Trade Organization

INTRODUCTION

Development Studies is an unusual enterprise (Corbridge, 2005: 1).

I.1. WHAT IS THIS BOOK ABOUT?

This book is about research and knowledge in 'development studies' (DS) or 'international development'.[1] Over the last 10–15 years there has been an expansion of interest in the subject and there are now significantly more taught courses focused on DS in schools and universities at various levels. However, over the same period, DS has faced a series of sustained critiques about its essential nature and its research quality and rigour. This has led to soul-searching within DS and in this book we are searching for answers to two overriding questions:

i. What is development studies? (i.e. what is its focus, aim and approach?)
ii. What constitutes rigorous research in development studies? (i.e. what are the characteristics of 'high quality' development research?)

The overall aim of this book is to address these two questions. The first question is about the distinctive features of DS as a field of study and of enquiry. The second question is about the range of analytical tools and approaches available at each stage of the research process, and how to 'build' credible or defensible research with which to inform policy and practice. However, this is not a book that attempts 'closure' (by which we mean *final* answers). Rather the opposite applies: we aim to contribute to ongoing discussion which we hope and expect will continue. We will seek to identify central questions and to provide possible pathways which will aim to provide further illumination.

One of the problems which we have faced in writing this book is that of how to refer to the parts of the world which are the main subject of DS. In many respects, as we argue in Chapter 1, DS is about 'development' (understood to a large extent as 'change') in the poorer countries of the world, but the concepts and approaches to the study of change in these countries are also relevant to higher- and middle-income countries. For consistency in this book we refer to 'developing countries' when relating to the 'poorer' countries and to 'industrialized countries' when relating to higher-income countries. This is not because we are happy with these particular terms (we discuss this in more detail in Chapter 1) but rather because we find other terms to be less satisfactory. In the contemporary world of the early twenty-first century there are many other terms which could be used to describe specific groups of countries with common basic characteristics, but we have tried to err in the direction of simplicity.

Another definitional question which requires clarification is 'what is meant by rigorous (or systematic) research (or study)'? We expand on this issue at some length in Chapter 5, but because we have used the words 'rigorous' and 'systematic' quite liberally it is appropriate to attempt definitions in this Introduction. In essence, the two words are used interchangeably to a large extent, and the meaning we take is closely related to two particular dimensions.[2] The first relates to approaching research, investigation or study using a number of discrete stages which follow a logical sequence – although a process of iteration may involve moving back and forth between stages as the research progresses. This 'process' has been placed in the context of a 'research cycle' and is discussed in Section 5.2a of Chapter 5, and the first essential stage is the clarification or definition of the 'research problem'. The second dimension consists of the utilization of appropriate methodology, methods and techniques, and data/information (including 'transparent' sources) within the research process. If the research, investigation or study is undertaken systematically the conclusions, results or outcomes will follow logically.

One of our major concerns in this book is to emphasize that 'research' (which we take to include not only academic research but also policy-related research, investigation and evaluation) and research methods are extremely relevant to development practice and to development practitioners. While some of the discussion about the nature of 'scientific' enquiry might initially appear remote from practical policy concerns, the overall approach of the book has attempted to focus on 'practice' as well as on more 'academic' activity.

Finally, there is an issue over the extent to which DS works mainly within the Social Sciences. One recurring question throughout this book is about the degree to which undertaking academic and policy-related research, investigation and studies in DS involves issues distinct from those associated with social science research, both generally and in industrialized country settings. We have attempted to address this question, but in places there is an obvious significant overlap between developing country and industrialized country method and practice. Another recurring question is about the extent to which the cross-disciplinarity of DS extends beyond the social sciences – the answer to this question must be 'quite a long way'. Understanding of agricultural, environmental and health-related research topics – to name but three – clearly involves the need for inputs from researchers with technical knowledge, a judgement which applies in both developing and industrialized countries. This means that the cross-disciplinary nature of DS must extend beyond the social sciences, and more detailed discussion may be found in Sections 3.3 and 3.4 of Chapter 3.

I.2. WHO IS THIS BOOK FOR?

This book is primarily intended for researchers (in both academic and practical contexts) and postgraduate students of DS. This is intended to include practitioners within 'international development' such as policy makers, those working in non-governmental organizations (NGOs), donor agencies and consultants who should find the book informative for the design, commissioning and review of research which are to inform decision-making.

One of the important features of the 'development community' is the inclusion of non-academic practitioners. Although it would be convenient if it was possible to make a clear distinction between those in the more academic/intellectual camp and those in a more practice-based camp (see Table I.1); in fact the borders between the two camps are actually highly 'porous'.[3] There is much crossing of the 'border' between the camps in both directions within any particular time period and over individuals' career paths (Bernstein, 2005). In fact, Woolcock (2007: 57) speaks of the DS community as composed of 'practical thinkers' and 'reflective doers' and argues students need to acquire three core competencies that arise from this which are the academic and non-academic skills of,

> 'detectives' (data collection, analysis and interpretation), 'translators' (reframing given ideas for diverse groups) and 'diplomats' (negotiation, conflict mediation, deal making) (ibid., 55).

The inclusion of non-academicians is a sign of the strength of the 'development community' in terms of 'getting research into practice'. However, the lack of a clear

Table I.1 A Stylized Depiction of the 'Development Community'

Academic/research-based group	Practice/policy-based group

• Researchers in universities, institutes and think tanks in the 'South' and 'North';
 • Research staff of Civil Society Organizations in the 'South' and 'North' such as trade unions, NGOs, voluntary bodies, church/religious groups, other pressure groups/campaigning bodies and the private sector including international business;
 • Researchers in governments and other public bodies in the 'South' and 'North' at various levels including bi-lateral donor agencies such as DfID, DANIDA, GTZ and USAID.
 • Research staff of supra-national agencies:
   - Multi-lateral agencies such as the IMF, World Bank and its subsidiaries; UNDP, UNICEF, FAO, ILO, UNCTAD and WTO.
	• Operational staff of Civil Society Organizations in the 'South' and 'North' such as trade unions, NGOs, voluntary bodies, church/religious groups, other pressure groups/campaigning bodies and the private sector including international business;
	 • Those working in the Media – in the 'South' and 'North';
	 • Politicians *and* bureaucrats in governments and other public bodies in the 'South' and 'North' at various levels including bi-lateral donor agencies such as DfID, DANIDA, GTZ and USAID.
	 • Operational staff of supra-national agencies:
	   - Multi-lateral agencies such as the IMF, World Bank and its subsidiaries; UNDP, UNICEF, FAO, ILO, UNCTAD and WTO.

distinction between research and practice has been one of the factors leading to a questioning of the 'rigour' of DS research. As Molteberg and Bergstrøm observe, 'the inclusion of non-academicians in the discourse renders the scientific status of Development Studies as ambiguous in the eyes of many academicians' (2000: 8). Also, the applied nature of much research in DS has led to a questioning of 'rigour' in DS due in part to the normative nature of any research that seeks to 'make a difference'. Central themes of this book are therefore the nature of DS, of 'rigorous' research and of the link between research and practice. The book reflects the elements of DS with a practical point of departure: the aim to use knowledge as a basis for societal change. This point of departure raises numerous ethical questions including whose knowledge 'counts', how to deal with conflicting claims to 'knowledge', recognition of bias and how values and assumptions shape what we think we 'know'. In short, the contested nature of 'knowledge' and of 'development' themselves.

The 'positionality' of this book also requires some explanation. Its origins lie, to a considerable extent, in two conference papers written in 2004 (Sumner and Tribe, 2004; Tribe and Sumner, 2004) which focus on the nature of DS and on issues associated with methodology and rigour in DS. We felt that although a considerable literature on research methodology, methods and techniques already existed, there was a gap relating to the precise clarification of what the subject DS consists of, and of distinctive features of academic and policy-related research in DS. The publishers of this book have themselves contributed significantly to the literature on research methods (Sage, 2007), and a recent book edited by Desai and Potter (2006) reviews – in a number of comparatively brief chapters – a range of specific issues associated with DS research. However, our aim in writing this book has been to provide both a broad overview of research and practice in DS and a more detailed discussion of methodological and epistemological issues linking DS to what we have termed 'constituent disciplines'.

I.3. WHO ARE THE AUTHORS?

One issue for development researchers to consider individually and collectively is that of 'positionality' or 'situationality'. By this we mean individual and group backgrounds or 'identities' (our race, gender, age, nationality, social and economic status, and other characteristics) which directly and indirectly influence our experiences, values, preconceptions, ideology, interpretations and research. For example, Haddad explains that:

> As an economist I have a taught tendency to the technocratic and to avoid messy reality, so look out for occasional apolitical and ahistorical perspectives. Concerns with social justice run deep in my psyche — so watch out for any downplaying of growth and efficiency (2006: 2).

'Positionality' goes to the heart of many of the criticisms of DS: it has often been suggested that DS imposes its – principally western or local elite – ideas on 'the Other' (the poor and marginalized). The 'positionality' or 'situationality' of the authors of this book is affected by their backgrounds in Economics (like Haddad) but both have a strong interest in cross-disciplinary research. It is widely argued that DS is, or should be, cross-disciplinary, and this book takes this position. Additionally, both of the authors are British, work within UK institutions and are influenced, as much of DS is, by the context of a post-colonial world. We are both male so that our understanding of one fundamental dimension of inequality – gender – is influenced by that. In sum, it can be made clear that we recognize that our backgrounds and experiences inevitably shape our writing. Perhaps the most important issue is that our writing should be reflective, open, with explicit recognition of our limitations.[4]

I.4. HOW IS THE BOOK STRUCTURED?

This book has seven substantive chapters following this Introduction. Each chapter begins with an introductory discussion of key themes and questions drawn from illustrative opening quotations. The structure of the book utilizes and adapts Bevan's (2006: 7–12) 'Foundations of Knowledge Framework' (see Table I.2). This is a 'road-map' for the book and provides a useful 'check-list' for thinking about 'knowledge' and its generation.

Chapter 1 discusses the focus of DS – the contested nature of 'development' itself. Chapter 2 addresses the purpose of DS – the normative point of departure and issues it raises. Chapter 3 is concerned with the question of what can we 'know' and how we can 'know' it in DS and we discuss differing perspectives on what constitutes legitimate academic goals, practices and claims to 'knowledge'. Chapter 4 looks at the 'big picture' in DS, in terms of theoretical and conceptual frameworks. Chapter 5 is about rigour, methodology and methods in DS, exploring the extent to which it is possible to answer the question what is 'really' happening? Chapter 6 is concerned with the link between research and practice in DS. Finally, Chapter 7 provides some conclusions and looks to the future.

Table I.2 Bevan's 'Foundations of Knowledge Framework'

1. The focus, domain, or problematic of study: what exactly are we interested in?	See Chapter 1
2. Values/standpoints/ideology: why are we interested?	See Chapter 2
3. Ontology and epistemology: what is the world assumed to be like? How can the world be known about?	See Chapter 3
4. Theories/conceptual frameworks and models: how can we explain and understand our object of study?	See Chapter 4
5. Research strategies, methodologies, research instruments, modes of analysis and empirical conclusions: how can we establish what is 'really' happening? What (kinds of) conclusions can we draw from our research?	See Chapter 5
6. Rhetoric and praxis: how are methods and techniques used and adapted within DS practice? How are DS research approaches relevant for DS practitioners?	See Chapter 6

Source: Adapted from Bevan (2005: 7–12).

To reiterate: our objective is explicitly not to establish 'closure' on any issue, rather it is to assist the reader in finding pathways through complex multi-dimensional contemporary issues relating to the nature of DS and rigorous research. We hope that the book will stimulate debate as a basis for a positive future for DS and international development. Comments will be very much welcomed.

Andy Sumner

a.sumner@ids.ac.uk

Michael Tribe

m.a.tribe@bradford.ac.uk and michael.tribe@strath.ac.uk

July 2007

NOTES

1   Study within the subject area of 'development' has a number of possible 'titles'. Typically, 'Development Studies' is used for teaching and 'International Development' is more associated with policy and practice. Other labels include, 'Third World Studies', 'World Development' and 'Global Perspectives'. Some have suggested, given the contemporary emphasis on poverty reduction and policy, that 'Poverty Studies' or 'Policy Studies' would be more appropriate (Apthorpe, 1999). We would propose a synthesis of 'Development Studies' and 'International Development' to produce 'International Development Studies'. However, in the text of this book we have referred to Development Studies (DS) throughout because this is a commonly understood label. One good reason for using DS is to avoid confusing the acronym produced from 'International Development Studies' – IDS – with the IDS at the University of Sussex, UK – the Institute of Development Studies.

2   However, as noted in Chapter 5, the word rigour can have a variety of interpretations.

3   An alternative characterization is Ravi Kanbur's (2001) which is based on his experiences with the preparation of the *World Development Report* 2000/1, from which he resigned following US Treasury attempts to censor the final text (Wade, 2001). He suggests that the development community can be seen as having a 'finance ministry' group and a 'civil society' group. The main contrast between the two groups for Kanbur was based on differences of opinion over market structure ('finance ministry' types see markets as generally competitive; 'civil society' types do not); on aggregation ('finance ministry' types rely on high levels of aggregate analysis; 'civil society' types do not) and on time horizons ('finance ministry' types are concerned with the medium term; 'civil society' types with the short and longer term).

4   A specific issue associated with positionality relates to the nature of Chapter 6, for example. In this chapter we set out the nature of, background to and experience with a number of methods and techniques which are regularly – but we would argue insufficiently – used in research, policy management and evaluation studies in DS. The selection of both the range of methods and techniques, and of the contexts within which they are used, has inevitably been influenced by our own professional backgrounds and experiences. If authors with different backgrounds and experiences had written the same type of chapter they would probably have selected a different range of methods and techniques and different contextualization. Although Chapter 6 is perhaps biased towards a development economist's view of the field, we would argue that it has adopted a broad perspective which is consistent with the cross-disciplinarity of DS, and that the methods and approaches which have been included can be utilized in much broader contexts than have been possible to encompass in the comparatively brief discussion presented in this book.

REFERENCES

Apthorpe, R. (1999) 'Development studies and policy studies: in the short run we are all dead', *Journal of International Development*, 11: 535–546.

Bernstein, H. (2005) 'Development studies and the Marxists', in Kothari, Uma (ed.), *A Radical History of Development Studies*. London: Zed Books.

Bevan, P. (2006) *Researching Wellbeing across the Disciplines: Some Key Intellectual Problems and Ways Forward*. Wellbeing in Developing Countries (WeD) Research Group Working Paper 25. Bath, UK: WeD.

Corbridge, S. (2005) *Queuing, Complaining, and Photocopying: Notes on the (Im)possibility of Development Studies*. Paper presented at the Development Studies Association Annual Conference, Milton Keynes, UK. Available at www.devstud.org.uk

Desai, V. and Potter, R. (eds). (2006) *Doing Development Research*. London: Sage Publications.

Haddad, L. (2006) *Reinventing Development Research: Listening to the IDS40 Roundtables*. Paper prepared for IDS40 Conference, 'Reinventing Development Research', 20–22 September.

Kanbur, R. (2001) 'Economic policy, distribution and poverty: the nature of disagreements', *World Development*, 29 (6): 1083–1094.

Molteberg, E. and Bergstrom, C. (2000) *Our Common Discourse: Diversity and Paradigms in Development Studies*. Centre for International Environment and Development Studies, Agricultural University of Norway (NORAGRIC) Working Paper Number 20. Ås, Norway: NORAGRIC.

Sage. (2007) *Sage Publications Catalogues (Books)*. Downloadable from http://www.sagepub.co.uk/books.nav

Sumner, A. and Tribe, M. (2004) *The Nature of Epistemology and Methodology in Development Studies: What do we Mean by 'Rigour'?*. Paper prepared for the DSA Annual Conference, Church House, London, 6 November. Available at http://www.devstud.org.uk/conference/workshops/3.2-devstud.htm

Tribe, M. and Sumner, A. (2004) *The Nature of Development Studies*. Paper prepared for the DSA Annual Conference, Church House, London, 6 November. Available at http://www.devstud.org.uk/conference/workshops/3.2-devstud.htm

Wade, R. (2001) 'Making the world development report 2000: attacking poverty', *World Development* 29 (8): 1435–1441.

Woolcock, M. (2007) 'Higher education, policy schools, and development studies: what should Masters degree students be taught?', *Journal of International Development* 19 (1): 55–73.

CHAPTER ONE

WHAT IS 'DEVELOPMENT'?

'Development' is a concept which is contested both theoretically and politically, and is inherently both complex and ambiguous ... ... Recently [it] has taken on the limited meaning of the practice of development agencies, especially in aiming at reducing poverty and the Millennium Development Goals. (Thomas, 2004: 1, 2)

The vision of the liberation of people and peoples, which animated development practice in the 1950s and 1960s has thus been replaced by a vision of the liberalization of economies. The goal of structural transformation has been replaced with the goal of spatial integration.... ... The dynamics of long-term transformations of economies and societies [has] slipped from view and attention was placed on short-term growth and re-establishing financial balances. The shift to ahistorical performance assessment can be interpreted as a form of the post-modernization of development policy analysis. (Gore, 2000: 794–5)

Post-modern approaches... see [poverty and development] as socially constructed and embedded within certain economic epistemes which value some assets over others. By revealing the situatedness of such interpretations of economy and poverty, post-modern approaches look for alternative value systems so that the poor are not stigmatized and their spiritual and cultural 'assets' are recognized. (Hickey and Mohan, 2003: 38)

One of the confusions, common through development literature, is between development as immanent and unintentional process... ... and development as an intentional activity. (Cowen and Shenton, 1998: 50)

If development means good change, questions arise about what is good and what sort of change matters... Any development agenda is value-laden... ... not to consider good things to do is a tacit surrender to... fatalism. Perhaps the right course is for each of us to reflect, articulate and share our own ideas... accepting them as provisional and fallible. (Chambers, 2004: iii, 1–2)

Since [development] depend[s] on values and on alternative conceptions of the good life, there is no uniform or unique answer. (Kanbur, 2006: 5)

1.1. INTRODUCTION

What is the focus of 'Development Studies' (DS)?[1] What exactly are we interested in? In this first chapter we discuss perhaps *the* fundamental question for DS: namely – what is 'development'? Following Bevan's approach (2006: 7–12), which has been outlined in our Introduction, this is the first 'knowledge foundation' or 'the focus or domain of study'.

In this chapter we discuss the opening quotations to this chapter in order to 'set the scene'. The writers who have been cited are, of course, not unique in addressing the meaning of development, but the selections have been made in order to introduce the reader to the wide range of perspectives which exists.

It would be an understatement to say that the definition of 'development' has been controversial and unstable over time. As Thomas (2004: 1) argues, development is 'contested, ... complex, and ambiguous'. Gore (2000: 794–5) notes that in the 1950s and 1960s a 'vision of the liberation of people and peoples' dominated, based on 'structural transformation'. This perception has tended to 'slip from view' for many contributors to the development literature. A second perspective is the definition embraced by international development donor agencies that Thomas notes. This is a definition of development which is directly related to the achievement of poverty reduction and of the Millennium Development Goals (MDGs).

There is a third perspective from a group of writers that Hickey and Mohan (2003: 38) broadly identify as 'post-modernists'.[2] The 'post-modern' position is that 'development' is a 'discourse' (a set of ideas) that actually shapes and frames 'reality' and power relations. It does this because the 'discourse' values certain things over others. For example, those who do not have economic assets are viewed as 'inferior' from a materialistic viewpoint. In terms of 'real development' there might be a new 'discourse' based on 'alternative value systems' which place a much higher value on spiritual or cultural assets, and within which those without significant economic assets would be regarded as having significant wealth.

There is, not surprisingly, considerable confusion over the wide range of divergent conceptualizations, as Cowen and Shenton (1998: 50) argue. They differentiate between immanent (unintentional or underlying processes of) development such as the development of capitalism, and imminent (intentional or 'willed') development such as the deliberate process to 'develop' the 'Third World' which began after World War II as much of it emerged from colonization.

A common theme within most definitions is that 'development' encompasses 'change' in a variety of aspects of the human condition. Indeed, one of the simplest definitions of 'development' is probably Chambers' (2004: iii, 2–3) notion of 'good change', although this raises all sorts of questions about what is 'good' and what sort of 'change' matters (as Chambers acknowledges), about the role of values, and whether 'bad change' is also viewed as a form of development.

Although the theme of 'change' may be overriding, what constitutes 'good change' is bound to be contested as Kanbur (2006: 5) states, because 'there is no uniform or unique answer'. Views that may be prevalent in one part of the development community are not necessarily shared by other parts of that community, or in society more widely.

In this chapter we discuss these issues and we seek to accommodate the diversity of meanings and interpretations of 'development'. In Section 2 we critically review differing definitions of 'development'. In Section 3 we ask what different definitions mean for the scope of DS (i.e. what is a 'developing' country). Section 4 then turns to indicators of 'development' with Section 5 summarizing the content of the chapter.

1.2. WHAT IS 'DEVELOPMENT'?

In this section we set up three propositions about the meaning of 'development' (see Figure 1.1). It is inevitable that some members of the development community will dismiss one or more of these, while others will argue strongly in favour. Even within individually contested conceptualizations there is space for considerable diversity of views, and differing schools of thought also tend to overlap. This over-all multiplicity of definitional debates includes a general agreement on the view that 'development' encompasses continuous 'change' in a variety of aspects of human society. The dimensions of development are extremely diverse, including economic, social, political, legal and institutional structures, technology in various forms (including the physical or natural sciences, engineering and communications), the environment, religion, the arts and culture. Some readers may even feel that this broad view is too restricted in its scope. Indeed, one might be forgiven for feeling that 'there is just too much to know now (as, indeed, there always was)' (Corbridge, 1995: x).

We would argue that there are three discernable definitions of 'development' (see Figure 1.1). The first is historical and long term and arguably relatively value free – 'development' as a process of change. The second is policy related and evaluative or indicator led, is based on value judgements, and has short- to medium-term time horizons – development as the MDGs, for example. The third is post-modernist, drawing attention to the ethnocentric and ideologically loaded Western conceptions of 'development' and raising the possibilities of alternative conceptions.

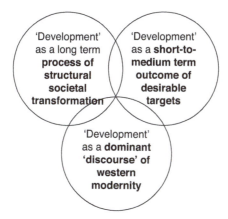

'Development' as a long term process of structural societal transformation

'Development' as a **short-to-** medium term outcome of desirable targets

'Development' as a **dominant** **'discourse'** of western modernity

Figure 1.1   What is 'Development'?

1.2a. 'Development' as a long-term process of structural societal transformation

The first conceptualization is that 'development' is a process of structural societal change. Thomas (2000, 2004) refers to this meaning of development as 'a process of historical change'. This view, of 'structural transformation' and 'long-term transformations of economies and societies', as Gore noted, is one that predominated in the 1950s and 1960s in particular. Today, one might argue that this definition of development is emphasized by the academic or research part of the development community but that there is less emphasis on this perspective in the practitioner part of the development community (as has already been broached in our Introduction).

The key characteristics of this perspective are that it is focused on processes of structural societal change, it is historical and it has a long-term outlook. This means that a major societal shift in one dimension, for example from a rural or agriculture-based society to an urban or industrial-based society (what is sometimes called the shift from 'traditional' to 'modern' characteristics), would also have radical implications in another dimension, such as societal structural changes in the respective positions of classes and groups within the relations of production for example (by which we mean the relationship between the owners of capital and labour). This means that development involves changes to socio-economic structures – including ownership, the organization of production, technology, the institutional structure and laws.[3]

In this conceptualization development relates to a wide view of diverse socio-economic changes. The process does not relate to any particular set of objectives and so is not necessarily prescriptive. Equally, it does not base its analysis on any expectations that all societies will follow approximately the same development process.

All countries change over time, and generally experience economic growth and societal change. This process has occurred over the centuries, and might be generally accepted as 'development' in the context of this discussion. This perspective on development is not necessarily related to intentional or 'good' change. Indeed, in some cases development involves decline, crisis and other problematical situations – but all of this can be accommodated within this wide perspective of socio-economic change.

Despite its generally non-prescriptive nature this approach has a strong resonance with the 'meta-narratives' (meaning overriding theories of societal change – refer to Chapter 4 for a more detailed treatment) that dominated DS during the Cold War. These were grand visions of societal transformation – either desirable transformation as modernization, or desirable transformation as a process of emancipation from underdevelopment. These are different perspectives which, generally, sought to prescribe their own one common pathway to an industrial society for newly independent countries. Although these meta-narratives have a strong resonance with the definition of development as structural societal change, they were deemed to be unsatisfactory in explanatory power in the late 1980s. Hickey and Mohan (2003: 4) argue that the failure of this approach to development theory is one reason why there has been a shift away from defining development as being coterminous with structural change.

Hickey and Mohan (2003) take the view that the pressure on international development research to be relevant has undermined this older established definition in favour of a more instrumental one (a fuller discussion of this issue appears in Chapter 2). A long-term, broad view may address the big picture but it may have a limited capacity to meaningfully guide development practice, such as policy-making, which typically focuses on a shorter time period such as a four-to-five-year government term or a three-year cycle in the case of Poverty Reduction Strategy Papers (PRSPs).

1.2b. 'Development' as a short- to medium-term outcome of desirable targets

A second perspective on 'development' can be seen in the light of some of the criticisms which have been outlined above. Thomas (2000, 2004) characterizes this second approach as 'a vision or measure of progressive change' and Gore (2000: 794) relates it to 'performance assessment'. This view is narrower in definition and is technocratic or instrumental – indeed, some might argue that it is too technocratic. At its most basic level it is simply concerned with development as occurring in terms of a set of short- to medium-term 'performance indicators' – goals or outcomes – which can be measured and compared with targets (for example changes in poverty or income levels). It therefore has a much more instrumental element which is likely to be favoured by practitioners within the development community notably in international development agencies.[4] Poverty reduction objectives in general, and the MDGs in particular, now play a major role in the thinking of the international agencies such as the Organization for Economic Cooperation and Development (OECD), Development Assistance Committee (2001), the United Nations Development Programme (UNDP), the World Bank (2000) or the bilateral aid agencies.

The key feature of this second perspective is that it is focused on the *outcomes* of change so that it has a relatively short-term outlook, leading some commentators, such as Gore, to label it as 'ahistorical'. This is somewhat problematic to many of the more academic members of the development community because it presupposes a set of (essentially bureaucratic or government) goals or objectives which may not be shared by many of the people who are supposedly benefiting from development. This means that there is a paternalistic assumption as to what is good for people's well-being based on a set of universal values and characteristics. This raises the question of 'ownership' not so much in the context of governments or of countries but more in the context of peoples, and the poor in particular. In other words there is an issue over whose objectives and values are expressed within the context of this second approach to development, and whether the articulation of the objectives is in any sense democratic or involves the effective participation of civil society (this issue is discussed in more detail in the edited collection of PRSP country case studies in Booth (2004)). There is a concern that this short-term and instrumental view of development loses the (grand) vision of societal transformation that Gore highlighted, and separates the conception of development from socio-economic structures, social relations and politics. Harriss, for example, argues that the separation of analysis

from the social processes of the accumulation and distribution of wealth... [lead-
ing to] ... depoliticisation. ...[What is required is a shift from] ... explanation of
individual deprivation to explanation of inequalities, the distribution of power,
wealth and opportunity. (2006: 5)

This echoes concerns that research can act to depoliticize development by taking a
technocratic approach (Ferguson, 1994: 19). There is also a major concern that a
focus solely on poverty (or, in earlier time periods, on economic growth) will lead to
neglect of other important and inter-related dimensions of development.

1.2c. 'Development' as a dominant 'discourse' of Western modernity

A third conceptualization of development takes a radically different approach so that
direct comparison with the other two outlined in this chapter is difficult. For this
reason we intend to give it more attention than the previous approaches.

The first two of our characterizations of development are based, respectively, on
visions of change and on outcomes. The third definition is based on the view that
development has consisted of 'bad' change and 'bad' outcomes through the imposition of Western ethnocentric notions of development upon the Third World. This is
the 'post-modern' conceptualization of development (one might also refer to this as
the 'post-development', 'post-colonial' or 'post-structuralist' position – see Chapter 3
for a more detailed discussion).

This third perspective emerged as a reaction to the deliberate efforts at progress
made in the name of development since World War II and was triggered in particular
by the 1949 Declaration by the US President Truman that:

> we must embark on a bold new program for making the benefits of our scientific
> advances and industrial progress available for the improvement and growth of
> underdeveloped areas. (cited in Esteva, 1992: 6)

The 'post-modern' approach is not so much a conceptualization of development as
a frontal onslaught onto the 'development industry' (including researchers, practitioners and aid institutions). Box 1.1 summarizes the 'post-modern' view.

The 'post-modern' approach draws upon, amongst others, Michel Foucault (1966,
1969). The key element of this approach is that, for post-modernists, development
(and poverty) are social constructs that do not exist in an objective sense outside of
the discourse (a body of ideas, concepts and theory) and that one can only 'know'
reality through discourse. In this approach there is no such thing as 'objective
reality'. Such a 'discourse' approach might be said to:

> examine how people use particular types of language and imagery to represent
> themselves and others in particular ways. The focus is on how these images are
> underlain by, and reproduced through, power relations, and on what their social,
> political and economic effects are – rather than whether or not they are 'true'... .....
> The power to define reality is a crucial aspect of power and one of the major means by
> which certain groups ... ... are silenced and suppressed. (Booth et al., 2006: 12–13)

Box 1.1 Post-Modern Conceptualization(s) of Development

[Development has been] a mechanism for the production and management of the Third World... ... organizing the production of truth about the Third World... ... Development colonized reality, it became reality... ... Instead of the kingdom of abundance promised by theorists and politicians in the 1950s, the discourse and strategy of development produced its opposite: massive underdevelopment and impoverishment, untold exploitation and oppression... ... Development was – and continues to be for the most part – a top down, ethnocentric, and technocratic approach, which treated people and cultures as abstract concept, statistical figures to be moved up and down in charts of progress ... ... The discourse [of development] actually constitutes the problems that it purports to analyse and solve. (Escobar, 1992: 413–4, 419; 1995: 4, 44–5)

The idea of development stands today like a ruin in the intellectual landscape. Its shadow obscures our vision... ... Delusions and disappointment, failures and crimes have been steady companions of development and they tell a common story: it did not work... ... But above all, the hopes and desires that made the ideas fly, are now exhausted: development has grown obsolete. (Sachs, 1992: 1)

Development is a label for plunder and violence, a mechanism of triage. (Alvares, 1992: 1)

Poverty is a myth, a construct and the invention of a particular civilization. (Rahnema, 1997: 158)

Culturally perceived poverty need not be real material poverty: subsistence economies which serve basic needs through self provisioning are not poor in the sense of being deprived. Yet the ideology of development declares them so. (Shiva, 1988: 10)

Our first conceptualization of development includes a broad view of structural change with two strands – one tending towards being prescriptive and the other non-prescriptive. The more prescriptive strand can be associated with development theories which include the concept of 'modernization' (i.e. having an 'ideal type' to which most countries are expected to develop to in the long-run) with significant contributions from political science (Apter, 1967) and from economics or economic history (Rostow, 1960). It is the first of these two strands (including an element of prescription) within our first conceptualization, and our second conceptualization, which post-modernists would argue imply that some people and countries are 'inferior' to other 'more developed' people and countries. The post-modernist view would suggest that those who construct the concept or the 'discourse' (as, for example, in the perception of the 'backwardness' of some rural communities in terms of agricultural production technology) have in mind this inherent element of inferiority-superiority. Indeed, central to the 'post-modern' critique is that development has been defined as synonymous with 'modernity' which is presented in the discourse as a superior condition.[5] This goes to the heart of the post-modern theorists' condemnation of development as a discourse constructed in the North as 'modernity' and imposed on the South.[6] The 'discourse' is socially constructed and places values on certain assets which the South does not have. Thus, it is argued, the South is viewed as 'inferior'. For example, 'traditional' or non-modern/non-Western approaches to medicine, or other aspects of society, are perceived as 'inferior'. Edward Said, who developed some of these ideas, argued that Western

---

Box 1.2   Edward Said and 'Orientalism'

Edward Said's major conceptual contribution (1993, 1995) was 'orientalism'. Said made an analysis of Western novels, anthropological and travel writing, operas and media. He linked Western imperialism with Western culture. He argued that the West's cultural representation and subjugation of the Third World pervades Western literature (notably that of Dickens, Austen, James and Hardy) as well as contemporary media representations of the Third World. Said argued that representations are not neutral. They contain a 'will to power'. Orientalism is

> the systematic discipline by which European culture [has been] able to manage – and even produce – the Orient politically, sociologically, militarily, ideologically, scientifically, and imaginatively'. (1995: 3)

'The Orient' is synonymous with all Third World or non-Western societies. For post-colonial and indeed post-development writers, the concern is that intellectuals and development workers, may be complicit in neo-colonial knowledge production or worse, their practices may silence the marginalized in developing countries.

---

political–intellectual representations of the 'Third World' have been integral to subordinating the Third World through the concept of 'Orientalism' (see Box 1.2).

Critiques of the post-modern conceptualization of development typically focus on its perceived nihilism, its celebration of severe deprivation as a form of cultural autonomy, its romanticized notion of the 'noble savage', and the assumption that all Southern social movements are emancipatory (for further discussion see Kiely, 1999; Parfitt, 2002; Pieterse, 2000). Post-modernism also suffers from an internal contradiction (Foucault called this 'the performative contradiction'): that is to say that if we can only know reality through discourse then why should we believe any one account (such as that of the post-modernists) more than any other – each account might be equally 'socially constructed'.

1.3. THE SCOPE OF DS

1.3a. DS and the 'Third World'

Any definition of development will shape the scope of DS and determine the definition of a developing country. Historically, DS has focused on developing countries, which have often been referred to as the Third World – a term which has never been precisely defined.[7] It was a loose grouping of newly independent countries in the 1950s and 1960s which became associated with the 'non-aligned movement' (countries aligned to neither the USA nor the USSR in the Cold War) launched in 1955. The term 'Third World' has also been associated with an alliance known as the G77 (Group of 77) which was formed within UNCTAD in the 1960s.[8] The term 'Third World' is dated by the Cold War, and by a time period when there was a First World (the industrialized countries) and a Second World (the communist block). When the Cold War ended the 'Third World' label became questionable. The use of the term implies that 'developing countries' and 'developed countries' are qualitatively different.

This positioning of the concept of development would appear to suggest that the scope of DS is limited to poor countries – however defined – such as those with high absolute poverty rates and low incomes per capita. This would be consistent with our second definition of development as being concerned with a set of short- to medium-term targets or outcomes related to objectives such as reducing poverty or raising income. Indeed, the use of the terms 'Third World' or 'developing country' might imply that developing countries and developed countries are sufficiently different that they cannot be directly compared. The South Commission, led by the former Tanzanian President, Julius Nyerere, argued that the common characteristics of developing countries transcended the differences. For Toye (1987) the characteristic which most developing countries share is the experience of colonization. Controversies include the appropriate terminology for references to the 'Third World' and the significance of the extent of heterogeneity within the 'Third World' (further elaboration may be found in Box 1.3). Post-modernists tend to argue that any labelling would implicitly or explicitly imply the inferiority of the developing countries, and would thus relate to the control exercised over them by developed countries. In short, the post-modernists would argue that the function of the 'development discourse' is to categorize people in order to control them through the creation of problematic categories (Foucault called this 'governmentality'). The accusation by the post-modernists is that DS has created such problematic categories in order to justify interventions (this issue is explored in more detail in Chapter 2).

A number of descriptions for groupings have emerged in the literature, most of which tend to differentiate between countries which are perceived to have experienced some form of 'good change' (i.e. they are 'developing') and those which have not (i.e. they are 'least developed') (for further elaboration see Box 1.4). These descriptions tend towards placing significance on economic elements of the groupings' characteristics.

Box 1.3   Common Labels for Developing Countries and Critiques

- Developing countries: too counterfactual or optimistic a term for many countries
- Less developed countries: too patronizing a term – strongly suggesting inferiority
- Low income countries: too economically determinist
- The South: not geographically perfect but the term used by both the 1980 Brandt Commission and the 1990 South Commission
- Majority world: too general to say the countries account for 80% of the world's population
- Post-colonial societies: too historically determinist – are countries that have had independence for, in some cases, several hundred years, still framed by that colonial experience
- Non-OECD countries: those countries that are not members of the OECD, the body which essentially represents the economic interests of the industrialized countries

---

Box 1.4   Groupings Used by International Development Agencies

Countries with low income per capita

> The World Bank groups countries by income based on Gross National Income per capita in 2005. Low income is below US$875 per person. Lower middle income is US$876 to US$3,465. Upper middle income is US$3,466 to US$10,725 and High income is US$10,726 or above. (World Bank, 2007: 285)

Countries with low 'human development'

> The UNDP has low, middle and high human development countries based on education and health criteria as well as income in their Human Development Index (a composite measure of income, health and education – see later discussion). (UNDP, 2006: 393–9, 413)

Countries which are 'least developed'

> UNCTAD has a 'Least Developed Countries' criteria (50 countries in 2006) based on three components – a) Gross National Income per capita or US$750-900 per capita (3 years average 2002-2004), b) indicators for human assets (including nutrition, child mortality, school enrolment, adult literacy) and c) an economic vulnerability indicator (including measures of the instability of agricultural production, population displaced by natural disasters, instability in exports, the share of agriculture in GDP and exports and proxies for economic 'smallness' (less than 75 million people) and 'remoteness'. (UNCTAD, 2006: 25–32)

There are many acronyms that emphasize this complexity – such as NICs, MICs and BRICs – and an attempt has been made to identify most of these in Box 1.5. By way of further clarification, the grouping described as 'Low Income Countries Under Stress' relates to countries which are fragile states with weak institutions as well as having low income per capita.

Since 1990 'transition countries' have been added as another category (World Bank, 1996). These are countries of Eastern Europe, former members of the Soviet Union, and others in transition from a state planned economy to some form of market economy – such as China, Mongolia, Vietnam, Cambodia and Laos.

Other categories include countries in conflict and post-conflict situations, countries with a high HIV/AIDS prevalence, and those with a high aid dependency (the 0.2% club and the 20% club – expressing aid as a percentage of GDP).[9]

Box 1.5   Acronyms Relating to International Development

BRIC	Brazil, Russia, India and China
BRICET	Brazil, Russia, India, China, Eastern Europe and Turkey
HIPC	Heavily Indebted Poor Country
LDC	Less Developed Country
LIC	Low Income Country
LICUS	Low Income Country Under Stress
LLDC	Land-locked Developing Countries
LMC	Lower Middle Income Country
MIC	Middle Income Country
NIC	Newly Industrializing Country
UMC	Upper Middle Income Country

1.3b. DS beyond the 'Third World'

The concerns of DS extend beyond developing countries. There is poverty and wealth in every country. Further, China is a 'developing country' and one of the world's largest economies, with high poverty levels. Inequalities within high income countries mean that the types of policy analysis applied to poverty reduction programmes in developing countries have a broader relevance. Life expectancy at the beginning of the twenty-first century in the Calton area of Glasgow in the United Kingdom at 53.9 years, for example, is lower than the average life expectancy in many developing countries.[10] The socio-economic impact of demographic and technological dynamics (as examples of structural change) requires careful policy-relevant research in industrialized countries just as much as in developing countries. All countries are developing in some sense of the term, and industrialized countries experience structural change of a socio-economic nature just as much as the developing countries. So cross-disciplinary analysis which is familiar to DS researchers is also relevant to industrialized countries (Bown and Veitch, 1986).

The demographic characteristics, to take a very relevant example, of developing countries tend to include comparatively high growth rates, low life expectancy, and a high proportion of children in the population. Industrialized countries tend to have low population growth rates, relatively high life expectancy, and a high proportion of older people in the population. Mortality rates tend to be high in developing countries, and the combination of factors causing deaths is very different to that in industrialized countries.[11] The implications of the differences in these structural features are of the utmost significance for education and health policy formulation, and changes in these features over time within developing and industrialized countries are also very policy significant. When combined with technological change the significance is even clearer although, of course, the technological levels in developing and industrialized countries are very different.

A number of other socio-economic issues in industrialized countries are also associated with the concerns of DS. For example, problems of 'over-development' in the industrialized countries, such as unhealthy diet and obesity, have complex socio-economic causes and effects. High consumption levels with their associated high CO_2 emissions in the industrialized countries not only have an impact on these countries, but also impact developing countries through the global environmental effects of the emissions. Other examples of increasing interconnectedness between industrialized and developing countries are represented by the globalization of terrorism, security issues and pandemics (HIV/AIDS and avian flu for example) and mean that a cross-disciplinary approach to research and policy analysis is increasingly relevant in an international context (Mehta et al., 2006).

Seers (1963) provided a seminal discussion of the diversity of developed country characteristics, and their divergence from the characteristics of developing countries. On this basis he could justify calling the developed, or industrialized, countries 'a special case'. The determining characteristics included factors of production (e.g. literacy and the mobility of labour), sectors of the economy (e.g. manufacturing much larger than either agriculture or mining), public finance (e.g. reliance on direct taxes), households (e.g. very few below subsistence level and a moderately equal distribution of income), savings and investment (e.g. well-developed financial intermediaries), and 'dynamic influences' (e.g. slow population growth and high urbanization). When Maxwell reviewed Seer's arguments 35 years later he suggested that they were really no longer appropriate because of the blurring of boundaries between developed and developing countries in recent years and although

> the poverty line in the UK... ... is 17 times the poverty line [the dollar-a-day] established by the World Bank for developing countries... the argument [for comparatives] rests not on levels of living, so much as on the economic, political and social characteristics of different groups of countries and on the tools of analysis deployed to study them. (1998: 25)

Widening the international scope of DS in this way is also consistent with a view of development as structural change and with the post-modern broad conceptualization of development within a discourse. It will be recalled that to a large extent the basis of the post-modernist critique of development is that the dominant discourse of Western modernity is imposed on the Third World. However, if 'development' is defined to encompass the entire planet (reminiscent of the approach of the Brandt Commission – Independent Commission on International Development Issues, 1980 – and of the Brundtland Commission – World Commission on Environment and Development, 1987), to include increased interconnectedness across the planet through globalization as well as diversity of value systems (for example cultural or spiritual) without any connotation of inferior or superior conditions, then the extent of inconsistency between the first and third conceptualizations, which we have established earlier in this chapter, would be considerably reduced. A possible response to this argument from the post-modernists might be that perspectives of socio-economic change in developing countries is best left to nationals of those countries and that the expansion of the scope of DS to cover global development is simply another way of imposing the values of the industrialized countries on developing countries. However, such a response would imply a remarkably compartmentalized view of international development at a time when boundaries are becoming less significant in many spheres of human activity.

1.4. INDICATORS OF 'DEVELOPMENT'

1.4a. A brief history of indicators

How do we assess whether development and change has occurred, and the extent to which it has occurred? Any attempt to answer these questions requires sets of statistics and other descriptive data which need to be handled in a systematic way. It is for this reason that the literature on development indicators has burgeoned over the last half century, with much of the concern being the need to treat all such indicators with caution (further discussion will be found in Chapter 5 – particularly in Box 5.8).

Development indicators have evolved considerably since the 1960s. The search has involved three particular problems. First, many of the developing countries for which secondary data is sought as a basis for indicators have non-existent, incomplete or unreliable data for several of the relevant series. Second, there has been a widely acknowledged mis-match between some of the economic series which are widely available (such as per capita income) and the concepts for which data is sought (such as development, welfare and poverty for example). Third, some of the concepts for which data are sought are inherently non-quantitative in nature so that it has been necessary to find alternative approaches for the identification of rigorous indicators.[12]

The publication of Kuznets' major series on the quantitative aspects of the economic growth of nations (1956, 1971, 1979, 1982, 1983), Bauer's Social Indicators (1966) and Seers' Limitations of the Special Case (1963), the Meaning of Development (1969) and What are we Trying to Measure (1972) led to a rethinking of development indicators away from reliance on growth in per capita income alone:

> The questions to ask about a country's development are therefore: What has been happening to poverty? What has been happening to unemployment? What has been happening to inequality? If all of these three have become less severe, then beyond doubt this has been a period of development for the country concerned...
> ... If one or two of these central problems have been growing worse, especially if all three have, it would be strange to call the result 'development', even if per capita income has soared. (Seers, 1972: 24)

Seers questioned the basic issue of whether growth in the average level of per capita incomes would be an adequate measure of development if development was defined in terms of the satisfaction of basic needs (for greater detail refer to Hicks and Streeten, 1979; ILO, 1976, 1977; Stewart, 1985; Streeten, 1980, 1984). Development indicators were needed for elements of basic needs – physical necessities such as food, shelter and public services, as well as the means to acquire these through employment and income. Progress with these broader measures was reflected in the greater availability of data on health and education, for example, for many developing countries during the 1970s. The fact that research related to distributional issues failed to show that the benefits of economic growth trickled down effectively to lower income groups in both urban and rural areas generated greater interest in this approach (Adelman and Morris, 1973; Chenery et al., 1974).

Much of the research was led by the International Labour Office, particularly through its World Employment Programme (see, for example, ILO, 1976, 1977). This coincided with the emergence in the 1960s and 1970s of levels of living indicators as a response to the dissatisfaction with the use of income per capita as a measure of welfare and of development. Steady development of statistical indicators of development is discernable from the 1960s into the 1970s and then into the 1990s. The work of Baster (1979), McGranahan et al., (1985), Morris (1979) and UNRISD (1970) set the foundations for Sen's work with the UNDP on the creation of human development indicators (UNDP, 1990).

1.4b. Contemporary universal and context specific development indicators

The UNDP *Human Development Report* was established in 1990 thanks to the influential work of Amartya Sen, Mahbub ul Huq, Richard Jolly, Frances Stewart and Meghnad Desai at the UNDP. It provided a new framework known as 'Human Development' or the 'Capabilities Approach' (see Box 1.6) and a related set of composite indicators led by the UNDP's Human Development Indices (see Table 1.1).[13] For Sen the focus is on the capabilities approach which consists of the means, opportunities or substantive freedoms which permit the achievement of a set of 'functionings' – things which human beings value in terms of 'being' and 'doing'. This, according to Sen, is the essence of Human Development.[14] However, because 'capabilities' are difficult to measure, many of the components of the Human Development Indices are actually based on 'functionings'.

The UNDP indices are amongst the most commonly cited development indicators, and the most widely used are the Human Development Index (HDI), the Gender

---

Box 1.6   The Human Development and Capabilities Approach

Sen (especially 1999), Nussbaum (especially 2000) and UNDP (1990–2007) have argued that development is not, as previously conceived, based on desire fulfilment (utility or consumption measured by a proxy for income – GDP per capita) because this does not take sufficient account of the physical condition of the individual and of a person's capabilities. Income is *only* an instrumental freedom – it provides a means for the achievement of other constitutive freedoms. Sen does not ignore income, rather he argues that too much emphasis can be placed on this dimension of development. Instead

> Development is the process of enlarging people's choices. (UNDP, 1990: 1)
> Development consists of the removal of various types of unfreedom that leave people with little opportunity of exercising their reasoned agency... ... Development can be seen... ... as a process of expanding the real freedoms that people enjoy... ... the expansion of the 'capabilities' of persons to lead the kind of lives they value - and have reason to value. (Sen, 1999: xii, 1, 18)

Sen has argued that there is a broad set of conditions (including being fed, being healthy, being clothed and being educated) that together constitute wellbeing. Individuals have a set of entitlements (command over commodities) which are created through a set of endowments (assets owned – physical and personal characteristics – financial, human, natural, social and productive) and exchange (production and trade by the individual). These entitlements are traded for a set of opportunities (capabilities) in order to achieve a set of functionings (outcomes of wellbeing). Sen resolutely refused to name the capabilities although he (1999: 38) did identify five basic freedoms. These are:

- political/participative freedoms/civil rights (e.g. freedom of speech, free elections);
- economic facilities (e.g. opportunities to participate in trade and production and sell one's labour and product on fair, competitive terms);
- social opportunities (e.g. adequate education and health facilities);
- transparency guarantees (e.g. openness in government and business and social trust);
- protective security (e.g. law and order, social safety nets for unemployed).

There have been numerous other attempts at constructing sets of capabilities (for discussion, see Alkire, 2002).

Table 1.1 Human Development Indicators

	Longevity	Knowledge	Living Standard
HDI	Life expectancy	Adult literacy and combined enrolment rate	Income per capita (US$ PPP)
GDI	Life expectancy (male/female)	Adult literacy (male/female) and combined enrolment rate (male/female)	Female and male earned income share
HPI-1	Probability at birth of not surviving to age 40 years	Adult illiteracy rate	Percentage of population without sustainable access to an improved water source and children underweight for age
HPI-2	Probability at birth of not surviving to age 60 years	Percentage of adults lacking functional literacy skills	Percentage of population below income poverty line (50% of median adjusted household disposable income); rate of long-term unemployment (lasting 12 months or more)

Source: UNDP (2006: 393–9).

Development Index (GDI) and the Human Poverty Index (HPI). In the case of the HPI two separate versions are provided: one for developing countries (HPI-1) and the other for industrialized countries (HPI-2). HPI-1 relates to absolute deprivation whilst HPI-2 relates to relative deprivation, and Table 1.1 summarizes the components of each. The HDI, GDI, HPI-1 and HPI-2 each take account of wellbeing, which is related to life expectancy, health, knowledge and education, and most of these indices include some form of purchasing-power-adjusted per capita income as an indicator of the standard of living. The UNDP also publishes a gender empowerment measure (GEM) which is a measure of gender equality in politics, business and wages.

Since the late 1990s there has been an internationally agreed set of development indicators in the form of the United Nations MDGs (see Box 1.7). The MDGs are the product of agreements at international conferences led by UN agencies, giving them some legitimacy as desirable development outcomes or targets. The signing of the Millennium Declaration (United Nations, 2000) by UN members at the UN Millennium Assembly in New York, on 18 September 2000 was the basis for a 'road map' – the MDGs – prepared for the UN General Secretary by a Working Group including the UNDP, other UN-specialized agencies, the IMF, the World Bank and the OECD (Poston et al., 2004). The Millennium Declaration (United Nations, 2000) lists six 'fundamental values' some of which are only partially represented in the MDGs (Maxwell, 2006: 3) consisting of: freedom (MDG 1, 2, 3, 4, 5, 6); equality (MDG 2); solidarity (MDG 8); tolerance (no corresponding MDG), respect for nature (MDG 7) and shared responsibility (MDG 8). The MDGs themselves comprise eight goals with 18 targets and 47 indicators (refer to Box 1.7 and United Nations, 2007).

Box 1.7   The United Nations Millennium Development Goals (MDGs)

MDG 1. Eradicate extreme poverty and hunger
MDG 2. Achieve universal primary education
MDG 3. Promote gender equality and empower women
MDG 4. Reduce child mortality
MDG 5. Improve maternal health
MDG 6. Combat HIV/AIDS, malaria, and other diseases
MDG 7. Ensure environmental sustainability
MDG 8. Develop a global partnership for development

Source: UN (2007).

The MDGs are, of course, not without critics. Saith (2007: 1184) has argued strongly that the MDG 'scaffolding' 'ghettoizes' the problem of development by locating it exclusively in the 'third world' with an agenda created almost exclusively by industrialized countries without adequate consultation and based entirely on absolute standards of living. As well as a trenchant methodological critique Saith argues that there is a potential distortionary MDG effect through a diversionary impact on the orientation of the social science research agendas – which are themselves largely dependent upon funds provided by government-funded research councils or from development agencies which are 'MDG driven'. He also argues that there is a potential distortion of practice through the behaviour of international aid agencies and government bureaucracies which tend towards the 'misuse and manipulation of statistics and the misrepresentation of outcomes... [so that] perverse incentives and behaviour can result' (Saith, 2007: 1174). He continues with the points that data availability and quality are very uneven or weak and that many of the MDGs fail to capture dimensions of wellbeing adequately (for example, what do primary enrolment/completion rates really say about educational achievement?). He suggests that the MDGs significantly understate the new dimensions of development (i.e. participation, democracy, sustainable livelihoods, vulnerability and risk). White and Black add the view that the MDGs deal problematically with gender equality and sustainability and have a general 'top-down' approach (2004).

A number of context-specific or 'specialist' development indicators have also been created in response to the realization that universal development indicators may contradict subjective perceptions of wellbeing and development. This approach is particularly associated with Chambers (1983, 1997) who argues that the perceptions of poor people (rather than of rich people, of aid agency officials, or members of the development community) should be the point of departure because top-down development indicators may not correspond with how poor people themselves conceptualize changes in their wellbeing. Security, dignity, voice, and vulnerability may be more important than consumption in some circumstances for example. These arguments have led to a significant increase in participatory research (discussed in more detail in Chapter 6) including the World Bank's *Voices of the Poor* study (which is discussed in Chapter 5). Kingdon and Knight argue that an approach which examines the individual's own perception of well-being is less imperfect, or more quantifiable, or both, as a guide to forming that value judgement than are the other potential approaches. (2004: 1)

These psychological elements of development indicators have shifted discussion from objective wellbeing to subjective wellbeing and from physiological conditions (namely the objective physical condition of the individual) to psychological conditions (the subjective psychological experience of the individual).[15] In short 'what a person has, what a person can do with what they have, and how they think about what they have and can do' (McGregor, 2006: 1).

1.5. SUMMARY

In this chapter we have addressed three areas:

1.5a. The meaning of development

The definition of development has been a major area of controversy. Implicit value assumptions and associated policy responses are logically linked to the nature of the definitions employed. Values are central to disputes about the definition of development – what to improve, how to improve it and, especially, the question of who decides? For much of the post-World War II period development has been defined in terms of a long-term view with an emphasis on socio-economic structural transformation (for example, the shift from an agrarian economy to an industrial economy). However, since the 1990s development has come to be defined with a shorter horizon related to policy objectives and performance indicators (such as growth of income per capita and poverty reduction). The United Nations poverty reduction goals for 2015, known as the MDGs, are prominent in this latter context amongst international agencies.

1.5b. The scope of DS

The context for international development has been changing fast. While previously reference was made to an apparently homogeneous Third World there is now an emphasis on diversity, including groupings such as the newly industrialized countries (NICs), middle income countries (MICs) and Brazil, Russia, India and China (BRICs). There is also a focus on the least developed countries and on low income countries under stress (LICUS). The study of development has often concentrated on the Third World, but we have argued that in a broader view the analysis of socio-economic change (including demographic, technical and cultural change) in higher-income industrialized countries is not analytically significantly different to comparable analysis in developing countries as well as in other global groupings, so that all countries are developing in this sense. There is a concern for poverty reduction in the industrialized countries as well as in developing countries, with a focus on the poor and the marginalized. In a broader view the rich and powerful within 'poor' countries have a disproportionate influence on the prospects for the adoption and implementation of robust poverty reduction policies just as the rich and powerful industrialized countries (and particularly the G8 countries) have a disproportionate influence on international prospects for the advancement of developing countries.

1.5c. Indicators of development

Development indicators have evolved considerably since the 1960s. This evolution has been inter-woven with disputes on the meaning of development. A major feature of this has been the contrast between economic indicators such as per capita income on one hand and broader views of development and wellbeing which include social and psychological dimensions at their centre on the other hand. Most recently a newly emerging focus is on the distinction between universal or objective wellbeing and subjective or context-specific wellbeing.

NOTES

1 Throughout this book we have abbreviated 'Development Studies' to the acronym 'DS'.
2 Post Modernism (see Chapter 3) can best be understood in contrast to, or as a reaction to, 'modernity'. It is an adverse reaction to rationality, faith in progress and the perception that science is precise. One main concern is that universalistic claims to 'truth' or 'meta-narratives' have a tendency to exclude and repress people (Parfitt 2002: 13).
3 For an example of this perspective see Deane (1965).
4 For example, this type of approach is written into the mission statements of the UK donor, the Department for International Development (DfID). DfID's Public Service Agreement with the UK Treasury sets out its key aims and objectives. These are 'to eliminate poverty in poorer countries in particular through achievement by 2015 of the Millennium Development Goals'. The full version of the DfID Public Service Agreement can be found on the DfID website http://www.dfid.gov.uk/aboutdfid/psa-sda.asp
   However, even within international development agencies there is some diversity of views. For example, the Drivers of Change approach used by the DfID has more resonance with the structural societal change definition of development. This is a framework for identifying factors that lead to country-specific 'change'. It has three components which are (i) structures ('underlying economic, social and political fabric of the country and its resource endowments as reflected in the distribution of assets, economic processes, social relations and ingrained political legacy and form of government'); (ii) institutions ('frameworks of rules governing the behaviour of agents – i.e. markets, cultural patterns, legal and administrative frameworks, and norms') and (iii) agents ('individuals and organisations that pursue particular sets of interests'). The full version of Drivers of Change can be found on the DfID website http://www.gsdrc.org/go/topic-guides/drivers-of-change
5 'Modernity' refers to a 'condition' of being modern or being like the industrialized countries of Western Europe and North America in particular. It encompasses industrialization, urbanization, increased use of technology and application of rational thinking and scientific principles to the understanding of progress and of medical, legal and political systems (Willis, 2005: 2–3).
6 In most of this book we have labelled the richer, developed countries as being 'industrialized', and the poorer countries as being 'developing'. All such labels have their limitations.

In the context of the discussion of the post-modernist school of thought we have thought it most effective to adopt the respective labels of 'North' and 'South'.

7   The term 'Third World' was coined by the French economist and demographer, Alfred Sauvy in 1952. It was based on the concept of the 'Third Estate' from the French revolution – a division of society between nobility, clergy and commoners. For Sauvy 'Third World' was intended to reflect 'exclusion' rather than 'inferiority' (Scheyvens and Storey, 2003: 13). We have generally avoided the use of this term, preferring to use the term 'developing countries'.

8   The Group of 77 has since grown to 131 countries but retains its original name. Further detail may be found on the G77 website: http://www.g77.org/

9   "The '20% Club' consists of countries which derive around 20% of GDP from aid. These countries will be major beneficiaries of the commitment in 2005 to double aid. Their agenda will cover such topics as absorptive capacity, political development and the use of aid to achieve both growth and human development. They will want to hold donors to account for delivery against commitments and will have a strong interest in streamlining the aid architecture. The '0.2% Club' consists of countries in which aid plays a much smaller role. Here, the issues are more to do with managing the changing challenges of globalization, with regional and inter-regional collaboration, and with linkages to non-aid development issues like security and the management of the global commons" (Maxwell, 2006: iv).

10 See http://politics.guardian.co.uk/publicservices/story/0,11032,1691742,00.html

11 The long-term change from the demographic characteristics of the developing countries to those of the developed countries is usually referred to as the 'demographic transition'.

12 Many of the technical questions associated with development and poverty indicators are comprehensively and rigorously reviewed in the Technical Notes in the appendices to Volume 1 of the PRSP Sourcebook (Klugman 2002: 405ff).

13 Since 1990 the original Human Development Index has been modified in the light of critique and has been joined by a wider range of specialized indices which are summarized in Table 1.1.

14 Some of the specialized terminology used in this context is that of Sen (1999).

15 A substantial amount of research based on this approach has been undertaken by the Wellbeing in Developing Countries (WeD) Research Group, Bath University, UK and information about publications and working papers can be found at http://www.bath.ac.uk/econ-dev/wellbeing/

REFERENCES

Adelman, I. and Morris, C. (1973) *Economic Growth and Social Equity in Developing Countries*. Stanford, CA: Stanford University Press.

Alkire, S. (2002) *Valuing Freedoms*. Oxford: Oxford University Press.

Alvares, C. (1992) *Science, Development and Violence*. New Delhi: Oxford University Press.

Apter, D. (1967) *The Politics of Modernization*. Chicago: University of Chicago Press.

Baster, N. (1979) 'Models and indicators', in Cole, S. and Lucas, H. (eds), *Models, Planning and Basic Needs*. Oxford: Pergamon.

Bauer, R. (ed.) (1966) *Social Indicators*. Cambridge, MA: MIT Press.

Bevan, P. (2006) *Researching Wellbeing across the Disciplines: Some Key Intellectual Problems and Ways Forward*. Wellbeing in Developing Countries (WeD) Research Group Working Paper 25. University of Bath, WeD: Bath, UK.

Booth, D. (ed.) (2004) *Fighting Poverty in Africa: Are PRSPs Making a Difference?* London: ODI.

Booth, D., Leach, M. and Tierney, A. (2006) *Experiencing Poverty in Africa: Perspectives from Anthropology*. Q-Squared Working Paper Number 25. Centre for International Studies, University of Toronto. Available at http://www.q-squared.ca (accessed 1 August 2006).

Bown, L. and Veitch, M. (eds) (1986) *The Relevance of Development Studies to the Study of Change in Contemporary Britain*. London: Economic and Social Research Council.

Chambers, R. (1983) *Rural Development: Putting the First Last.* London: ITDG.

Chambers, R. (1997) *Whose Reality Counts? Putting the First Last.* London: ITDG.

Chambers, R. (2004) *Ideas for Development.* IDS Working Paper 238. Sussex: IDS.

Chenery, H., Ahluwalia, M., Bell, C., Duloy, J. and Jolly, R. (1974) *Redistribution with Growth.* Oxford: Oxford University Press for the World Bank.

Corbridge, S. (ed.) (1995) *Development Studies a Reader.* London: Arnold.

Cowen, M., and Shenton, R. (1998) *Doctrines of Development.* London: Routledge.

Deane, P. (1965) *The First Industrial Revolution.* Cambridge: Cambridge University Press.

Escobar, A. (1992) 'Planning', in Sachs, W. (ed.), *The Development Dictionary.* London: Zed.

Escobar, A. (1995) *Encountering Development: The Making and Unmaking of the Third World.* Princeton: Princeton University Press.

Esteva, G. (1992) 'Development', in Sachs, W. (ed.), *The Development Dictionary,* London: Zed.

Ferguson, J. (1994) *The Anti-politics Machine: 'Development', Depoliticisation and Bureaucratic Power in Lesotho.* Cambridge: Cambridge University Press.

Foucault, M. (1966) *The Order of Things: An Archaeology of the Human Sciences.* Paris: Gallimard.

Foucault, M. (1969) *The Archaeology of Knowledge.* London: Routledge.

Gore, C. (2000) 'The rise and fall of the Washington consensus as a paradigm for developing countries', *World Development,* 28 (5): 789–804.

Harriss, J. (2006) *Why Understanding of Social Relations Matters More for Policy on Chronic Poverty than Measurement.* UK: Chronic Poverty Research Centre, IDPM, University of Manchester and the Overseas Development Institute.

Hickey, S. and Mohan, G. (2003) *Relocating Participation within a Radical Politics of Development: Citizenship and Critical Modernism.* Draft working paper prepared for conference on 'Participation: From Tyranny to Transformation? Exploring new approaches to participation in development', 27–28 February 2003, University of Manchester, Manchester.

Hicks, N. and Streeten, P. (1979) 'Indicators of development: the search for a basic needs yard-stick', *World Development,* 7 (6): 567–580.

Independent Commission on International Development Issues. (1980) *North-south: A Programme for Survival (the Brandt Commission).* London: Pan Books.

ILO (International Labour Organization). (1976) *Employment, Growth and Basic Needs: A One-world Problem.* Geneva: ILO.

ILO (1977) *Meeting Basic Needs: Strategies for Eradicating Mass Poverty and Unemployment.* Geneva: ILO.

Kanbur, R. (2006) *What's Social Policy got to do with Economic Growth?* Available at http://www. arts.cornell.edu/poverty/kanbur/ (accessed 1 August 2005).

Kiely, R. (1999) 'The last refuge of the noble savage? A critical assessment of post-development theory', *European Journal of Development Research,* 11: 30–55.

Kingdon, G. and Knight, J. (2004) *Subjective Wellbeing Poverty versus Income Poverty and Capabilities Poverty?* GPRG Working Paper 3. Global Poverty Research Group, Centre for the Study of African Economies, University of Oxford and Institute for Development Policy and Management, University of Manchester.

Klugman, J. (2002) *A Sourcebook for Poverty Reduction Strategies.* Washington: World Bank.

Kuznets, S. (1956) 'Quantitative aspects of the economic growth of nations', *Economic Development and Cultural Change,* 5 (1): 5–94.

Kuznets, S. (1971) *Economic Growth of Nations: Total Output and Production Structure.* Cambridge, Mass: The Belknap Press of Harvard University Press.

Kuznets, S. (1979) *Growth, Population and Income Distribution: Selected Essays.* New York: W.W. Norton.

Kuznets, S. (1982) 'The pattern of shift of labor force from agriculture 1950-70', in Gersovitz, M., Diaz-Alejandro, C., Ranis, G. and Rosenzweig, M.R. (eds), *The Theory and Experience of Economic Development: Essays in Honor of Sir W. Arthur Lewis.* London: George Allen and Unwin. pp. 43–59.

Kuznets, S. (1983) 'Modern economic growth: findings and reflections', in Todaro, M. (ed.), *The Struggle for Economic Development: Readings in Problems and Policies.* New York: Longman. pp. 56–67. Reprinted from *American Economic Review,* June 1973, 63 (3): 247–258.

Maxwell, S. (1998) 'Comparisons, convergence and connections: development studies in North and South', *IDS Bulletin,* 29 (1): 20–31.

Maxwell, S. (2006) *What's Next in International Development? Perspectives from the 20% Club and the 0.2% Club*. Working Paper 270, Overseas Development Institute, London.

McGranahan, D., Pizarro, E. and Richard, C. (1985) *Measurement and Analysis of Socio-economic Development: An Enquiry into International Indicators of Development and Quantitative Interrelations of Social and Economic Components of Development*. Geneva: UNRISD.

McGregor, J. (2006) *Researching Wellbeing: from Concepts to Methodology. Wellbeing in Developing Countries (WeD) Research Group*. Working Paper 20. Bath University, UK: WeD Research Group.

Mehta, L., Haug, R. and Haddad, L. (2006) 'Reinventing development research', *Forum for Development Studies*, 33 (1): 1–6.

Morris, D. (1979) *Measuring the Condition of the World's Poor: The Physical Quality of Life Index*. Cass: London.

Nussbaum, M. (2000) *Women and Human Development: The Capabilities Approach*. Cambridge: Cambridge University Press.

OECD (Organization of Economic Co-operation and Development). (2001) *Development Assistance Committee Poverty Guidelines*. Paris: OECD.

Parfitt, T. (2002) *The End of Development: Modernity, Post-Modernity and Development*. London: Zed.

Pieterse, J.-N. (2000) 'After post-development', *Third World Quarterly*, 21: 175–191.

Poston, M., Conway, T. and Christiansen, K. (2004) *The Millennium Development Goals and the IDC: Driving and Framing the Committee's Work*. London: ODI.

Rahnema, M. (1997) 'Towards post-development: searching for signposts, a new language and new paradigms', in Rahnema, M. and Bawtree, V. (eds), *The Post-Development Reader*. London: Zed.

Rostow, W.W. (1960) *The Stages of Economic Growth: A Non-Communist Manifesto*. Cambridge: Cambridge University Press.

Sachs, W. (ed.) (1992) *The Development Dictionary*. London: Zed.

Said, E. (1993) *Culture and Imperialism*. New York: Vintage.

Said, E. (1995) *Orientalism*. London: Penguin.

Saith, A. (2007) 'From universal values to MDGs: lost in translation', *Development and Change*, 37 (6): 1167–1199.

Scheyvens, R. and Storey, D. (2003) *Development Fieldwork: A Practical Guide*. London: Sage.

Seers, D. (1963) 'The limitations of the special case', *Bulletin of the Oxford Institute of Economics and Statistics*, 25 (2): 77–98; reprinted in Martin, K. and Knapp, J. (eds) (1967) *The Teaching of Development Economics: Its Position in the Present State of Knowledge*. London: Frank Cass. pp. 1–27.

Seers, D. (1969) 'The meaning of development', *International Development Review*, 11: 2–6.

Seers, D. (1972) 'What are we trying to measure?' *Journal of Development Studies*, 8 (3): 21–36; reprinted in Baster, N. (ed.) (1972) *Measuring Development: The Role and Adequacy of Development Indicators*. London: Frank Cass. pp. 21–36.

Sen, A. (1999) *Development as Freedom*. Oxford: Oxford University Press.

Shiva, V. (1988) *Staying Alive: Women, Ecology and Development*. London: Zed.

Stewart, F. (1985) *Basic Needs in Developing Countries*. Baltimore, MA: Johns Hopkins University Press.

Streeten, P. (1980) 'Basic needs and human rights', *World Development*, 8 (2): 107–111.

Streeten, P. (1984) 'Basic needs: some unsettled questions', *World Development*, 12 (9): 973–980.

Thomas, A. (2000) 'Development as practice in a liberal capitalist world', *Journal of International Development*, 12 (6): 773–787.

Thomas, A. (2004) *The Study of Development*. Paper prepared for DSA Annual Conference, 6 November, Church House, London.

Toye, J. (1987) *Dilemmas of Development: Reflections on the Counter-Revolution in Development Economics*. Oxford: Blackwell.

UNCTAD (United Nations Conference on Trade and Development). (2006) *Least Less Developed Countries Report*. Geneva: UNCTAD.

UNDP (United Nations Development Programme). (1990) *Human Development Report 1990*. New York: Oxford University Press for the UNDP.

UNDP (2006) *Human Development Report*. New York: Oxford University Press for the UNDP.

United Nations (2000) *Millennium Declaration*. New York: United Nations. Available at http://www.ohchr.org/english/law/millennium.htm (accessed 15 June 2007).

United Nations (2007) *The UN Millennium Development Goals*. New York: United Nations. Available at http://www.un.org/millenniumgoals/ (accessed 15 June 2007).

UNRISD (United Nations Research Institute on Social Development). (1970) *Contents and Measurement of Socioeconomic Development*. Geneva: UNRISD.

White, H. and Black, R. (2004) 'Millennium development goals: a drop in the ocean', in Black, R. and White, H. (eds), *Targeting Development: Critical Perspectives on the Millennium Development Goals*. London: Routledge. pp. 1–24.

Willis, K. (2005) *Theories and Practices of Development*. London: Routledge.

World Bank (1996) *World Development Report 1996 – from Plan to Market*. New York: Oxford University Press for the World Bank.

World Bank (2000) *World Development Report 2000/1 – Attacking Poverty*. New York: Oxford University Press for the World Bank.

World Bank (2006) *World Development Report 2007 – Development and the Next Generation*. New York: Oxford University Press for the World Bank.

World Commission on Environment and Development. (1987) *Our Common Future (the Brundtland Commission)*. Oxford: Oxford University Press.

CHAPTER TWO

WHAT IS THE PURPOSE OF DEVELOPMENT STUDIES?

Research on development... ... seeks to make a difference. This makes it even more loaded and contested than other kinds of research. (Mehta et al., 2006: 1)

Development Studies is research committed to improvement. Knowledge generation is not an end in itself ... An implication of this is that Development Studies addresses current, actual problems, focusing on solving them – it tends to be applied and action – or policy-orientated. (Molteberg and Bergstrøm, 2000: 7)

Researchers in international development care more than most about turning their research into policy. (Court and Maxwell, 2005: 714)

Who are we – who am I to intervene in other people's lives when we know so little about any life, including our own? (Rahnema, 1997: 395)

Development Studies has been accused in recent years of being irrelevant, of being hopelessly evolutionary, of being colonial in intent, of being masculinist, of being dirigiste, and of being a vehicle for depoliticisation and the extension of bureaucratic state power. It stands accused of being the source of many of the problems of the so-called Third World. (Corbridge, 2005: 1)

Development Studies crucially involves issues of positionality. Those studying development must be critically aware of their own position: the 'viewpoint' from which they are undertaking their analyses. It is important to recognize the difference between studying processes of change as though they are 'out there' and studying processes which we are involved in. (DSA, 2006: 1)

2.1. INTRODUCTION

In this second chapter we discuss the purpose of DS and in doing so address Bevan's (2006: 7–12) second 'knowledge foundation' which is 'values and ideology'. As in Chapter 1 the opening quotations are discussed in this introductory section. These quotations are only intended to 'set the scene', and we do not mean to suggest that there are not other writers who have made equally significant contributions to the subject.

Many people are attracted to DS by some sense of concern and commitment about social justice and the prevailing levels of global poverty and inequality (Mehta et al., 2006: 1; Molteberg and Bergstrøm, 2000: 7). One avenue for this commitment is a focus on informing policy – as Court and Maxwell (2005: 714) note 'researchers in international development care more than most about turning their research into policy'.[1]

Definitions of DS typically identify some level of instrumentality, as in Molteberg and Bergstrøm's (2000: 7) proposition that 'knowledge generation is not an end in itself'. This makes DS, in the words of Mehta et al. (2006: 1) 'more loaded and contested than other kinds of research'.

Indeed, instrumentality in DS has been a central factor in many critiques of DS. It has led many to contend that DS is 'the source of many of the problems of the so-called Third World' (Corbridge, 2005: 1). The point at issue relates particularly to the nature of interventions in the lives of the people who are the 'subjects' or 'participants' of DS research who are often from a different social and cultural background to that of the researcher. Rahnema's (1997: 395) remark that 'who are we... ....to intervene in other people's lives?' is typical of this viewpoint.

In short, if the purpose of DS research is often instrumental or applied it should be clear that issues of legitimacy are raised by this orientation towards 'good intentions'. The ethics-related (and methodological) issues associated with this legitimacy are discussed in this chapter. In Section 2 we consider the past and present configurations of DS. In Section 3 we go into greater depth discussing the purpose of DS. In Section 4 we focus on the question of 'positionality' and the consequences for the researcher and the researched being part of the same 'reality'. Section 5 summarizes the chapter.

2.2. THE NATURE OF DS

2.2a. DS: The past?

When did DS emerge and why? Harris (2005: 17) notes 'quite when "development studies" began... ... is a matter for debate... ...[it] emerged in a particular intellectual and political context in the 1960s'. The term DS only came into being as a teaching course title relatively recently – in the 1960s and 1970s – and many well-known journals and institutions date from this time period (see Box 2.1).

A number of key development research and training institutes were established in the 1960s, including the Overseas Development Institute (London) and the Institute of Development Studies (at the University of Sussex) in the United Kingdom. One issue which tends to recur is where to situate DS institutes and courses. Some would argue that to have DS research and training institutes located in developing countries is an anachronism since virtually all socio-economic and associated research and training in these countries would be expected to be 'development oriented'. On the other hand the location of DS research and teaching in industrialized countries would be consistent with the maintenance of hegemony in the subject area, and with the development of policy-related concerns of 'metropolitan' country governments and of aid institutions. However, notwithstanding these issues and concerns a number of

---

Box 2.1   Selected Development Studies Journals

- Economic Development and Cultural Change (US, 1952);
- Development (US, 1957);
- Journal of Development Studies (UK, 1965);
- Development and Change (Netherlands, 1970);
- Oxford Development Studies (UK, 1996, previously known as Oxford Agrarian Studies and est. 1972);
- World Development (Canada, 1973);
- Forum for Development Studies (Norway, 1974);
- Third World Quarterly (UK, 1979);
- Canadian Journal of Development Studies (Canada, 1980);
- Development Policy Review (UK, 1983, previously known as ODI Review and est. 1974);
- Journal of International Development (UK, 1989, previously known as the Manchester Papers on Development established in 1981);
- European Journal of Development Research (UK, 1989).
- Development in Practice (UK, 1991);
- Progress in Development Studies (UK, 2001);

Note: This list is not intended as exhaustive. There are also numerous regional and disciplinary journals related to 'development'. Place refers to current location of editorial office and date of establishment.

---

notable DS institutions have been established in developing countries, and are still active and respected – examples being the Institute of Development Studies in Nairobi University, Kenya and the Bangladesh Institute of Development Studies in Dhaka.[2]

However, the issue of when DS emerged as a coherent and explicit subject area for study and research is, of course, more complex than identifying the first use of the term DS for teaching programmes or journal titles or in institutional names. The emergence of DS has traces in both colonial and post-colonial eras. Kothari (2005: 47–8), for example, has argued that DS emerged out of colonial studies but that DS 'rarely acknowledges [its] colonial roots...... and the variety of ways in which the west produces knowledge about other people in other places'.

There is certainly a continuity between colonial studies, the period of colonial administration, and quite a number of the anthropological and economic studies which were undertaken for example, in British colonies in the late 1940s and 1950s with funding and other support from the UK Colonial Office (for example, Gulliver, 1957; Lewis, 1953; Mayer, 1951; Peacock and Dosser, 1958). Some of those who worked for the colonial administrations before independence became academics, development researchers and practitioners after independence.

It has also been argued that DS is a product of the post-colonial period and of the de-colonization process in the 1950s and 1960s (Bernstein, 2005; Loxley, 2004; Molteberg and Bergstrøm, 2000; Shaw, 2004). The 1960s also witnessed the first UN 'Development Decade' with the establishment of new UN institutions (such as UNCTAD) and the conversion of other institutions towards a more development-oriented role.

Other features of the 1960s were influential on thinking and activism as Harriss noted in the quotation in the opening of this section (2005: 17). European events of 1968 (including the Paris uprising) had a major effect on intellectuals, and there was a resurgence of Marxist socio-economic theory together with the articulation of neo-Marxist dependency theory in a development context (Frank, 1969; Roxborough, 1979).

Revolution was in the air. The independence of most African colonies had recently taken place and declarations of 'African Socialism' were popular (Kwame Nkrumah in Ghana, Julius Nyerere in Tanzania, and Leopold Senghor in Senegal as well as black liberation movements in South Africa fighting Apartheid such as the African National Congress (for discussion see Meredith, 2005)). We might also note the importance of Nkrumah's book *Neo-colonialism: The Last Stage of Imperialism* (1965) and of the collection of Nyerere's speeches (1966, 1968). In West Africa Senghor's political writings were very influential (1964) although he also contributed significantly to African creative writing together with North African authors such as Fanon (1970) and Camus (1966). From India, Nehru's leadership of the non-aligned movement together with Gandhi's pacifist philosophy and anti-colonial standpoint played a considerable international role. There was also radical thinking and political action in Europe at the time, an influential civil rights movement in the USA, and the Indo-China experience (including the Vietnam War). These influences all gave a political dimension to writing and thinking about international development and to the independence of former colonies.

In the 1960s and 1970s there was an internationalization of influences on academic establishments affecting teaching and research, and many nationals of newly independent countries studied in countries other than the former metropolitan colonial powers. For example, before independence in East and West Africa most of the expatriate staff in universities were British, and after independence North Americans (US and Canada in particular), Dutch, Scandinavians, Hungarians, and others joined in making the endeavour more international in both personnel and in thinking (see for example Sicherman, 2005). The development of new and expanded universities in developing countries created a significant demand for academic staff, and in the first instance this demand was largely met by expatriates. With the movement towards localization of academic staff the displaced expatriate staff needed to find a place in their home countries (for the most part) and so many academics working in a development context of a certain age are 'returnees' from this development process. The increased number of indigenous academics in developing countries was also of significance, with the evolution of developing country socio-economic research and research institutions.

Intellectually, as noted above, neo-Marxism as well as non-Marxist Structuralism was a major feature in the development literature at that time. Andre Gunder Frank and leading Latin American intellectuals such as Celso Furtado had a major influence on development thinking (Frank, 1969; Furtado, 1967, 1970).

Thomas Kuhn's *The Structure of Scientific Revolutions* (1962) added to a sense of intellectual revolution with his discussion of 'paradigms' (the issues around Kuhn's approach are discussed in Chapter 3). Kuhn argued that science does not evolve but that key anomalies build up against the dominant theory. These anomalies eventually lead to a 'scientific revolution', paradigm change (a structural shift in theory) resulting in a new world view.[3]

Since the 1960s DS has experienced some major changes. Examples of these changes include the shifting concepts and interpretations of 'development' which we discussed in Chapter 1 and the stronger emergence of cross-disciplinarity that we will discuss in Chapters 3, 4 and 5. A more instrumental approach in DS has also been evident since the mid 1980s following concerns about an alleged lack of relevance of DS to development practitioners and to poor people (Simon, 2005). The debate of the 1980s was triggered by pieces written by Booth (1985) and Edwards (1989). Edwards' critique was written during a period as an Oxfam field director in Lusaka, Zambia and was a plea for research that could provide practical solutions rather than high theory. Since this time DS has encompassed an approach that is more instrumental and which more directly informs policy/practice/action through research rather than emphasizing high theory (further discussion of this issue will be found in Chapter 4).

2.2b. DS: The present?

There is a growing literature on the nature of DS (Box, 2007; DSA 2004, 2006; Harriss, 2002; Hulme and Toye, 2006; Loxley, 2004; Molteberg and Bergstrøm, 2002a, 2002b; Schmitz, 2007; Tribe and Sumner, 2004).[4] Across this literature, three common dimensions emerge. One way to visualize this is to imagine a matrix in the form of a 3 x 3 x 3 *Rubik* cube (see Figure 2.1). This cube, with 27 elements, could be viewed as DS in its entirety,[5] individual pieces of research being located at different points within the cube:

- DS is about development (however defined – refer to Chapter 1).
- DS is (to a greater or lesser extent) about cross-disciplinary insights. DS increasingly seeks to draw on the insights of more than one discipline but does not necessarily always achieve this satisfactorily (see discussion in Chapters 3 and 4).
- DS is (to a large extent) about applied or instrumental research.[6] DS tends not to be interested in knowledge generation for its own sake but for its applied or instrumental value. DS is concerned with real-world problems (even when theorizing). Many members of the DS 'community' seek to 'make a difference' (Mehta et al., 2006: 1).

Each of these three characteristics are elements within the 3 x 3 x 3 cube. The first, about the dimensions of development can be, as has been discussed in Chapter 1, sub-divided into development as a process of change, as a policy/practice-related evaluative outcome or as a dominant discourse. This could be viewed as a continuum from arguably value-free (development as change) at one end of the continuum to research which is more explicitly value laden (development as a policy/practice-related evaluative outcome) at the other end.

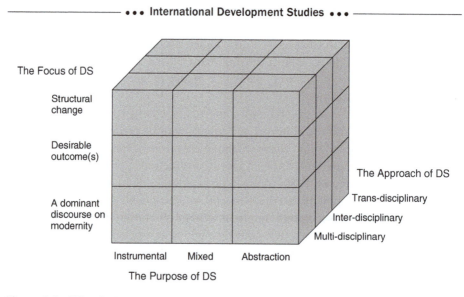

The Focus of DS

Structural
change

Desirable
outcome(s)

A dominant
discourse on
modernity

The Approach of DS

Trans-disciplinary

Inter-disciplinary

Multi-disciplinary

Instrumental   Mixed   Abstraction

The Purpose of DS

Figure 2.1   What is Development Studies?

The second, can again be placed within a continuum of purpose – from research with limited instrumentality (such as theory/abstraction) at one end of the continuum to research with high instrumentality at the other (research which is focused on policy, practice, or on an action-based approach) with combinations of the two in between.

The third, about cross-disciplinary insights, can also be placed in a continuum of approaches – multi-disciplinary, inter-disciplinary, or trans-disciplinary research – denoting an increasing level of integration between constituent disciplines (which is discussed in considerably more detail in Chapters 3 and 4).

Another issue relating to the nature of contemporary DS is to compare it with Area Studies, with which DS is often linked. Area Studies has some common features with DS – a shared cross-disciplinary approach and a concern with developing countries for example and Table 2.1 attempts a systematic comparison between DS and Area Studies. One of the main differences is that Area Studies has an emphasis on languages and on cultural/historical studies which are not emphasized in DS to the same extent. Another is that Area Studies focuses on the study of specific countries and global regions rather than on international comparative studies and the interrelationships between countries and regions. DS also has a concern with purely international aspects of development which do not focus on any specific countries or regions. The more policy-related and instrumental concerns of DS are not shared directly with Area Studies. Finally, and very significantly, DS has a body of development theory, albeit contested (as will be discussed in more detail in Chapter 4) while Area Studies does not have any such distinctive body of theory.

Table 2.1   Comparison of Development Studies and Area Studies

	Development Studies	Area Studies
Focus	Cross-regional and cross-country comparative foci and an emphasis on development	Individual country and regional foci with an emphasis on culture, history and language
Purpose	Theoretical, policy related and instrumental	Neutral
Approach	Cross-disciplinary	Cross-disciplinary

In summary, Area Studies focuses on studies of particular countries and global regions, does not include international comparative studies, is not concerned with the development and application of theories with broad global application, and is not concerned with international institutions, economic affairs and other relations. Many of the concerns of people working in Area Studies are shared by those working in DS. Indeed, there is a significant degree of overlap between the two which will be made clearer in our discussion in Chapter 3.

2.3. THE PURPOSE OF DS

2.3a. What are ethics?

The word 'ethics' comes from the Greek word *ethos* meaning character, custom or usage. There is, of course, a branch of philosophy which deals with ethics and the rightness and wrongness of actions. Ethics (see Box 2.2) is concerned with questions such as what *should* we do and how *should* we conduct ourselves. Ethical issues arise when researchers need to choose between courses of action on the grounds of what is 'morally' right or wrong rather than using efficiency or expediency criteria (Mikkelsen, 2005: 325).

Whose ethics do researchers abide by in their research? Denzin (1997) argues there are two models in social science. On the one hand, one might take the Kantian

---

Box 2.2   Defining Ethics

- A system of moral principles: *the ethics of a culture*.
- The rules of conduct recognized in respect to a particular class of human actions or a particular group, culture, etc.: *medical ethics; Christian ethics*.
- Moral principles, as of an individual: *his ethics forbade betrayal of a confidence*.
- That branch of philosophy dealing with values relating to human conduct, with respect to the rightness and wrongness of certain actions and to the goodness and badness of the motives and ends of such actions.

Source: dictionary.com (accessed 1 December 2006).

position – an absolutist or universal model – a set of principles which are inflexibly applied. Alternatively, one could adopt the postmodernist position of flexibility in ethical decisions with local meanings attached to the conceptualization of ethics. It may be theoretically possible to resolve the tensions between these two extremes (universal versus local) and the tensions between constituent disciplines within DS through negotiation leading to what Hølm (2003) called a middle ground of 'negotiated universalism'. How this is actually done in practice is a much more difficult question.[7]

Aristotle, in the 10 books of *Nicomachean Ethics* (350 BCE), focused on the importance of being ethical or virtuous. For him the highest good was *eudaimonia* – happiness or having a good spirit or 'human flourishing'. He also believed that context was an essential factor. It is possible to apply questions based on Aristotle's principles to DS. Is having (self-defined) 'good' intentions enough for development researchers? What role does context play in the ethics of DS? DS is an ethically complex field of enquiry. Consider for example the following:

- DS has an ethical and instrumental point of departure for many involved as researchers or practitioners – they seek to 'do good', and they risk the possibility of misinterpretation of complex situations and creating outcomes which are very different to what they intended, or of intervening in the lives of others without understanding the objectives and value systems of the 'researched' or of research 'participants' completely.
- DS involves researchers and practitioners who operate at completely different levels of social, economic, political, and cultural power to those who are the 'researched' or research 'participants', such as researchers and practitioners from the IFIs or Universities in industrialized countries interacting with smallholder farmers' households.
- DS addresses sensitive issues – war, corruption, inequality, HIV/AIDS, and poverty – within which there are substantial divergences of objectives, value judgements and opinions.
- DS is cross-cultural and cross-disciplinary with the possibility of conflicts between different ethical systems – to what extent should researchers and practitioners acknowledge 'local' ethical principles as opposed to 'universal' ethical principles?

DS has yet to explore fully many of the ethical dilemmas raised by undertaking research in developing countries. Many researchers in DS have a strong sense of social justice, but the recent increased interest in ethics within the social sciences has not yet featured strongly in their concerns. However, some constituent disciplines of DS have been far more reflective than others. As Brown et al. (2004: 4) put it:

> It is fair to say that there is a notable paucity of literature that deals specifically with the ethical dimensions of social science in developing contexts... Of the few disciplines to more directly reflect on these issues, anthropology has been engaged in sustained debate, especially since the early 1970s.

Table 2.2   What are the Ethics of Development Studies?

If development studies is...	Questions for researchers
about development or about researching development	*Who decides what development is?* *Who decides research priorities and approaches?*
about cross-disciplinary insights	*To what extent do the approaches of different disciplines to development research contrast and conflict?* *Which discipline's ethics are adopted?* *How should the ethical interfaces between social science and the physical sciences be handled?* *Should universal or local ethics be adopted?*
about applied or instrumental research or about informing policy/practice/ action which involves interventions in the lives of 'the researched'	*How should research relating to change and reform be conducted?* *What kind of relationships should researchers have with the elite and policymakers who have decision-making power?* *How can researchers seek to build non-hierarchical relationships and to recognize power asymmetries in their relationships with participants?* *What do 'outsiders' bring to research and writing on development?* *What is the impact of research on non-participants?*

Source: Adapted from Sumner (2007).

DS research and practice raises a wide range of ethical questions and an attempt has been made to summarize them in Table 2.2. First, as has been discussed in Chapter 1, the definition of development clearly involves ethical issues relating to alternative conceptualizations of 'development'. Significantly the main criticism of DS by 'post-modernists' and 'post-developmentalists' has been that it imposes its own (principally Western) ideas on the subjects of writing (on 'the Other'[8]).

If DS is instrumental to a greater or lesser extent, and if it is increasingly about informing policy, practice and action, ethical considerations are crucial because it inevitably entails intervening in the lives of 'the Other' in two respects. First, DS research is not undertaken by those who are responsible for policy decision-making, so that the relationship between researchers and policy- and decision-makers raises ethical issues. Second, DS research (and many other areas of research) involves an inter-relationship between the researchers and the 'researched' (who may be respondents to surveys within primary data collection, or who may be the targets of policy change based on research) which has ethical dimensions.

2.3b. What are the ethics of DS?

It is possible to conceptualize the ethics of DS within three approaches, each of which overlap, and each relating to the discussion in the earlier parts of this chapter and in Chapter 1 (see Figure 2.2).

The ethics of the idea of development are closely associated with ethical issues relating to the definition of human wellbeing and of development itself (refer to the

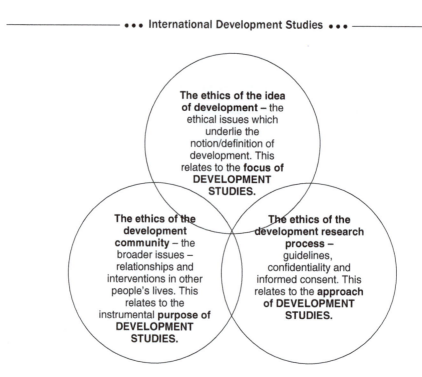

Figure 2.2 What are the Ethics of Development Studies?

discussion in Chapter 1 and to Sen, 1999 in particular). In short, notions of development can be traced to discussion of human wellbeing dating from antiquity.[9]

The second approach – which considers the ethics of the research *process* – tends to
focus on a somewhat narrow list of technical but important issues relating to the
research process itself – such as reciprocity, anonymity, confidentiality, informed
consent, and safety (Brydon, 2006; Laws et al., 2003; Mikkelsen, 2005). There are
several sets of ethical guidelines from which DS can select from its constituent
disciplines (see Box 2.3).

Box 2.3   Ethics Guidelines of Academic Associations Relevant to Development Studies

Association of Social Anthropologists:
   www.anthropology.ac.uk/ethics2.html
Political Studies Association:
   www.psa.ac.uk/Publications/Professional_Conduct.htm
Social Research Association:
   www.the-sra.org.uk/index.htm
Developing Areas Research Group (DARG), Royal Geographic Society:
   www.gg.rhul.ac.uk/DARG/ethical.htm
International Development Ethics Association:
   www.development-ethics.org

It can be argued that one of the principal functions of research ethics guidelines is to create 'distance' between the researcher and the 'researched' – an ethical safety zone. Guidelines are intended to facilitate research which is perceived to be objective (where the researcher and researched are separable) rather than subjective (with a 'fuzzy' demarcation between researcher and participants). Participatory and action research, which are predicated on the non-separability of researcher and the researched, require a much clearer definition of the 'ethical safety zone'. Care is necessary in interpreting and using guidelines due to the differences between alternative sets of guidelines and to the differences between the contexts within which guidelines have been created and within which they are applied. For example, obtaining informed consent for the use of information has different meanings in different cultures.

The Developing Areas Research Group (DARG) guidelines referred to in Box 2.3, which are a set of broad principles complemented by specific guidance relating to identified issues, are directly relevant for DS (see Box 2.4).

David and Sutton (2004) argue that ethics should be considered at all stages of the research process, starting with the question of what 'deserves' to be researched, moving on to the conduct of research and then on to the utilization of research findings. Ethics need to be applied most emphatically to the whole research process rather than simply to the data collection stage, on which most attention has been focused in the past. Earlier discussion in this chapter has suggested that the questions to be asked include: who decides on research priorities? Whose voice counts? Who controls the research process? Who owns the research output? Who benefits from the research? Scheyvens and Storey (2003: 234) argue that 'ethics goes beyond ... regulations to the very heart of appropriate conduct and respect for the norms and values of other people'.

This brings us to the third, and arguably most fundamental approach to the relation between ethics and DS. This might be characterized as the community-wide issues – that is to say the ethics of the development *community* itself (see Tables 2.2 and 2.3).

Box 2.4   The DARG Guidelines

Broad Principles: Members of DARG should endeavour to incorporate the following broad principles in their work in and on the developing world: honesty, integrity, sensitivity, equality, reciprocity, reflectivity, morality, contextuality, non-discriminatory, fairness, awareness, openness, altruism, justice, trust, respect, commitment.

Specifics: Permission; access, disclosure, consent; risks; confidentiality, anonymity; privacy, intrusion; awareness; contextuality; reciprocity and partnerships; discrimination and exploitation; gifts, bribes, corruption; honesty, realism; power, responsibility; altruism, priority; positioning; outcomes; authentication; ownership; non-academic contexts; consultancy; distasteful organizations; government; professional reputation.

Source: DARG (2003).

Table 2.3   The Ethics of the 'Development' Community: Questions for Reflection

Ethical issues raised	Questions for researchers
The role of outsiders	*Do outsiders 'crowd out' or 'crowd in' local researchers?*
Capacity	*Does research 'build' capacity – and should it aim to do so?*
Accountability	*To whom should researchers be accountable and what process of accountability should occur?* *To whom are researchers actually accountable and what process of accountability occurs in practice?*
Control of the research agenda	*Who controls the research agenda in principle, and what process of control occurs?* *Who controls the research agenda in practice, and what process of control occurs?*
The role of research institutions outside of developing countries	*What is the role of developed country institutes for research in developing countries? What should this role be?*
Independence	*Are researchers independent, independent from whom, and how is independence assured?*
Policy relevance	*Is DS policy relevant?* *What does policy-relevant research mean?* *Should all DS research be policy relevant?* *Do DS researchers have responsibility for the policy outcomes arising from their research?*
Relationship between researchers and decision-makers	*What kind of relationships should researchers have with the decision-makers, policymakers and elites which their research may influence?*

Source: Extracted from text in Haddad (2006).

These issues question the *role* of the researcher in international development, and in particular what responsibilities and accountabilities researchers have for their work. What should be the role of the researcher? In more instrumental policy/practice/ action-based research to what extent do researchers have a responsibility for the outcomes from their research, or are these the responsibility of the decision-makers? Applying resources to development-related research may increase the knowledge base, but it is necessary to demonstrate that resources allocated to research have higher returns than with alternative uses.[10] The basic question is which has more impact – resources spent on development research or resources used in development programmes directly?

This debate around the issue of ethics goes to the heart of DS. It is about the ethics of *being a development researcher* – that is the ethical and moral issues associated with interventions into the lives of others. These ethical and moral issues arise for all researchers and practitioners working in their home environment, and the fact that a considerable body of DS researchers and practitioners work in countries and environments which are not 'home' and where they are non-indigenous makes the issues more critical.

2.4. 'POSITIONALITY' AND DS

2.4a. What is the 'problem'?

To what extent is our research in the development context shaped by our own individual and personal viewpoint? To what extent is research in the development context shaped by the collective but contestable viewpoint of an institution? How should we approach research when we are a part of the reality being researching? In this section we discuss 'positionality' or 'situationality', which relates to these issues.

What is the 'problem' to which we are referring? It is not possible to conduct research about developing countries without carrying a lot of what is probably best referred to as 'baggage'. Both DS researchers from industrialized countries and indigenous researchers encounter development in a way that is affected by a) their own preconceptions, and b) the preconceptions of people in developing countries with whom they come into contact through their research. These preconceptions are partly influenced by history (which has gone before) but is also influenced by contemporary and non-historical perceptions. All researchers, particularly those in the social sciences, are almost always 'outsiders' in some sense. They are likely to differ in economic, social and cultural status from the 'researched', that is from the 'participants' or 'subjects' of the research. This issue of 'outsiderness' applies to indigenous researchers within developing countries, just as much as it applies to Western social scientists performing research in their own country. Thus when researchers encounter the 'Other' (those who are the research 'participants' or 'subjects') the relationship is affected in part by the researchers' own economic, social and cultural background and how researchers might fail to recognize how they see research 'participants' or 'subjects' is shaped by the researchers' own roles and background. Therefore the interrelationships experienced by DS researchers are a function of what can be termed 'positioning'.[11]

It has been shown in Chapter 1 that DS has faced sustained criticisms from postmodernists for its representations of development. The overriding theme for postmodernists is that outsiders – or even insiders – can never 'know' anything in an absolute or objective sense since to 'know' anything is a subjective experience, as Rahnema (1997: 395) makes clear in her question in the quotation at the beginning of this chapter. Rahnema explores ways in which researchers and writers get involved and can get to 'know' (albeit in their own subjective ways), but she stresses the importance of reflecting on positionality and questioning 'knowledge' which is gained through research. For post-modernists the concern is that intellectuals and 'development' workers may be complicit in 'neocolonial knowledge production' or worse, that their practices may 'silence' the Third World 'subaltern'.[12]

2.4b. What might researchers do differently?

How have DS researchers responded to this critique? For a field of enquiry predicated on an ethical point of departure – improving peoples lives in the 'Third World' – DS has been surprisingly slow at addressing the ethical implications of intervening in people lives and claiming to 'know' what is 'good' for them. This has led to what Scheyvens and Storey (2003: 2) have called a 'crisis of development researcher's legitimacy'. It has led some people to abandon development research altogether, others to take a relativist position that 'privileges' local knowledge, and yet others to pursue participatory research as means to overcome criticisms of DS researchers in the Third World as 'academic tourists' or 'research travellers' where the process of research is beneficial only to the researcher's career (Lather, 1988: 570).

The suggestion that research between Western and Third World people is always exploitative is, however, difficult to sustain as Scheyvens and Storey note because it:

> is based on the assumption third world people have no power... [but] ..the reality is that researchers rarely hold all the control of the research process. (2003: 5)

Post-modernist theorists recognize that representations of marginalized 'Third World' groups are intimately linked to their 'positionality' and propose 'hyper-self reflexivity' (a heightened self-awareness by the researcher as situated within the research). In Section 5.4b (and particularly Table 5.5) of Chapter 5 we shall explore these issues further.

Chambers (1983, 1997, 2006) also writes of the mechanisms through which certain visions of reality are filtered, raising the need for perpetual self-scrutiny and critical reflexivity when assessing development and poverty. Chambers (1983: 2) argues that outsiders are attracted to, and are trapped, in urban cores which generate and communicate their own sort of knowledge, while rural peripheries are isolated and neglected. The direct rural experience of most urban-based outsiders is said to be limited to brief visits from urban centres in the form of 'rural development tourism'. Chambers (1983, 1997, 2006) has identified a number of biases of development researchers (Box 2.5). His message is that 'many biases impede outsiders' contact with rural poverty in general and with the deepest poverty in particular... ... the solution

---

Box 2.5   Chamber's 'Biases of Development Researchers'

A spatial bias – researchers tend to go to urban areas, places with roads and places with airports;

A project bias – researchers tend to go where it is known something is being done – where money is being spent on projects;

A person bias – researchers tend to talk to elites (village leaders, headmen, religious leaders, paraprofessionals and so on); to men (most local level government staff are men for example) and to users and adopters (of services, practices) rather than non-users and non-adopters. Researchers rarely talk to the old and children;

A seasonal bias – researchers tend to go in the dry season;

A diplomatic bias – researchers tend to avoid sensitive questions due to politeness and timidity;

A professional bias – professional training, values and interests – researchers look for what fits their ideas. For example, researchers tend to miss the interconnectedness of poverty;

A security bias – researchers tend to go where it is safe and thus lack experience of being personally insecure.

Source: Chambers (2006: 28–33).

is to make more visits, not fewer, and to enjoy them better... ... get out, visit, and offset the biases' (2006: 17, 3, 33).

So, what might researchers do differently? Two inter-related issues present themselves. First, reflecting more *openly* about ethical dilemmas rather than sanitizing research for publication. This entails greater openness in reflecting on positionality, explicitly situating the researcher in the research and being transparent about possible conflicts of interest between participants, funders and collaborators, and about 'baggage'. Here DS can learn from anthropologists and sociologists in particular, who have questioned academic distance and authority.

The merits of DS and of cross-cultural research – research which crosses the bounds of culture, sex and class – lie in the diversity of perspectives which it can present. The real issue is who speaks (or claims to speak) for whom? Escobar (1995) criticized DS for legitimizing Western 'experts' and undermining local knowledge. However, there are different forms of 'representation'. Spivak (1988a, 1988b) argued that when researchers represent 'the Other' they fail to recognize their own role in shaping that representation.

Spivak (1988a: 275–76) differentiates between 'speaking for' (as a political representation) and 'speaking about' (as a representation of the 'participant', the 'researched' or the 'subject' of the research). Perhaps we may add a third – 'speaking with' (that is engaging in dialogue). For post-modern writers, the aim is to write 'history from below' or to write for 'those most consistently exiled from episteme' (respectively, from Kapoor, 2002: 653; Spivak, 1990: 102–3), which might be taken as a fourth form of representation.

The second issue, and strongly related to the first, is that it is necessary to place greater weight on the significance of the impact of interventions on the lives of other people. This is Lather's 'catalytic validity' of research and 'the degree to which the research process reorients, focuses, and energizes participants towards knowing reality in order to transform it' (1988: 272). This issue also implies thinking about the accountability of DS researchers in the manner which has been set out in Table 2.3. Who should decide the research agenda? What kinds of collaboration models (non-hierarchical) are appropriate? What kind of research reduces poverty? What are the transmission channels between knowledge and societal change?

In countering the post-modernist critique Parfitt (2002: 6–7, 83) provides an ethical exploration of why DS exists. He argues that it is not inevitable that DS is an imperialist discourse. Indeed, he argues that members of 'social minorities' (i.e. those with relatively more power) are ethically obliged to assist the 'social majorities' (i.e. those with less power) wherever they live. This draws heavily on Emmanuel Levinas (in particular 1969, 1998) whose work was concerned with the ethics of 'the Other'. Levinas argued that the question is not 'why do we exist?' but 'how do we justify our existence?'. Levinas contended that human beings have an infinite responsibility for 'the Other' because the sense of identity is constructed from 'positionality' regarding, and relationships with, other human beings. His central proposition is that relationships with 'the Other' are associated with self-identity to a large extent. Indeed, human beings only have a sense of identity through the existence of others, and there is therefore a fundamental obligation to treat other human beings well because of dependence on them for a sense of identity. Levinas' ethics thus provide a basis, but not an inevitable imperative, for engaging in DS because of its role in establishing an identity as a constituent element in universal human characteristics.

DS raises a surprising depth of ethical complexity. It would seem that researchers need some flexible, open and guiding principles rather than precise guidelines within which to frame research and practice. A fundamental question relates to why the researcher or practitioner has any legitimacy at all. Why does DS exist? If DS research does not contribute to catalytic change in some form, what ethical basis is there for its existence? These questions raise the issue of the relationships which researchers form with the subjects of their research and also with their collaborators and funders, and with policymakers and elites. Significant issues extend into the accountability of researchers (to whom? and how?), the independence of researchers (from whom? and how?), and the ownership of research (who decides the agenda? how? and who decides what should be done with the results of research?).

These are big questions with no easy answers. What could researchers do more immediately? In the context of the point about guiding principles rather than guide-lines, Pham and Jones (2006: 2–3, 5) propose four dimensions of social-justice-related research as follows:

> [The four dimensions are] self-reflexivity in the research process; reciprocity dialogue with research participants; uncovering marginalised knowledges; and rethinking definitions of research design and validity.

2.5. SUMMARY

In this chapter we have addressed three areas:

2.5a. The nature of DS

DS emerged in the 1960s in a specific intellectual and activist context. The origins of DS can be traced to colonial studies. Since the 1960s DS has gone through major changes including shifting meanings attached to development, the stronger emergence of cross-disciplinarity and the evolution of the purpose of DS. The shift in DS towards greater instrumentality raises issues related to ethics that require further reflection on the part of the researcher.

2.5b. The purpose of DS

DS has been surprisingly slow at addressing the ethical implications of intervening in people's lives and claiming to 'know' what is 'good' for them. If DS is about development, there is a question of who decides what 'development' consists of. If DS is to a greater or lesser extent cross-disciplinary (and cross-cultural) there is a question of whose ethics should be taken. If DS is increasingly, to a greater or lesser extent, instrumental and has an interest in knowledge generation not only for its own sake but for its instrumental use, there are ethical questions regarding the generation and use of research and researchers' relationships with the subjects of researched and with the powerful.

2.5c. Positionality and DS

To what extent is research shaped by the biases and viewpoints of the researchers and practitioners? How should we approach development when we are part of the same reality? When researchers represent 'the Other' they do so from their particular viewpoint and that representation is framed in part by the researchers' own economic, social and cultural background. Perpetual self-scrutiny and critical reflexivity is needed when analyzing development.

NOTES

1 A recent survey of 43 heads of European development research institutes found that 88% saw the research community itself as an important audience, but 82% also said that policy-makers in their own country were an important audience (EADI, 2006: 6).

2 The University of Nairobi's Institute for Development Studies was founded in 1965, and further information can be obtained from the website (http://www.uonbi.ac.ke/departments/dept_page.php?dept_code=NH&fac_code=45). The Bangladesh Institute of Development Studies (BIDS) was originally established in 1957, and was moved to Dhaka in 1971 after the separation of East and West Pakistan and the foundation of the state of Bangladesh. Further details can be found on the BIDS website (http://www.bids-bd.org/about/index.htm).

3 See Chapter 1 of Easlea (1973).

4 Over the period since 2004 a number of country-based papers on the nature and role of development studies have been added to the EADI dossier at http://www.eadi.org/detail_page.phtml?page=dossier_devstudies

5 Of course, if the matrix was increased to 4 x 4 x 4 it would contain 72 elements – so the matrix may be thought of as being generic rather than being constrained to the 3 x 3 x 3 of the *Rubik* cube.

6 Some scholars refer to DS using the word 'normative'. This is clear in the sense of meaning a commitment to practice-oriented work and to welfare improvements but can easily be confused with the meaning of 'normative' as being the obverse of 'positive' economics in the sense of being 'value-free'. A problem in this context is the 'hidden' bias towards the status quo (or towards contemporary power relations) represented by 'value-free' neo-classical economics. To say that DS is applied or instrumental is not the same as saying that DS is entirely normative because there are both positive and normative points of departure to practice-oriented work. The distinction between positive and normative is that the positive approach aspires to be 'value free' in the sense that biases and values are explicitly excluded from the analysis. Normative analysis explicitly or implicitly includes these biases and values. Many researchers would argue there will always be some form of bias or implicit inclusion of values in both research and analytical writing and that the issue is how to exercise control and to be aware of bias (Chapter 5 contains further discussion of this issue). Some researchers and writers would, of course, argue that their work is completely objective and value free or bias free.

7 An interesting area of speculation is that of how the ethical approaches of anthropologists and economists differ. Many economists view conventional economic analysis as 'objective' with no consideration of potential misrepresentation of alternative world views, value systems, or ethical positions. This 'economistic' approach might be characterized as taking

the view that there is only a type of human being – economic man or *homo economicus* – who is a rational, utility-maximizing individual. However, the 'heterodox economics' tendency takes a more complex and segmented approach to economic analysis (further discussion will be found in Chapters 3 and 4). A useful reference point for heterodox economics is www.HETecon.com

8   As noted in our Introduction and in Chapter 1, the term 'the Other' is used to signal difference. In this context we mean the 'objects' of research and writing – for example, the people of developing countries in the context of studies of those countries, or to 'the poor' in the context of studies relating to poverty. Many, or perhaps most, researchers are likely to be highly educated and middle class and the extent to which they can ever fully understand the poor is worthy of reflection. A similar issue applies to researchers from developed countries conducting research in developing countries.

9   A useful reference point is the International Development Ethics Association which is a cross-cultural group of philosophers, social scientists, and practitioners who apply ethical reflection to global development goals and strategies and to North/South relations. See http://www.development-ethics.org

10 Surr et al. (2002: 8–9) list many studies that purport to demonstrate the strength of research in reducing poverty. Agricultural research in particular would seem to have a high rate of return. Surr et al. note that research suggests that the cost of lifting one person out of poverty through agriculture research was US$180–190 per person, compared with US$2,304 per person for lifting one person out of poverty through aid spending in general.

11 In a PhD thesis reflection is a vital part of the process of learning to undertake research. However, the readers of a consultancy report or of a policy document may unlikely to be interested in the authors' ethical dilemmas. One of the issues here is that a DS PhD thesis is likely to have been written by one individual, while a consultancy report or a policy document will probably have been produced by a 'team'. Perhaps this is something which we should discuss more openly in DS where research is increasingly undertaken by teams, and the funding system is such that there is now less difference between a consultancy report – which has externally determined terms of reference – and research funded by a donor body such as DFID.

12 'Subaltern' is a term from cultural studies. It emerged from the Indian school of history known as 'Subaltern Studies' which challenged the study of history as that written for and about the elite. The term 'subaltern' refers to the non-elite – the masses, the marginalized and the oppressed.

REFERENCES

Aristotle. (350 BCE) Nicomachean Ethics. Available at http://virtuescience.com/nicomacheanethics.html (accessed 7 July 2007).

Bernstein, H. (2005) 'Development studies and the Marxists', in Kothari, U. (ed.), A *Radical History of Development Studies*. London: Zed Books.

Bevan, P. (2006) *Researching Wellbeing across the Disciplines: Some Key Intellectual Problems and Ways Forward*. Wellbeing in Developing Countries (WeD) Research Group Working Paper 25. Bath, UK: WeD.

Booth, D. (1985) 'Marxism and development sociology: interpreting the impasse', *World Development*, 13 (7): 761–787.

Box, L. (2007) *Understanding Development(S): The Development of Understanding. Mimeograph*. The Hague: Institute of Social Studies.

Brown, N., Boulton, M. and Webster, A. (2004) *Social Science Research Ethics in Developing Countries and Contexts*. ESRC Research Ethics Framework. Discussion Paper 3. ESRC Research Ethics Framework Project. Science and Technology Studies Unit (SATSU), Department of Sociology, University of York and School of Social Studies and Law, Oxford Brookes University.

Brydon, L. (2006) 'Ethical practices in doing development research', in Desai, V. and Potter, R.B. (eds), *Doing Development Research*. London: Sage.

Camus, A. (1966) *The Plague*. Translated by S. Gilbert. Harmondsworth: Penguin Books.

Chambers, R. (1983) *Rural Development: Putting the First Last*. London: ITDG.

Chambers, R. (1997) *Whose Reality Counts? Putting the First Last*. London: ITDG.

Chambers, R. (2006) *Poverty Unperceived: Traps, Biases and Agenda*. IDS Working Paper 270. Sussex, UK: IDS.

Corbridge, S. (2005). *Queuing, Complaining, and Photocopying: Notes on the (Im)possibility of Development Studies*. Paper presented at the Development Studies Association Annual Conference, Milton Keynes, UK. Available at www.devstud.org.uk

Court, J. and Maxwell, S. (2005) 'Policy entrepreneurship for poverty reduction: bridging research and policy in international development', *Journal of International Development*, 17 (6): 713–725.

DARG (Developing Areas Research Group). (2003) *DARG Ethical Guidelines*. Available at www.gg.rhul.ac.uk/DARG/ethical.htm (accessed 24 April 2007).

David, M. and Sutton, C. (2004) *Social Research: The Basics*. London: Sage.

Denzin, N. (1997) *Interpretative Ethnography: Ethnographic Practices for the 21st Century*. London: Sage Publications.

DSA (Development Studies Association, UK). (2004) *Unit of Assessment in the Research Assessment Exercise 2008 for Development Studies*. Available at www.devstud.org.uk/consultation.htm (accessed 1 August 2005).

DSA. (2006) *Draft Benchmarking Statement for Development Studies*. Available at http://www.devstud.org.uk/consultation/benchmark.htm (accessed 1 May 2007).

EADI (European Association of Development Institutes). (2006) *European Development Research Survey 2006*. Bonn: EADI.

Easlea, B. (1973) *Liberation and the Aims of Science: An Essay on Obstacles to the Building of a Beautiful World*. London: Chatto and Windus.

Edwards, M. (1989) 'The irrelevance of development studies', *Third World Quarterly*, 11 (1): 116–135.

Escobar, A. (1995) *Encountering Development: The Making and Unmaking of the Third World*. Princeton: Princeton University Press.

Fanon, F. (1970) *Toward the African Revolution*. Harmondsworth: Pelican Books.

Frank, A.G. (1969) 'The development of underdevelopment', in A.G. Frank (ed.), *Latin America: Underdevelopment or Revolution*. New York: Modern Reader. pp. 3–17. Reprinted from Monthly Review, September 1966.

Furtado, C. (1967) *Development and Underdevelopment: A Structural View of the Problems of Developed and Underdeveloped Countries*. Berkeley and Los Angeles: University of California Press.

Furtado, C. (1970) *Economic Development of Latin America: A Survey from Colonial Times to the Cuban Revolution*. Cambridge: Cambridge University Press.

Gulliver, P. (1957) *Interim Report on Land and Population in the Arusha Chiefdom*. London: UK Colonial Office, HMSO.

Haddad, L. (2006) *Reinventing Development Research: Listening to the IDS40 Round tables*. Paper prepared for IDS40 Conference, 'Reinventing Development Research', 20–22 September.

Harriss, J. (2002) 'The case for cross-disciplinary approaches in international development', *World Development*, 30 (12): 487–496.

Harriss, J. (2005) 'Great promise, hubris and recovery: a participants history of development studies', in Kothari, U. (ed.), *A Radical History of Development Studies*. London: Zed Books.

Hølm, S. (2003) 'Moral Pluralism' in 'the Ethical Aspects of Biomedical Research in Developing Countries'. Proceedings of a Roundtable (1 October 2002), Luxembourg: Luxembourg Office for Official Publications of the European Communities.

Hulme, D. and Toye, J. (2006) 'The case for cross-disciplinary social science research on poverty, inequality and wellbeing', *Journal of Development Studies*, 42 (7): 1085–1107.

Kapoor, I. (2002) 'Capitalism, culture, agency: dependency versus postcolonial theory', *Third World Quarterly*, 23 (4): 647–664.

Kothari, U. (2005) 'A radical history of development studies: individuals, institutions and ideologies', in Kothari, U. (ed.), *A Radical History of Development Studies*. London: Zed Books.

Kuhn, T. (1962) *The Structure of Scientific Revolutions*. Chicago: University of Chicago Press.

Lather, P. (1988) 'Feminist perspectives on empowering research methodologies', *Women's Studies International Forum*, 11 (6): 569–581.

Laws, S., Harper, C. and Marcus, R. (2003) *Research for Development: A Practical Guide*. London: Sage.

Levinas, E. (1969) *Totality and Infinity: An Essay on Exteriority*. Pittsburgh, PA: Duquesne University Press.

Levinas, E. (1998) *Otherwise Than Being: Or Beyond Essence*. Pittsburgh, PA: Duquesne University Press.

Lewis, W.A. (1953) *Report on Industrialization in the Gold Coast*. Government Printing Department: Accra.

Loxley, J. (2004) 'What is distinctive about international development studies?' *Canadian Journal of Development Studies*, 25 (1): 25–38.

Mayer, P. (1951) *Colonial Research Studies: Two Studies in Applied Anthropology in Kenya*. London: UK Colonial Office, HMSO.

Mehta, L., Haug, R. and Haddad, L. (2006) 'Reinventing development research', *Forum for Development Studies*, 33 (1): 1–6.

Meredith, M. (2005) *The State of Africa: A History of Fifty Years of Independence*. London: Free Press.

Mikkelsen, B. (2005) *Methods for Development Work and Research*, 2nd ed. London: Sage.

Molteberg, E. and Bergstrom, C. (2000) *Our Common Discourse: Diversity and Paradigms in Development Studies*. Centre for International Environment and Development Studies, Agricultural University of Norway (NORAGRIC) Working Paper Number 20. Ås, Norway: NORAGRIC.

Nkrumah, K. (1965) *Neo-colonialism: The Last Stage of Imperialism*. London: Heinemann.

Nyerere, J. (1966) *Freedom and Unity: Uhuru na Umoja: A Selection from Writings and Speeches 1952-1965*. Nairobi: Oxford University Press.

Nyerere, J. (1968) *Freedom and Socialism: Uhuru na Ujamaa: A Selection from Writings and Speeches 1965-1967*. Nairobi: Oxford University Press.

Parfitt T. (2002) *The End of Development? Modernity, Post-Modernity and Development*. London: Pluto.

Peacock, A. and Dosser, D. (1958) *The National Income of Tanganyika 1942-1954*. Colonial Research Study No. 26. London: Colonial Office, HMSO.

Pham, Thi Lan and Jones, N. (2006) *The Ethics of Research Reciprocity: Making Children's Voices Heard in Poverty Reduction Policy Making in Viet Nam*. Young Lives Working Paper. London: SCF.

Rahnema, M. (1997) 'Towards post-development: searching for signposts, a new language and new paradigms', in Rahnema, M. and Bawtree, V. (eds), *The Post-Development Reader*. London: Zed.

Roxborough, I. (1979) *Theories of Underdevelopment*. London: Macmillan.

Scheyvens, R. and Storey, D. (2003) *Development Fieldwork: A Practical Guide*. London: Sage.

Schmitz, H. (2007) 'The rise of the East: what does it mean for development studies', *IDS Bulletin*, 38 (2): 51–58.

Senghor, L. (1964) *On African Socialism: A Report to the Constitutive Congress of the Party of African Federation*. Translated and edited by M. Cook. New York: Praeger.

Shaw, T. (2004) 'International development studies in the era of globalization… and unilateralism', *Canadian Journal of Development Studies*, 25 (1): 17–24.

Sicherman, C. (2005) *Becoming an African University: Makerere 1922-2000*. Trenton: Africa World Press.

Simon, D. (2005) *Dilemmas of Development and the Environment in a Globalising World: Theory, Policy and Praxis*. Inaugural Lecture Series. Department of Geography. Royal Holloway, University of London.

Spivak, G. (1988a) *In Other Worlds*. New York: Routledge.

Spivak, G. (1988b) 'Can the subaltern speak?' in Nelson, C. and Grossberg, L. (eds), *Marxism and Interpretation of Culture*. Chicago: University of Illinois Press.

Spivak, G. (1990) 'Poststructuralism, marginality, postcoloniality and value', in Collier, P. and Greyer-Ryan, H. (ed.), *Literary Theory Today*. London: Polity Press.

Sumner, A. (2007) 'The ethics of development research', *IDS Bulletin*, 38 (2): 59–68.

Surr, M., Barnett, A., Duncan, A., Speight, M., Bradley, D., Rew, A. and Toye, J. (2002) *Research for Poverty Reduction*. Department for International Development (DFID) Research Policy Paper. London: DFID.

Tribe, M. and Sumner, A. (2004) *The Nature of Development Studies*. Paper prepared for DSA Annual Conference, Church House, London, 6 November. Available at the Conference section of the DSA website: www.devstud.org.uk

CHAPTER THREE

WHAT CAN WE 'KNOW' IN DEVELOPMENT STUDIES?

Knowledge is formed by the interplay of what is outside, and what is inside, our-selves... ...[this means] being aware of the external processes of observation and inter-action which inform us; and inside ourselves, this concerns trying to be aware of our own predispositions to select, interpret and frame. (Chambers, 2005: 83)

At every point in our research – in our observing, our interpreting, our reporting, and everything we do as researchers, we inject a host of assumptions. (Crotty, 2004: 17)

Any scientific enterprise is a result... ... of underlying... ... assumptions, values, and beliefs that shape the problems focused on, the approaches used, and the analyses made. (Molteberg and Bergstrøm, 2000: 13, 25)

Every scientific statement must remain tentative forever. (Popper, 1968: 280)

Practicing in different worlds, the two groups of scientists see different things when they look from the same point in the same direction... ... Truth does not tri-umph by convincing its opponents and making them see the light, but rather because its opponents eventually die, and a new generation grows up that is familiar with it. (Kuhn, 1962: 150, 161)

Different disciplines have different ways of problematizing issues and they use different languages. The easiest thing for a researcher is to work with someone who understands their way of thinking and the language they use. (Haddad et al., 2006: 2)

Every academic knows the experience of reading something from outside his or her discipline and knows the unsettling feeling it induces. (Brint, 2000: 210)

Inter-disciplinary research is both lauded and ignored across the social sciences, which exhibit their own languages, methodologies, and assumptions... ... Challenging the domination of disciplines is hard even at the multidisciplinary level, let alone in a trans-disciplinary way. (McGregor, 2006: 33)

3.1. INTRODUCTION

In this chapter we take Bevan's next two 'knowledge foundations' (2006: 7–12) which have been outlined in Table I.2. These are ontology (what is the nature of 'reality'?) and epistemology (what can we 'know'?). We explore the nature of 'reality', the relationship between the researcher and 'reality', and how the researcher can 'know' about 'reality'.

Research in DS, as arguably in all areas of enquiry, is shaped and framed by our underlying assumptions about 'reality' and 'knowledge'. In short, we have 'predispositions to select, interpret and frame', because we 'inject a host of assumptions' and in consequence 'any scientific enterprise is a result... ... of underlying ontological and epistemological assumptions, values, and beliefs' (respectively, Chambers, 2005: 83; Crotty, 2004: 17; Molteberg and Bergstrøm, 2000: 13). This begs the questions of what is science and of what is knowledge?

There has been a major debate, which has become known as the 'battle for science' (or 'science wars'), over the last 50 years which has primarily been about challenges to the notion that science (both physical and social sciences) is an objective and value-free quest for the 'truth'. Kuhn argued that science is ideological and value laden, and is driven by a dominant idea at any particular time within the scientific community. This dominance only changes when 'a new generation grows up' (1962: 161). This contradicts the position of the dominant school of thought at the time when Kuhn was writing – Positivism – which was associated with Karl Popper in particular. Popper was concerned with making a clear distinction between 'science' and 'non-science'. He argued that only those theories which are testable and falsifiable by observation and experiment are scientific. The growth of human knowledge proceeds from this point: nothing can ever be proven beyond doubt so that 'every scientific statement must remain tentative for ever' (Popper, 1968: 280).

What are the implications of this for DS, a cross-disciplinary field of enquiry? Different disciplines have different basic assumptions about the nature of 'reality' and about what we can 'know'. Economics, for example, often claims to have more in common with the objectivity and approach of the physical sciences while others, notably anthropology, may take a fundamentally different position. As Haddad (2006: 2) and McGregor (2006: 33), respectively, note 'different disciplines have different ways of problematizing issues and they use different languages' and 'the social sciences ... exhibit their own languages, methodologies, and assumptions'. In fact the differences between constituent disciplines within DS are so significant that a feeling of unease can be induced by reading outside one's home discipline (Brint, 2000: 210). This chapter aims to provide a point of departure for further discussion of issues associated with knowledge and cross-disciplinarity.

In this chapter we reflect critically on how our basic assumptions frame our research and practice and how they might create 'blind spots'. In Section 2 we consider the fundamental issues relating to the nature of knowledge and science. In Section 3 we focus on the nature of disciplinarity before turning in Section 4 to the issues associated with doing cross-disciplinary research in DS. In Section 5 we summarize the content of the chapter.

Box 3.1   Philosophy of Knowledge: Key Terms and Questions

Ontology: What actually exists? What is the nature of 'reality'?
Epistemology: How can we know 'reality'?
Theory: What are the basic assumptions about inter-relationships between phenomena which are the subject of the research?
Methodology: What is the strategy behind choice of methods?
Methods: What are the techniques which are used to gather and analyze data?

3.2. KNOWLEDGE AND SCIENCE

3.2a. A brief history of knowledge

There is a range of terms used in any discussion about knowledge (see Box 3.1). The most common are those related to the branches of philosophical enquiry that deal with the nature of reality itself (ontology) and the nature of knowledge itself (epistemology). Ontology is best described as a theory or set of assumptions concerning what 'exists' and thus *what is* and *what is 'knowable'*? Epistemology is best described as a set of assumptions concerning *how we can 'know'* that which 'exists' (see Box 3.1).

Researchers need to be aware of the basic assumptions which they make because of the impact of these assumptions on their research and especially on their findings and conclusions. In fact, ontology and epistemology are the first two steps in a 'scaffold of learning' (see Box 3.2). Epistemology informs our choice of theory/conceptual framework which in turn informs our methodology and methods.

The questions of what is knowledge, what constitutes knowledge, and the foundation for knowledge and belief has been a major area of (Western) philosophical inquiry since at least the time of Plato's *Theaetetus* dialogue (Plato, 360 BCE) (see Table 3.1).[1]

Box 3.2   The 'Scaffold of Learning'

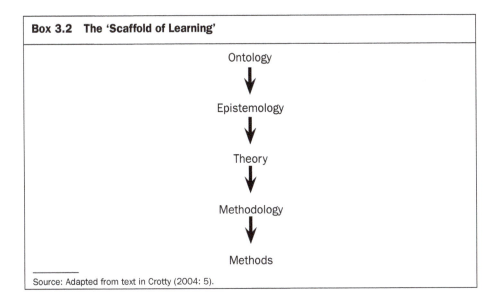

Source: Adapted from text in Crotty (2004: 5).

Table 3.1 Selected (Western) Philosophers' Thinking on 'Knowledge' and 'Reality'

Name	Contribution
Socrates (469–399 BCE)	Proposed the Socratic method of *elenchus* – the eliciting and questioning of beliefs in order to establish truths and reveal inconsistencies. Developed inductive reasoning (considering many cases as a basis for generalization) as the means to knowledge
Plato (427–347 BCE)	Proposed the dialectic method – an exchange of propositions (theses) and counter-propositions (anti-theses) resulting in a synthesis of opposing assertions. The aim of the dialectic method is to resolve disagreement through rational discussion. Argued that reality is an imitation of a perfect, eternal world
Aristotle (384–322 BCE)	Proposed that logic and induction were the tools for knowledge acquisition. Argued that there are four 'causes' that explain why and how something exists: (i) material cause (the matter comprising it); (ii) formal cause (the pattern or law defining its development); (iii) efficient cause (the agent or initiator of the process); and (iv) final cause (its end or result)
Francis Bacon (1561–1626)	Argued that human perceptions have a tendency to distort what is before them because of a person's prepositions and prejudices ('the idols of the tribe'). The proposed method to overcome this was induction – general laws and principles derived from a number of particular instances – with caution before jumping to generalizations. Negative instances were to be sought through comprehensive data assembly
Galileo Galilei (1564–1642)	Argued for the need to measure and quantify which would reveal the structure and laws of the universe through deductive reasoning. The primary properties of things – their 'real properties' – can be measured, counted, and quantified and the scientific world is abstract from the 'lived' world
Thomas Hobbes (1588–1679)	Argued for deductive reasoning and boldly applied mathematics to human affairs
René Descartes (1591–1650)	Argued for mathematic models as a basis for knowledge. A rationalist and empiricist. Proposed 'method of doubt' – our senses can be deceptive and anything that is subject to doubt cannot be accepted as 'truth'

John Locke (1632–1704)
Argued knowledge comes from sense experience. We have 'degrees of certainty' (some knowledge is better than others). A rationalist and empiricist. Argued that there are primary qualities of phenomena (observed in the same way to all) and secondary qualities of phenomena (observed differently – subjectively – by different people)

Gottfried Wilhelm Leibniz (1646–1716)
Proposed a principle of 'sufficient reason' – there is always a reason for everything to be as it is. An empiricist. Argued that the process of reasoning is an adequate foundation for knowledge

George Berkeley (1685–1753)
Argued there is no such thing as matter and that all perception exists in our minds. The external world is produced by our minds. All that we know is based on sensations which are based on purely mental phenomena

David Hume (1711–1777)
Argued knowledge may be a priori (before experience) and a posteriori (after experience)

Immanuel Kant (1724–1804)
Argued human knowledge is founded on the application of reason to our experience of the world. We fit information into a priori categories. The world is not independent of us. What we know depends on our sense and how we interpret them. It is not necessarily true that every event has a cause

John Stuart Mill (1806–1873)
Causation is rarely based on a single cause, but is the result of a juxtaposition of factors. Argued for inductive reasoning and generalization from experience

Friedrich Nietzsche (1844–1900)
Attacked the belief that there is an objective world structured independent of human comprehension. He argued that we make rather than discover values and meanings. The most powerful define what counts as knowledge

Karl Popper (1902–1994)
Argued that a 'falsification' rather than a 'verification' principle should be at the heart of scientific method

Michel Foucault (1926–1984)
Argued that one can only know reality through a 'discourse' (a body of ideas, concepts and theory). There is no such thing as objective reality. The power to define reality – through controlling the discourse – is a crucial aspect of power. Argued a 'discourse' categorizes people and creates the problematic categories that it claims to deal with

Thomas Kuhn (1922–1996)
Argued that 'truth' is a product of the dominant 'paradigm'. Scientists are not objective

Source: Adapted from relevant entries in Collinson and Plant (2006).

Examples of broad approaches are Descartes' 'search for certainty' (implying that anything subject to doubt cannot be accepted as 'truth') or the competition to find a 'criterion of truth' between Greek sceptics, the Stoics and the Epicureans. Further examples can be provided by Leibnitz' and Kant's 'principles of sufficient reason' (the idea that everything has an underlying cause). The key conceptual issues in this connection are concerned with what is 'knowable', the extent to which we can 'know' anything, and how we can assess claims to 'know'.

There have been several notable strands in the evolution of philosophy. The first strand, the seventeenth-century 'birth of reason', was a radical questioning of religious or mythical accounts of natural processes which triggered greater reflection on the physical and social world. This included the work of Socrates, Plato, and Aristotle. For these writers the foundation of knowledge was an inductive method (drawing generalizations – making theory – from evidence).

The second strand, the rise of empiricism, covers the work of Bacon, Locke, Hume and Mill. For these writers the foundation of knowledge was empiricism (observation) and the application of the principles of science and mathematics to the social world. The evolution of science as the basis for knowledge and human progress (as opposed to explanations based on religious belief) accelerated in the period known as the 'Enlightenment' in Europe (during the late seventeenth and early eighteenth centuries). For Galileo, Hobbes, and Descartes too, the foundation of knowledge was mathematics through a deductive method (using theory as a basis for making generalizations and as a basis for collecting evidence).[2]

The dominant position in the early part of the nineteenth century – namely that knowledge should be sought through empiricism and mathematics – became known as Positivism (and is associated with Karl Popper amongst others). The rise of post-modernism (associated with Nietzsche, Foucault, Kuhn and others) in the 1900s questioned whether there is any 'truth' and argued that all knowledge is constructed or relative (rather than being discovered). This became known as Relativism.

3.2b. Positivism, Relativism and Realism

Positivism and Relativism are two opposing perspectives about what constitutes 'knowledge' and 'science'. Between these two perspectives Realism seeks to provide a 'middle-ground'. Each of these three approaches covers a wider diversity of viewpoints. For example, Relativism is often used interchangeably with constructivism, constructionism, interpretivism, post-modernism, and hermeneutics (see discussion in Crotty, 2004). Positivism is often used interchangeably with science although this is highly contentious. There are various forms of Realism – naïve, scientific, transcendental, subtle and critical (see Spencer et al., 2003: 46).

Kanbur and Shaffer (2005: 5) suggest a characterization of epistemology within DS. They distinguish between positivist/empiricist approaches at one extreme (based on observation which establishes knowledge claims) and relativist/hermeneutics/interpretative approaches (based on 'discourse' for the establishment of knowledge through 'inter-subjective meanings') at the other. Increasingly, the middle ground of

Realism is also evident, based on the argument that some of our perceptions or 'sense-data' can and do accurately represent external phenomena and some do not. This draws on Locke and Descartes. There is a knowable Reality independent of humans, but perceptions of that Reality are subjective.

One way of conceptualizing the difference between Positivism, Relativism, and Realism is to ask whether we are looking for a single truth (associated with Positivism) or many truths (associated with Relativism) or something in between (Realism). In this context there is a distinction between certainty (associated with the positivist approach) and a more informed understanding of reality (associated with Relativism) or again, something in between (associated with Realism).

Each epistemological perspective makes assumptions about the nature of reality, about the aim of knowledge enquiry, and about the relationship between the researcher and the researched. Table 3.2 outlines stylized tendencies (these are not absolutes) in these three main approaches. What does this all mean for research in DS? Researchers need to be critically aware and need to reflect upon their underlying assumptions regarding what there is to know and how researchers can know about it. However, this differs across the constituent disciplines within DS.

Positivism emerged in England and France during the Enlightenment of the seventeenth and eighteenth centuries but can be traced back to Francis Bacon and Galileo, who argued in favour of quantification. At this time European philosophers proclaimed the individual to be autonomous and no longer a part of 'nature', or of 'god', as had previously been thought. There was optimism that the benefits arising from knowledge and science would help to improve the 'human condition'.

Auguste Compte is seen by many as the founder of Positivism. Compte argued that the scientific method of the physical sciences should be applied in the social sciences. He also argued for observation, experiment, and comparison but warned against the dangerous overuse of mathematics. Locke, Hume and Mill can also be regarded as contributors to Positivism through their work on empiricism. Hobbes, Descartes, and Spinoza also contributed to Positivism through their use of mathematics.

Table 3.2 Stylized Tendencies in Epistemological Assumptions

	Positivism	Realism	Relativism
What is reality?	There is one reality, which is observable	There is a reality which exists independently of the researcher and which can be described	There are multiple realities, which can be experienced
What is the aim of knowledge enquiry?	Acquisition of a single truth – in the form of a universal, general law	To describe reality. It is not possible to establish the truth about reality	A more informed construction or understanding
How does the researcher relate to the researched?	The researcher is objective and independent of the researched	The researcher and their thoughts are part of reality. The researcher is a dependent observer	The researcher is subjective and is not independent of the researched

In the 1920s and 1930s Positivism evolved into Logical Positivism (also called Logical Empiricism) amongst a group of philosophers known as the 'Vienna Circle' (which had related counterparts in Warsaw and Berlin). This was a group consisting of Otto Neurath, Rudolf Carnap, Hans Reichenbach, Kurt Godel, Friedrich Waisman, and Moritz Schlick. In 1936 Ayer's *Language, Truth and Logic* was seen as a 'milestone' publication for Logical Positivism, not so much for what it added intellectually but because it popularized Logical Positivism in the English-speaking world.

Logical Positivism argues that there are two approaches to the acquisition of knowledge: first, applying logical reasoning and second, using empirical evidence for the testing of refutable propositions. The former (logical reasoning) is a priori being derived through reasoning without reference to experience (i.e. it is deductive), and the latter is a posteriori being derived from observed facts (i.e. it is inductive). Logical Positivists held that statements must be tested by verification (the 'principle of verification') and that research must satisfy the standard natural or physical science model and the method of observation of phenomena.

Karl Popper was one of the most famous philosophers of the twentieth century. He had an early association with the 'Vienna Circle' but had a slightly different view to that of the Logical Positivists. Popper argued that the central problem of philosophy is that of the demarcation between science and non-science. He argued that a theory is 'scientific' if it can be tested. However, he also argued that at the heart of scientific method should be a 'falsification' principle rather than a 'verification' principle. Scientists should seek to disprove – to falsify – their hypotheses rather than seek to verify them. Further, all hypotheses should, in principle, be falsifiable by observation. Popper was part of the twentieth-century 'Science Wars' (see Box 3.3).

In sum a Positivist approach assumes that:

- An objective reality exists;
- Reality is accessible through sensory experience;
- Reality is measurable;
- Reality is one unambiguous reality;
- There is independence between the 'reality', the researcher and the instruments of research (none may influence any other).

These assumptions reflect the importance placed upon the replicability of experiments and the objective position of the researcher in the natural or physical sciences. Positivism today is still linked closely to empirical science. It retains an optimistic faith that scientific discovery is the driving force of progress, that scientific method is accurate and certain, and argues for 'objectivism' implying that objects have meaning priori to knowledge and exist independently of our consciousness.

Post-positivism (not to be confused with post-modernism) is a recent formation and is a humbler form of Positivism. It argues that knowledge acquisition should be based on the establishment of probabilistic propositions rather than certainty; for relative objectivity rather than absolute objectivity; and for the achievement of approximate truth rather than of 'total' truth. Post-positivism is associated with

Werner Heisenberg (and Niels Bohr) and is linked to the 'uncertainty principle' (Bohr, 1958; Heisenberg, 1927). The 'uncertainty principle' is based on the fact that there is a mathematical limit to the accuracy with which things can be observed in the physical world. For example, Heisenberg (1927) argued that it is impossible to determine both the position and momentum of subatomic particles with any real accuracy *and* furthermore, that the observed particle is altered by the very act of being observed. This therefore challenges the notion that the observer (researcher) and the observed (researched) are independent.

Further, many fundamental theoretical constructs within science have never been observed at all but usefully serve as explanatory devices (Heisenberg noted that no one has actually observed a particle or a wave). There are some interesting parallels with research in DS. For example, has anybody ever observed a perfectly competitive market? Or has anybody ever observed a perfectly functioning democracy? Or has anybody ever observed good governance?

Further, drawing on quantum physics further, the very act of research may change the behaviour of the subjects of research – an issue which will be discussed in more detail in Chapter 5.

The direct relevance of the 'uncertainty principle' to DS research is also relevant to its cross-disciplinary nature. If DS seeks to combine insights from different disciplines there is an issue around the significance of epistemological differences between Economics (traditionally viewed as more positivistic) and Social Anthropology (traditionally viewed as more relativistic) and whether these differences can be accommodated where these disciplines are combined. There is a danger that in combining differing views about reality, and about what we can know, that intellectual legitimacy is challenged (this issue will be discussed further in Sections 5.4a and 5.4b).

Relativism represents a completely different view of reality and what we can know. Key thinkers in the Relativism school of thought include Berger, Derrida, Foucault, Kuhn, Latour, Luckmann, and Nietzsche. Relativism emphasizes the social constructions of meaning and is premised on the idea that reality does not exist independently from our experiences. Multiple realities exist which are intangible, local and specific in nature. Meaning is not discovered or created; it is constructed. In short, the concept of a single 'truth' is meaningless, as is any project which aims to uniquely and accurately describe the world. All claims to 'closure' – to know with certainty – are suspect. Academic research should strive towards ever more sophisticated, informed, and inclusive constructions of the world through the interaction between the researcher and the researched.

The relativist approach is particularly associated with the 1962 publication of Thomas Kuhn's *The Structure of Scientific Revolutions* which triggered the 'Science Wars' referred to in the introductory section of this chapter (see Box 3.3).[3] Kuhn challenged Popper's view of objective science arguing that 'human interests, human values, human fallibility, human foibles, all play a part' (1962: 36). His thesis was written in the extreme circumstances of political repression in the USA, when people including many academics were sacked or victimized for 'un-America activities' in the context of anti-communist paranoia.

Box 3.3   Science Wars: Kuhn Versus Popper

In 1962 Thomas Kuhn published *The Structure of Scientific Revolutions* which was to become one of the bestselling academic books of the twentieth century. Selling over a million copies it has been translated into 20 languages.

The Structure of Scientific Revolutions triggered what has become called the 'Science Wars' because it was perceived as an attack on the dominant thinking in science at that time epitomized in Karl Popper's 1959 (2nd edition, 1968) English publication *The Logic of Scientific Discovery* (originally published in German some 25 years earlier).

Kuhn was a historian of science (although originally a theoretical physicist) and Popper was concerned with the philosophy of science. Kuhn was largely defined by the single book, but Popper published much more widely.

Kuhn's book was viewed as revolutionary and Popper's work as reactionary. However, in reality, Kuhn was a conservative mistaken as a radical or a subversive and Popper a socialist mistaken as a conservative. Both were strong defenders of science, but they differed over their characterization of the nature of science.

Essentially 'Science Wars' was about a challenge to the power and authority of 'science' based on the questioning of its objectivity. Two prominent flash-points for the 'Science Wars' were a meeting of Kuhn and Popper in 1965 at the University of London and the 1996 special issue of the journal *Social Text* which was a response to aggressive attempts to mount a defence of science.

Source: Fuller (2005).

Kuhn was concerned with how ideas evolve and how they are 'thinkable' or 'unthinkable' at any particular time, and he argued that knowledge is not simply accumulated but is a product of the intellectual time and environment. Kuhn developed the idea of a 'paradigm'.[4] Kuhn's original point of reference for a 'paradigm' was 'the entire constellation of beliefs, values and techniques, and so on shared by the members of a given community' (1962: 175).

Kuhn (1962) argued that one of the main causes of paradigm changes is the natural turnover of the membership of generations of scientists. He argued there are three phases to a paradigm shift. The first is 'the pre-scientific phase' – with no consensus but rather a number of incompatible competing theories. The second phase is 'normal science' – when one of the competing frameworks becomes a dominant consensus in terms of methods, terminology, and ways of seeing the world. 'Normal science' consists of unpacking the 'promise of success' of new ideas. The third phase is the 'scientific revolution' when key anomalies build up against a body of theory leading to its rejection and to a paradigm shift. The shift changes the questions of enquiry and the rules of the game. Change occurs when the weight of key anomalies builds up to a crisis and a revolution occurs switching to a new world view in a new paradigm (1962: 103). The weight of anomalies relates to internal inconsistencies and failure to answer the questions seen as important to the dominant group of practitioners.

Kuhn's contribution to systems of knowledge creation has been complemented by post-modernist writers who have more recently drawn on Foucault's work (see Chapter 1). Post-modernism and post-structuralism are notoriously difficult to define precisely and writers, Foucault included, have often disassociated themselves from the labels

(Parfitt, 2002). Post-modernism can be summarized as the idea that 'there are no abso-lute truths and no objective values. There may be local truths and values' (Rue, 1994: 272–273). Post-modernism can best be understood in contrast to, or as a reaction to, modernity. It consists of an adverse reaction to rationality, faith in progress and the perception that science is precise. One concern is that any universalistic claims to truth tend to exclude those who are marginalized by this truth or who do not fit the narrow defining characteristics of the framework (Lyotard, 1984). We should avoid 'closure' – knowing with certainty. This effectively deprives us of the ability to make 'truth' claims that are universal. In sum, a relativist approach takes the position that:

- No objective reality exists;
- There are many ambiguous 'realities';
- There is only meaning, and this meaning may be different for every interpreter;
- There is no independence between any perception of reality, the researcher, the researched, and the instruments of research.

In recent years the positivist-relativist division has been questioned and new schools of thought have emerged which, as noted earlier, are broadly known as 'Realism'. Realism has a more relaxed approach to epistemology. The basis of Realism is that there is a physical reality which exists independently of our cognition but that we cannot appraise it – we can only describe it due to the fact that we are dependent observers – and we are not independent of events. Thus knowledge is a social construct, but one which aims to explain a physical reality (Molteberg and Bergstrøm, 2000: 21). Realism

> provides an alternative to both hopes of a law-finding science of society modelled on natural science methodology and the anti-naturalist or interpretivist reductions of social science to the interpretation meaning. (Sayer 2000: 2–3)

To summarize, Realism takes the position that:

- Reality exists independently of the researcher;
- What the researcher thinks is a small part of reality;
- It is impossible to establish 'the truth' about what is real (the structures and powers of objects deriving from their nature, which, depending on circumstances, may or may not be actualized).

3.3. DISCIPLINARITY

3.3a. Is DS a discipline?

DS seeks to be cross-disciplinary (DSA, 2004; Harriss, 2005; Hulme and Toye, 2006; Loxley, 2004; Molteberg and Bergstrøm, 2000; Tribe and Sumner, 2004). However, different disciplines may have quite different ontologies and epistemologies.

Box 3.4   Hedgehogs and Foxes

Gould, drawing on seventh-century Greek poetry, argues that scholars are either hedge-hogs or foxes. Hedgehogs stick to a single effective strategy throughout their academic careers. In contrast, foxes devise many strategies throughout their academic career. Foxes are thus more likely to cross disciplines. However, the fox within many academics remains hidden because scholarly career structures are typically built for hedgehogs because work within closely defined disciplinary boundaries is most rewarded. The fox within may emerge in the later stages of an academic career after a researcher is estab-lished or is at least likely to remain somewhat hidden in earlier stages.

Source: Gould (2003).

How should development researchers proceed? Gould (2003) draws parallels with foxes and hedgehogs, and this is summarized in Box 3.4.

There are significant intellectual and professional or institutional barriers between disciplines. These barriers are both ontological and epistemological, and are also based on the structure of universities and of university politics. Haddad (2006: 3) and McGregor (2006: 33) have both referred to the fact that different disciplines have distinct ontological and epistemological approaches – to problem definition, to axioms and assumptions concerning the nature of reality and of human beings, to analytical methods and techniques. Indeed, some disciplines even have language (or jargon) which is almost incomprehensible to those 'outside' the discipline. Brint (2000: 210) notes the 'unsettling feeling' associated with the crossing of disciplinary boundaries because 'disciplines in fact provide a core element to the identity of most intellectuals'.

This raises the question of the nature of a discipline, and whether DS, as an area of study which synthesizes several disciplines, can itself be regarded as a discipline. Most of those who would describe themselves as being involved in the DS 'commu-nity' would not regard it as a discipline, having their own home discipline within which they also work – such as economics, sociology, political science, or civil engi-neering. This implies that DS is an umbrella area of study – covering a range of con-stituent disciplines – rather than being a discipline in itself. A more appropriate conception of DS is perhaps as a 'subject'.

As Canning (2005: 38) points out, 'although the words "subject" and "discipline" are often used interchangeably, the discipline is different to the subject: a subject is a knowledge base whereas as the discipline is a "tribe", culture, a "guild"'.

However, Strober suggests that

> using knowledge criteria alone (e.g. the existence of a distinctive theory, paradigm, body of information, methodology or scholarly journal) to decide whether a branch of knowledge is a discipline... is a hopeless task... Knowledge criteria alone do not result in agreement among academics on these matters... in part because partici-pants in the debate are not impartial spectators. (2006: 5–6)

Strober goes on to argue that departmental status (i.e. a department associated with a named subject area) in a sufficient number of universities could be a proxy for whether a field is thought to be a discipline. She sums up what many have noted, that what counts as a discipline is as much a 'political' consideration as a purely epistemological one. It reflects the departmental structure of universities, university career and reward structures, and the nature of professional associations, journals, library classifications, and research funding bodies that shape and frame career and organizational incentives.

Turner (2000) argues that in order for a field to become a discipline it requires 'identity' and 'exchange': 'identity' as a discipline comes from achieving 'political' status (for example as a university department) and in doing so 'exchange' relates to the creation of a market for applications from intending students. In short, a discipline is a field of study which has departmental status in a sufficient number of universities. Turner's (2000: 51) definition of a discipline illustrates this argument succinctly – disciplines are 'cartels that organize markets for the production and employment of students by excluding those job seekers who are not products of the cartel'.

If we pursue the knowledge-based nature of disciplines, most of us would understand a discipline as involving a body of theory, and perhaps, discipline-specific assumptions on the nature of reality and knowledge and possibly favoured methodological approaches and methods or techniques.

DS is considered by many to have a 'body of theory' which will be explored in a little more detail in our Chapter 4. Some of the key issues are therefore: (a) is there general agreement on the nature and content of this body of DS theory?; (b) can Development Theory be said to belong to a discipline?; c) to what extent are some theories shared between constituent disciplines of DS?; and d) how does Development Theory relate to theories used by constituent disciplines within DS? Several of the disciplines which are well represented in the DS community themselves have a distinct sub-area of study relating to Development with its own specialized (and adapted) body of theory, such as Development Economics.

Figure 3.1 shows that Development Economics is an example of a sub-discipline within the Economics discipline, and that it also has a clear location within DS. The logic of Figure 3.1 would also hold if Anthropology, Sociology, or Political Science were to be substituted for Development Economics in the diagram as the 'home' discipline. The figure also shows a relationship between Area Studies, DS and Development Economics, with Area Studies having a similar status to DS – being a 'subject' rather than a 'discipline'. Economists, whether regarding themselves as development economists or not, regularly work within the ambit of both Area Studies and DS.

Fine (2002) and Kanbur (2002) have specifically suggested that there have been intellectual tensions over the years between development economists and economists, between development economists and non-economist DS specialists, and between mainstream economists and DS specialists. Economists have often been criticized for being discipline oriented rather than being problem oriented. This implies that they

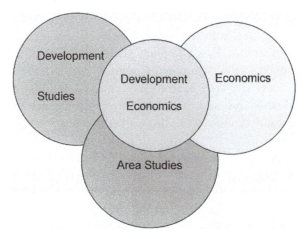

Figure 3.1 The Relationship between Development Studies, Development Economics and Area Studies

have been accused of being concerned more with finding circumstances to which they can apply conventional economic theories, methods and, techniques as purely intellectual exercises rather than with bringing intellectual power to bear on major societal problems through the use of appropriate theory, methods, and techniques as a basis for increased understanding of the problem or issue.[5]

DS is, of course, more inclined to be problem oriented than to be discipline oriented, and there are numerous highly regarded contributions from the DS community which fall into the problem-oriented category. For example, the work of the Nobel Laureate in Economics, Amartya Sen. He has seminal publications on poverty and famines (Sen, 1980, 1982a), on development indicators (for example some of the articles reprinted in Sen, 1982b, 1984) and on the nature of development (Sen, 1999 and 2001).

Typically contemporary DS is thought to be some combination of one or more Social Science disciplines and subjects such as Economics, Sociology, Anthropology and Politics plus Human Geography and perhaps Philosophy and Psychology too (Jackson, 2002; Kanbur, 2002). Hulme and Toye (2006) however, prefer to speak of 'knowledge communities':

> A knowledge community is defined here as a network of knowledge-based experts who share an interest in a subset of knowledge issues, and who accept common procedural protocols as criteria to judge the success of their knowledge creation activities. What is essential here is not that all members of a knowledge community know or communicate with each other, but that they have common intellectual interests and aims, and a shared understanding and acceptance of the methods by which their sort of knowledge is successfully created... the legitimate methods or 'procedural protocols' of each knowledge community provides it with its intellectual discipline, determining among other things the content of the training thought to be appropriate for those aspiring to become members. (2006: 1094–5)

DS might be thought of as a 'knowledge community' in itself but it also draws on several cross-cutting 'knowledge communities' including social policy, environmental studies, gender studies, and post-colonial studies.[6] Molteberg and Bergstrøm (2000) go so far as to argue that DS is defined by the fact that it

> addresses complex problems at the nature-society interface and thus has to deal with issues in which phenomena of different ontological status are inter-linked. (2002a: 25)

There is an issue over the extent to which DS is regarded as having an intellectual location principally within the Social Sciences. DS specialists working on agricultural and rural development emphasize the significance of agricultural sciences (including soil science and ecological studies) in determining development potential. Those working on issues associated with the environment and development also emphasize the significance of science and technology as part of a broader definition of DS.[7] So, how should DS seek to bring together this huge array of disciplines and subjects?

3.3b. What is cross-disciplinarity?

There appears to be only limited consensus over how the differing conceptualizations and terminologies within cross-disciplinary study should be handled (Bergstrøm and Molteberg, 2000: 9; Kanbur, 2002: 483). The adjectives which are most commonly used are 'cross-disciplinary' studies, 'interdisciplinary' studies, 'multidisciplinary' studies, and 'transdisciplinary' studies – with the associated respective nouns being interdisciplinarity, multidisciplinarity and transdisciplinarity (see Box 3.5 for definitions).

In short, cross-disciplinarity is a generic term meaning *any* kind of mixing of disciplines. Multi-disciplinary entails researchers in teams conducting research from their own disciplinary viewpoint but where the team as a whole includes researchers from a number of disciplines. Interdisciplinarity is a step further towards integration rather than co-existence and means that the different disciplines are still discernable but some level of deeper integration is evident. Individuals (or teams) seek to integrate

---

Box 3.5   Definitions of Cross-disciplinary Terms

Cross-disciplinarity is a generic term referring to any analysis or policy recommendations based substantially on analysis and methods of more than one discipline.

Multidisciplinarity refers to work in which individual discipline-based researchers (or teams) do their best, within their disciplinary confines, to examine an issue and subsequently collaborate to develop together an overall analytical synthesis and conclusions.

Interdisciplinarity refers to research that attempts a deep integration of two or more disciplinary approaches from the beginning and throughout an entire research exercise.

Source: Kanbur (2002: 483).

---

concepts and methodologies from the outset. Most of the individual researchers will have familiarity with at least a second discipline.

Transdisciplinarity relates to complete integration of two or more disciplines with the possibility of forming a new discipline. As an example the field research method known as ethnography originates in anthropology but took insights from psychology, philosophy, sociology, and other disciplines. A final option in this classification is 'non-disciplinarity', which is not the same as trans-disciplinarity and represents a deliberate attempt to ignore the notion that one should work within well-defined disciplinary boundaries, a position which might be taken by those working in a postmodernist perspective.

These conceptualizations of DS have been represented in Figure 3.2 reflecting Bergstrøm and Molteberg's perception of cross-disciplinary concepts as being within a continuum, with 'additive' approaches at one end (multi-disciplinarity) and fully 'integrative' approaches at the other end (transdisciplinarity) (2000: 11).

An illustrative example can perhaps be given from the area of water supply – focusing on potable water for direct human consumption rather than irrigation water or 'commercial' water. For civil engineers (i.e. technical people) concerns about potable water supply and public water policy tend to relate to major engineering projects. To economists they relate to costs (capital and recurrent) of provision, to costs associated with water collection by households and to pricing policy. For the rural development specialist in developing countries they are likely to relate to boreholes and protected springs. For the social development specialist the social implications of improved water supply systems would be the principal concern. It is clear from this that water supply is too important to be left to the sole attention of people specialized in a single discipline (such as civil engineers), and that a multidisciplinary, interdisciplinary, or transdisciplinary approach is always going to be superior. Such studies which combine the insights provided by a range of disciplines are just as relevant to an understanding of many areas of society in industrialized countries or transition economies as they are for developing countries which have no monopoly in their need for such studies.

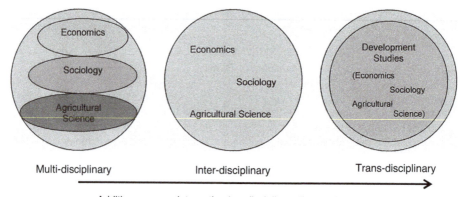

Additive --- some integration but disciplines discernable --- Integrative

Figure 3.2   Diagrammatic Presentation of Cross-disciplinarity in Development Studies

3.4. DOING CROSS-DISCIPLINARY RESEARCH IN DS

3.4a. DS, knowledge and science

This section will focus on the issues of how DS should approach the underlying assumptions which researchers make about the nature of reality and knowledge, and whether a positivist, relativist, or realist approach should be adopted.

Although contemporary DS draws on the full range of epistemological stances, there has been a noticeable shift in emphasis from Positivism towards Relativism in recent years (Scheyvens and Storey, 2003: 132). In the post-Second World War period Positivism was dominant, visible in the grand theories of development that proposed one common linear pathway to industrialization for example (these issues will be explored in more detail in Chapter 4). This is perhaps reflected in the comparative strength of development economists at the time relative to non-economists in the study of socio-economic development in developing countries. Contemporary DS has a tendency towards Relativism (visible in participatory poverty assessments for example), which reflects a relative decline in the strength of the economists and the involvement of other disciplines including some researchers who might describe themselves as DS researchers rather than as being associated to any particular discipline.

DS as a field of study has epistemological diversity which reflects its cross-disciplinary nature. To recap, the model of DS which we proposed in Chapter 2 was that:

- The focus of DS: DS is about 'development' (however defined – refer to Chapter 1);
- The purpose of DS: DS is (to a large extent) about applied or instrumental research: DS tends not to be interested in knowledge generation for its own sake but for its applied or instrumental value. DS is concerned with real-world problems (even when theorizing). Many members of the DS 'community' seek to 'make a difference' (Mehta et al., 2006: 1);
- The approach of DS: DS is (to a greater or lesser extent) about cross-disciplinary insights: DS increasingly seeks to draw on the insights of more than one discipline but does not necessarily always achieve this satisfactorily.

There are thus a number of potential epistemological contradictions at the heart of DS. The *focus* could suggest a tendency towards Positivism due to the implicit assumption that all developing countries share some common characteristics, or alternatively it might tend towards relativist approaches because of the highly diverse political, social, economic, and cultural contexts. The *purpose* might suggest a tendency towards relativist approaches because of an applied or instrumental point of departure, but the search for policy or solutions could suggest a tendency towards Positivism and generalizable laws. The *approach* then has a tendency to seek to reconcile these differing epistemological positions through bringing disciplines together.

In contemporary DS both Positivism and Relativism have a clear influence. Positivism, with a descriptive function in measuring and quantifying phenomena (as presented, for example, in numerous annual reports and statistical publications of governments and international agencies), and also with an analytical function in the type of quantitative modelling which is particularly prominent in the research output of the IMF and the World Bank clearly has an important role. Relativism also has a strong influence in the interpretation and understanding of development through discourses such as the post-development critique, and also in the rise of participatory approaches to research in DS.

Comparison of two recent well-known studies, Dollar and Kraay's *Growth is Good for the Poor* and Narayan et al.'s *Voices of the Poor* illustrates how broad DS is epistemologically (see Box 3.6 – in which the literary citations are recorded). The Dollar and Kraay study is based on quantitative analysis of secondary data and on an experimental, natural or physical science type method of mathematical regression analysis. In contrast the Narayan et al. study is based on qualitative analysis of both secondary data and primary data from Participatory Poverty Assessments (PPAs). Dollar and Kraay's study is a descriptive-explanatory study (what is the relationship between x and y?), while Narayan's study is an interpretative study (what are x and y?). In short, within the same academic field and focus of study (poverty) the epistemological (and methodological) perspectives are at opposite ends of the spectrum which we are discussing.

In sum, it is important that, whatever approach is adopted, there should be an awareness of the basic assumptions and what they rule in and rule out. High-quality DS research is usually concerned with levels of probability rather than of certainty, which requires subjectivity-awareness and control rather than absolute objectivity,

---

Box 3.6   Comparison in Development Studies: 'Dollar and Kraay' and 'Narayan'

David Dollar and Aart Kraay are two World Bank economists, who have published a number of studies using cross-country quantitative analysis based on econometrics. The first version of *Growth is Good for the Poor* appeared in the World Bank Policy Research Working Paper series and the paper was then revised (Dollar and Kraay, 2000, 2001) before being published in another version in the *Journal of Economic Growth* (2002) and again as a chapter in a book (Dollar and Kraay, 2004). The Working Paper was a background document for the World Bank's *World Development Report* 2000–2001 on Poverty (World Bank, 2000). *Growth is Good for the Poor* (2002) argues that it has provided 'evidence' (the word is used 37 times in the study) to support the proposition that not only is growth good for the poor, but that the policies pursued by the IMF and World Bank have been good for the poor because they have led to growth. The paper has faced sustained methodological criticism (see for details Amann et al., 2006; Nye et al., 2002; Rodrik, 2000).

The Narayan et al. (2002) participatory poverty assessment was also carried out by the World Bank, and much of the analysis was included in the *World Development Report* 2000–2001 (World Bank, 2000). It is one of the World Bank's most ambitious studies to date covering 60,000 poor people in more than 60 countries. The study has two components and was carried out with help from non-governmental organizations (NGOs) and independent research centres. The first component is a literature review of 75 participatory poverty studies from the late 1990s with coverage of 40,000 people in 41 countries. The second component is a set of new studies in 23 countries covering 20,000 people. The studies sought to elicit poor households' perspectives on wellbeing.

and for approximate truth rather absolute 'closure'. While diversity across DS is welcome, researchers constantly need to bear in mind the three questions which dictate their underlying assumptions on the nature of 'reality' and knowledge:

- What is 'reality'?
- What is the goal of enquiry?
- Are the researcher and the 'researched' independent?

3.4b. DS and cross-disciplinarity

DS seeks to be cross-disciplinary, but the basic assumptions of reality and knowledge differ between disciplines. An attempt has been made to summarize these differences in Table 3.3 following Bevan (2006). Cross-disciplinary work involving disciplines with similar underlying assumptions is, of course, likely to be easier than where there are significantly different assumptions. For example, in a very general sense Politics and Sociology share an assumption that reality exists independently of our thoughts. Other disciplines are likely to be much harder to mix. For example, Economics and Social Anthropology have contrasting assumptions on the nature of reality and even the goal of research (see Table 3.3 and related discussion). This discussion is based on a stylized or ideal-type (in the Weberian sense) depiction. It is through, highly contentious because there is considerable diversity within disciplines.

In Economics there is arguably less intra-discipline diversity than in Anthropology. However, what is often neglected is that even within economics there are major differences between heterodox/radical/structural economists and the more conventional neo-classical economists.

Hulme and Toye (2006) have also raised the issues of disciplinary 'cultures' and in particular the differing meanings of 'rigour' (which are discussed in more detail in Chapter 5):

> Disciplines arguably share not just aims, interests and methodological norms, but also a distinctive culture – made up of attitudes, aspirations and social values ... [and] many poverty researchers claim to recognise such cultural differences as shaping the work that people within a discipline undertake. Arguably, economists (and, to a lesser degree political scientists) mix well with more powerful people and feel relatively confident about explaining the implications of their findings to politicians and high-level bureaucrats. By contrast, anthropologists and sociologists are less ready to mix and empathise with people in power and much less likely to be confident about arguing for the implications of their work for public policy. They are more likely to mix and relate well to the less powerful and even the powerless and marginalized...
>
> Cross-disciplinary research would be suspected of lack of rigour if its practice required participants to abandon conceptual and methodological standards that their knowledge communities had previously regarded as essential... For some pairings of knowledge communities, for example econometrics and critical realist sociology ... the 'rigour' of each group is seen as fundamentally flawed by the other.

Table 3.3 Ideal-type Depiction of Disciplines and Underlying Assumptions on 'Reality' and 'Knowledge'

	Economics	Politics	Sociology	Social Anthropology
What is reality?	One reality exists. Reality is independent of our thoughts What is observable is real	One reality exists. Reality is independent of our thoughts	One reality exists. Reality is independent of our thoughts Much of reality is unobservable	There are different realities associated with different standpoints and cultures
What is the goal of enquiry?	Acquisition of a single 'truth' – a universal, general law	We can establish truths or generalizations about human beings	Truth needs to be understood in terms of practical adequacy	Interpretation of local meanings. There is no universal truth
How are the researcher and the 'researched' related?	The researcher is objective and is independent of the 'researched'	The researcher is subjective and is not independent of the 'researched'	The researcher is subjective and is not independent of the 'researched'	The researcher is subjective and is not independent of the 'researched'

Source: Adapted from Bevan (2006: 15).

While cross-disciplinary criticism can sharpen work it is unlikely to be something that can be built on, if the criticisms are that a collaborator, who is respected within his/ her discipline, has produced 'nonsense'. (2006: 1095, 1097)

Contrasting Economics and Social Anthropology offers particular insights because they can be seen as being at opposite ends of a social science continuum (see Box 3.7) and have been the focus of an ongoing 'conversation' between anthropologists and economists (Bardhan, 1989). In spite of using the word 'conversation' Cosgel (2006) notes that the main problem would appear to be that economists and anthropologists do not talk to each other very much. Part of the evidence for this is the limited cross-citation between disciplines. Cosgel argues that this occurs because of methodological differences and also (and significantly) because of different behavioural assumptions and modes of inquiry.[8]

Many economists regard their research as being an objective search for simple, universal laws within a positivist approach. In contrast, many social anthropologists see their research as a subjective search for context-specific understandings of complexity within a more relativist approach.

In short, there are very real tensions between some disciplines which reinforce barriers and make cross-disciplinary collaboration difficult. Within DS this has especially been the case between Economics and other social sciences where tensions are palpable. Economists have often regarded their discipline as having a dominant and more rigorous position in development thinking and within development agencies in particular (Harriss, 2002; Kanbur, 2002, 2006; Loxley, 2004).[9] Woolcock (2007: 64) goes as far as to note 'there can be little doubt that, for better or worse, economics is the lingua franca of international development'.

Box 3.7 Conversations between Anthropologists and Economists

In Bardhan's edited collection (1989) the clash between the differing methodologies and interpretations of anthropologists and economists were explored. The aim was to learn from the toolkits, conceptual categories, and methods of inquiry of other disciplines. The entire collection discussed the strengths and weaknesses of alternative methods of measuring economic change, and was the continuation of a process started at a workshop held in 1985 entitled 'Rural Economic Change in South Asia: Differences in Approach and in Results between Large-Scale Surveys and Intensive Micro Studies' which sought to increase awareness of the limitations that the standard methods of the respective disciplines often imposed.

Bardhan, in introducing the text, argued some of the disputes between anthropologists and economists were insoluble. Debate has recently been re-ignited by a series of papers (Bardhan and Ray, 2006; Cosgel, 2006; Kanbur and Riles, 2006). However, almost two decades after the original publication, there has been only limited progress towards reconciliation due to what Bardhan and Ray term the three 'foundational dichotomies' between mainstream economists and social and cultural anthropologists. These are autonomy versus embeddedness; outcomes versus processes; and, parsimony versus complexity.

Economics has been accused of 'imperialist' tendencies not only in DS but across the social sciences as a whole (Fine, 2002) and it has been argued that the onus is on the economists to change (Bardhan and Ray, 2006: 2). As Kanbur notes:

> While the discipline of economics is unified (pretty much) by a single paradigm and method, 'non-economics' is not. Economics has been accused of 'imperialist' tendencies not only in DS but across the social sciences as a whole (Fine, 2002) and it has been argued that the onus is on the economists to change and accommodate non-economists (Bardhan and Ray, 2006: 2). And, within each of these disciplines one does not find the paradigmatic unity that there is in economics. At least in the context of development policy studies, what seems to unite these disciplines, and their sub-branches, is viewing themselves as an alternative paradigm to the economic method, each in its own different way. (2006: 9)

In this context, and given the expressed views of some non-economists working within DS, it is perhaps surprising that many of the fundamental advances over the last 40 years in the course of the evolution of DS into a form of cross-disciplinarity have been led (rather than resisted) by development economists. The work of Gunnar Myrdal, Amartya Sen, Dudley Seers, and Paul Streeten is perhaps particularly notable in this respect. Many of the criticisms of 'mainstream' economics have come from within the economics profession and notably from development economists, Sen's major work on 'Development as Freedom' (1999) and Toye's earlier contributions (1987 and 1993) being particularly notable in this regard. In this context it is, of course, necessary to distinguish between research papers and journal articles which can be regarded as representing the 'theoretical frontiers' of DS, and the content of entry-level (or even advanced) teaching texts.

Ultimately successful cross-disciplinarity may require relaxation of some of the assumptions which divide disciplines, or which restrain the development of what some would regard as a new discipline (rather than as a subject) such as DS. It has been argued that there is a risk of losing the intellectual strengths of individual disciplines within cross-disciplinary research through the weakening of assumptions. Harriss argues:

> 'Discipline' in research is productive.. ... But equally it is extremely important that academic disciplines, or the particular 'sets of rules' that predominate within any one of them ... ... are subject to critical scrutiny from other approaches ... ... there is a sense in which 'disciplines' need to be saved from themselves. (2002: 494)

It may be necessary to take small steps within a modest approach to these controversial issues. Kanbur argues (2002: 484) that, although genuine inter-disciplinarity may be worth striving for, it is possible that the best that can be hoped for is multidisciplinarity. It is necessary to distinguish between the positive contributions which each individual discipline brings to a research problem and the aspects of the research problem to which each discipline can offer only limited insights.

There are several stages in the process of fostering and encouraging interdisciplinarity and cross-disciplinarity. The first, an awareness and understanding stage,

---

Box 3.8   Myerson's 'Code of Practice' for Cross-disciplinary Research

The pre-requisites for productive cross-disciplinary research are;

- People should be disposed to communicate ideas, and this requires contexts within which it is safe and easy to do so.
- Ways of thinking which favour comparisons, which are relative in that sense, and are not necessarily relativistic.
- Creative forms of negation, which present new possibilities, or which supplement previous propositions.
- Active tolerance of difficult emotions involved in the exchange of ideas and opinions.

Source: Myerson (1994: 1515).

---

might involve each discipline learning and sharing the axioms of other disciplines. The second, a conceptualizing stage, taking a general or specific problem and deciding which disciplines are most relevant to the research question and establishing the basic assumptions of those disciplines about the nature of reality. What methodologies – overall research strategies and methods including individual data collection techniques – are commonly used in the disciplines which are being considered? Are there substantial areas of agreement about the similarities and complementarities between disciplines or are there outright conflicts? The third stage, a 'team stage', relates to the formation of an appropriate research team which depends upon multi-, inter-, or trans-disciplinarity, and involves a degree of relaxation of disciplinary assumptions and the matching of methods (these issues are discussed further in Chapter 5). The exploitation of complementarities between disciplines remains one of the most challenging areas for DS. Researchers need shared (but not identical) beliefs about reality, goals of enquiry and language, as well as mutual respect and 'space' within which a dialogue (or discourse) can take place. This involves issues of the process rather than of the content of research. Myerson suggests a code of practice for cross-disciplinary research which is summarized in Box 3.8.

3.5. SUMMARY

In this chapter we have addressed three areas:

3.5a. Knowledge and science

The question of what is knowledge and science have been a matter of some controversy. Positivism and Relativism are two (seemingly) opposing perspectives about what constitutes knowledge and science. A third approach, Realism, seeks to provide a middle ground. All three approaches include a variety of perspectives with significant diversity within each.

3.5b. Disciplinarity

Most of those involved in DS would probably not regard it as a discipline, and most also have their own home discipline – such as economics, sociology, political science or civil engineering. This implies that DS is an umbrella area of study – covering a range of disciplines – rather than being a discipline in itself. It can be suggested that a more appropriate conception of DS is as a 'subject'. Within cross-disciplinarity it is important to be clear about the distinction between multidisciplinary, interdisciplinary, and 'transdisciplinary' studies.

3.5c. Doing cross-disciplinary research in DS

Although contemporary DS draws on a full range of epistemological stances, there has been a distinct shift of emphasis from Positivism towards Relativism in recent years. If DS seeks to be cross-disciplinary it is necessary to recognize that different disciplines have quite different epistemologies. An overriding issue is the need for a rigorous approach in DS research and awareness of basic assumptions and what they include and exclude within the relevant disciplines. It can be argued that DS research seeks a level of probability rather than certainty, a level of subjectivity-awareness and control rather than absolute objectivity and approximate truth rather than 'totality'. Research outcomes in DS aim to make 'knowledge' claims without claiming absolute 'closure'.

NOTES

1   It is not that Eastern philosophy has not dealt with epistemology, but rather that the separation of philosophical endeavour from religious endeavour has only recently appeared in eastern philosophy (for further discussion see Collinson et al., 2000). One significant factor in the process of the dissemination of knowledge is the dominance of the English language initially as a by-product of British colonial history.
2   In short, for induction the starting point is evidence, and for deduction the starting point is theory.
3   The significance of Kuhn's work has been introduced in Section 2a of Chapter 2.
4   Kuhn later dropped the word 'paradigm' following criticism in favour of more restrictive terms. Masterman (1970) had noted that Kuhn's definition of a 'paradigm' had been defined or interpreted in 21 different ways, and argued that these could be reduced to three. He re-defined a paradigm as the '(world) vision' – the meta-physical view and its ontological foundations; the 'exemplar' – the model or 'vehicle' which is being pursued; and the 'body of professionals'.
5   It should be noted that John Maynard Keynes was particularly concerned, in developing his 'General Theory ...' with finding a theoretical basis for macroeconomic management which could sustain full employment of the labour force in industrialized countries. Equally, Roy Harrod and Evsey Domar were concerned with finding a theoretical basis for understanding the nature of economic cycles so that fluctuations of economic activity (levels of employment) could be avoided through more sophisticated macroeconomic management in industrialized countries. In the context of developing countries there are many economists – Gunnar Myrdal, Hans Singer, Dudley Seers, and even Ian Little are examples – who could be regarded as being concerned with honing theoretical approaches to the understanding of socio-economic development 'problems'.

6. While poverty is – for many in DS – the be all and end all of DS as we discussed in Chapter 1 there are broader definitions. That said one might argue that DS is very much concerned with standards of living and human conditions.
7. On the nature-society interface refer to Molteberg and Bergstrøm (2000) and Morton and Martin (2004).
8. One extensive study of 42 economics and 20 non-economics journals from 1995 to 1997 noted that there was some very limited cross-citation between economics and political science and sociology and that cross-citation between economics, anthropology and psychology was nil (Pieters and Baumgartner, 2002: 504).
9. Some economists might go so far as to suggest that economics should not be regarded as a social science in the same sense as the other disciplines included within Table 3.3 and in the discussion in this book. Evidence for the dominance of economics might be Broad's (2006) exploration of the World Bank's research department's activities over the last few years. Notably the Bank-initiated Global Development Network was 'dominated by the economics discipline' (Clift, 2002: 475).

REFERENCES

Amann, A., Aslanidis, N., Nixson, F. and Walters, B. (2006) 'Economic growth and poverty alleviation: A reconsideration of Dollar and Kraay', *European Journal of Development Research*, 18 (1): 22–44.

Bardhan, P. (1989) 'Introduction', in Bardhan, P. (ed.), Conversations Between Economists and Anthropologists: Methodological Issues in Measuring Economic Change in Rural India. Delhi: Oxford University Press. pp. 1–12.

Bardhan, P. and Ray, I. (2006) *Methodological Approaches in Economics and Anthropology*. Q-Squared Working Paper Number 17. Centre for International Studies, University of Toronto. Available at http://www.q-squared.ca (accessed 1 August 2006).

Bevan, P. (2006) *Researching Wellbeing Across the Disciplines: Some Key Intellectual Problems and Ways Forward*. Wellbeing in Developing Countries (WeD) Research Group Working Paper 25, University of Bath, Bath, UK.

Bohr, N. (1958) *Atomic Physics and Human Knowledge*. Chichester, UK: Wiley Interscience.

Brint, S. (2000) *The City of Intellect*. Stanford, MA: Stanford University Press.

Broad, R. (2006) 'Research, knowledge, and the art of 'paradigm maintenance': The World Bank's Development Economics Vice-Presidency (DEC)', *Review of International Political Economy*, 13 (3): 387–419.

Canning, J. (2005) 'Disciplinarity: a barrier to quality assurance? The UK experience of area studies', *Quality in Higher Education*, 11 (1): 37–46.

Chambers, R. (2005) 'Critical reflections of a development nomad', in U. Kothari (ed.), *A Radical History of Development Studies*. London: Zed Books.

Clift, C. (2002) Foreword to cross-disciplinarity in development research. *World Development*, 30 (3): 475–476.

Collinson, D. and Plant, K. (2006) *Fifty Major Philosophers*. London: Routledge.

Collinson, D., Plant, K. and Wilkinson, R. (2000) *Fifty Eastern Thinkers*. London: Routledge.

Cosgel, I. (2006). *Conversations between Anthropologists and Economists*. Q-Squared Working Paper Number 18. Centre for International Studies, University of Toronto. Available from http://www.q-squared.ca (accessed 1 August 2006).

Crotty, M. (2004). *Foundations of Social Research: Meaning and Perspective in the Research Process*. London: Sage.

Dollar, D. and Kraay, A. (2000) *Growth is Good for the Poor*. World Bank Policy Research Working Paper Number 2587. Washington: World Bank.

Dollar, D. and Kraay, A. (2001) *Growth is Good for the Poor*. World Bank Policy Research Working Paper Number 2587 (revised). Washington: World Bank.

Dollar, D. and Kraay, A. (2002) 'Growth is good for the poor', *Journal of Economic Growth*, 7: 195–225.

Dollar, D. and Kraay, A. (2004) 'Growth is good for the poor', in Shorrocks, A. and Van Der Hoeven, R. (eds), Growth, Inequality, and Poverty: Prospects for Pro-poor Economic Development. Oxford: Oxford University Press. pp. 62–80.

DSA (Development Studies Association, UK) (2004) *Unit of Assessment in the Research Assessment Exercise 2008 for Development Studies*. Available from www.devstud.org.uk/consultation.htm (accessed 1 August 2005).

Fine, B. (2002) 'Economics imperialism and the new development economics as Kuhnian paradigm shift?' *World Development*, 30 (12): 2057–2070.

Fuller, S. (2005) *Kuhn versus Popper: The Struggle for the Soul of Science*. Cambridge: Icon.

Gould, J. (2003) *The Hedgehog, the Fox and the Magister's Pox*. New York: Harmony Books.

Haddad, L., Rowsell, H., Gee, C., Lindstrom, J. and Bloom, M. (2006) *Mapping Development Research among UK Organizations and Their Partners*. Report To The ESRC. Sussex: IDS.

Harriss, J. (2002) 'The case for cross-disciplinary approaches in international development', *World Development*, 30 (12): 487–496.

Harriss, J. (2005). 'Great promise, hubris and recovery: a participant's history of development studies', in Kothari, U. (ed.) *A Radical History of Development Studies*. London: Zed Books.

Heisenberg, W. (1927) 'Über den anschaulichen Inhalt der quantentheoretischen Kinematik und Mechanik', *Zeitschrift für Physik*, 43: 172–198. (English translation: Wheeler, J.A. and Zurek, H. (1983) *Quantum Theory and Measurement*. New Haven, Conn: Princeton University Press.

Hulme, D. and Toye, J. (2006) 'The case for cross-disciplinary social science research on poverty, inequality and wellbeing', *Journal of Development Studies*, 42 (7): 1085–1107.

Jackson, C. (2002) 'Disciplining gender?' *World Development*, 30 (12): 497–509.

Kanbur, R. (2002) 'Economics, social science and development', *World Development*, 30 (12): 477–486.

Kanbur, R. (2006) *What's Social Policy Got To Do With Economic Growth?* Available from http://www.arts.cornell.edu/poverty/kanbur/ (accessed 1 August 2005).

Kanbur, R. and Riles, A. (2006) *And Never the Twain Shall Meet? An Exchange on the Strengths and Weaknesses of Anthropology and Economics in Analyzing the Commons*. Q-Squared Working Paper Number 22. Centre for International Studies, University of Toronto. Available from http://www.q-squared.ca (accessed 1 August 2006).

Kanbur, R. and Shaffer, P. (2005) *Epistemology, Normative Theory and Poverty Analysis: Implications for Q-Squared in Practice*. Available from http://people.cornell.edu/pages/sk145/papers.htm (accessed 1 August 2006).

Kuhn, T. (1962) *The Structure of Scientific Revolutions*. Chicago: University of Chicago Press.

Loxley, J. (2004) 'What is distinctive about international development studies?' *Canadian Journal of Development Studies*, 25 (1): 25–38.

Lyotard, J. (1984) *The Postmodern Condition*. Manchester, UK: Manchester University Press.

Masterman, M. (1970) 'The nature of a paradigm', in Lakatos, I. and Musgrave, A. (eds), *Criticism and the Growth of Knowledge*. Cambridge: Cambridge University Press.

McGregor, A. (2006) *Researching Wellbeing: From Concepts To Methodology*. Wellbeing in Developing Countries (WeD) Research Group Working Paper 20. Bath, UK: University of Bath.

Mehta, L., Haug, R. and Haddad, L. (2006) 'Reinventing development research', *Forum for Development Studies* 33 (1): 1–6.

Molteberg, E. and Bergstrøm, C. (2000) Our Common Discourse: Diversity and Paradigms in Development Studies. Centre for International Environment and Development Studies, Agricultural University of Norway (NORAGRIC) Working Paper Number 20. NORAGRIC: Ås, Norway.

Morton, J. and Martin, A. (2004) *Natural Resources Research and Development Studies*. Paper prepared for DSA Annual Conference. Church House, London, 6 November.

Myerson, G. (1994) *Rhetoric, Reason and Society: Rationality as Dialogue*. London: Sage.

Narayan, N., Patel, R., Schafft, K., Rachemacher, A. and Koch-Schulte, S. (2002) *Voices of the Poor: Can Anyone Hear us?* Washington, DC: World Bank.

Nye, H., Reddy, S. and Watkins, K. (2002) *Dollar and Kraay on 'Trade, Growth and Poverty: A Critique'*. Columbia University: Mimeograph.

Parfitt, T. (2002) *The End of Development: Modernity, Post-Modernity and Development*. London: Zed.

Pieters, F. and Baumgartner, H. (2002) Who talks to whom? Intra- and interdisciplinary communication of economics journals. *Journal of Economic Literature*, 40 (2): 483–509.

Plato (360 BCE) Theaetetus (translated by Benjamin Jowett). Available from http://classics.mit.edu/ Plato/theatu.html (accessed 7 November 2004).

Popper, K. (1968) *The Logic of Scientific Discovery*, 2nd ed. London: Hutchinson.

Rodrik, D. (2000) *Comments on "Trade, Growth, and Poverty,"* by D. Dollar and A. Kraay. Available from http://ksghome.harvard.edu/~drodrik

Rue, L. (1994) *By the Grace of Guile: The Role of Deception in Natural History and Human Affairs*. New York: Oxford University Press.

Sayer, A. (2000) *Realism and Social Science*. London: Sage.

Scheyvens, R. and Storey, D. (2003) *Development Fieldwork: A Practical Guide*. London: Sage.

Sen, A. (1980) *Famines. World Development*, 8 (9): 613–741.

Sen, A. (1982a) *Poverty and Famines: An Essay on Entitlement and Deprivation*. Oxford: Clarendon Press.

Sen, A. (1982b) *Choice, Welfare and Measurement*. Oxford: Blackwell.

Sen, A. (1984). *Resources, Values and Development*. Oxford: Blackwell.

Sen, A. (1999 and 2001) *Development as Freedom*. Oxford: Oxford University Press.

Spencer, L., Ritchie, J., Lewis, J. and Dillon, J. (2003) *Quality in Qualitative Evaluation: A Framework for Assessing Research Evidence*. London: Government Chief Social Researcher's Office.

Strober, M. (2006) 'Habits of the mind: challenges for multi-disciplinary engagement', *Social Epistemology*, 20 (4): 315–331.

Toye, J. (1987) *Dilemmas of Development: Reflections on the Counter-Revolution in Development Theory and Policy*. Oxford: Basil Blackwell.

Toye, J. (1993) *Dilemmas of Development. Reflections on the Counter-Revolution in Development Economics*. 2nd ed. Oxford: Basil Blackwell.

Tribe, M. and Sumner, A. (2004) *The Nature of Development Studies*. Paper prepared for the DSA Annual Conference, Church House, London, 6 November. Available from http://www.devstud.org.uk/conference/workshops/3.2-devstud.htm (20 June 2007).

Turner, S. (2000) 'What are disciplines? And how is interdisciplinarity different?' in Weingart, P. and Stehr, N. (eds), *Practicing Interdisciplinarity*. Toronto: University of Toronto Press.

Woolcock, M. (2007) 'Higher education, policy schools, and development studies: what should Masters degree students be taught?' *Journal of International Development*, 19: 55–73.

World Bank. (2000) *World Development Report 2000/2001: Attacking Poverty*. New York: Oxford University Press for the World Bank.

CHAPTER FOUR

WHAT IS THE 'BIG PICTURE' IN DEVELOPMENT STUDIES?

How can seemingly the same objective reality be interpreted so differently? ... ... at least some of the disagreement can be understood in terms of differences in perspective and framework. (Kanbur, 2001: 1084)

The business of social theorizing encompasses a wide variety of activities... ... theorizing can be understood to comprise complex 'package deals' which combine inter-linked claims in respect of the nature of the social world itself (ontology), [and] the nature of knowledge in respect of that social world which might be obtained (epistemology). (Preston, 1996: 5, 339–40)

For most of [development studies'] life, focus has been on building grand theories. In recent years, grand theory ambitions have largely been criticized and left... ... and attention is increasingly given to a more empirically grounded understanding of problems in view of their situation-specificity and complexity. Critical reflection on the development/modernization project continues to be a central activity... ... The objective of theory building is largely redefined from the promotion of development and growth to understanding processes of change and differentiation. (Molteberg and Bergstrøm, 2000: 6)

Much of the theory construction in development studies has been introduced with no explicit considerations concerning basic ontological, epistemological and methodological positions. I perceive this as a serious shortcoming. (Martinussen, 1997: 346)

4.1. INTRODUCTION

In this chapter we focus on what we call the 'big picture' in DS research. By the 'big picture' we mean theory in DS, which includes grand theory (meta-narratives) as well as 'context-specific' theory (micro-narratives), both of which can guide empirical research. It is through this approach that we address the elements of Bevan's (2004: 5; 2006) knowledge foundations which are related to theories, conceptual frameworks and models.

DS has it own indigenous theories but its cross-disciplinary nature means that much of the theory used by researchers is adopted and adapted from constituent disciplines within DS (within the context of Figures 3.1 and 3.2). It is not the objective of this chapter to review all available theories which have been formulated within DS or which are regularly used in DS research and writing. This is ground which has been well covered by Preston (1996), by Martinussen (1997), and more recently by Willis (2005), and we refer the reader to these texts. Rather, this chapter is concerned with discussion of the state of theory formation in DS and how researchers can draw upon existing bodies of theory, or approach the construction of innovative theoretical frameworks, for their own research.

In the first instance we again discuss the quotations which open the chapter in order to set the scene. These opening quotations are not by any means exhaustive of the relevant literature but we would argue that they are representative of the issues and concerns which arise in this context.

Theory has been, and remains, a major area of controversy for DS. Frameworks chosen for the study of development can be highly deterministic in terms of the kinds of conclusions that may be reached, or in terms of the kinds of conclusions that are ruled out from the outset. In fact, as Kanbur (2001: 1084) has noted, disagreements regarding development policy may themselves be predicated on 'differences in perspective and framework' (i.e. ways of seeing the world rather than reality itself).

Preston notes (1996: 5, 339–40) that 'the business of social theorizing encompasses a wide variety of activities' or 'package deals' that make a variety of assumptions relating to the theoretical framework within which inter-actions between the phenomena which are being researched take place. In recent years there has been little attempt to develop or adapt grand theories in DS, so Molteberg and Bergstrøm (2000: 6) note that 'attention is increasingly given to a more empirically grounded understanding of problems in view of their situation-specificity and complexity' – in other words greater attention has been paid to 'micro-theory' than to 'macro-theory'. Martinussen (1997: 346), has been very critical about theory formation in DS and particularly for the lack of self-awareness concerning 'basic ontological, epistemological and methodological positions'.

In this chapter we seek to encourage greater awareness of the underlying assumptions of DS theories and of their limitations and omissions.

In Section 2 we discuss the need for theory and the nature of theory. In Section 3 we discuss theory formation in DS. In Section 4 our concern is with frameworks for the guidance of development research. In Section 5 we summarize the chapter.

4.2. THE IMPORTANCE OF THE 'BIG PICTURE'

4.2a. Why do we need theory?

All theory consists of abstractions which are an essential aid to systematic thought and analysis of the phenomena which are being studied.[1] Theory is the framework or basis for the identification of the relevant data which needs to be collected for the analysis of the 'research problem', and for the organization and processing of this data.

Theory can provide the basis for claims to causation, explanation and predictions of future events which are essential elements of policy analysis and planning for development practitioners. Although there are disputes within and between intellectual disciplines about the nature of the theory which is most appropriate for the study of 'development', there should be no dispute about the need for theory as part of a systematic approach to study.

We need theories of development in order to obtain a better overall understanding of development and as a basis for specific pieces of research. We need theories to guide and to order empirical enquiry. Without theory research studies are likely to be highly descriptive with limited explanatory claims. Theory involves explicit statements about the simplifying assumptions which are a major part of the 'abstraction'. For example, research on poverty needs to take account of intra-household welfare distribution which is related to the gender and age factors which influence the distribution of consumption within the household. Any assumption that intra-household welfare distribution is independent of gender and age would defeat the objectives of research in this area. Another example in the context of poverty would be the assumption that an income-based, or economic, definition of poverty is a sufficient basis for research, with no regard for health, education and psychological issues for example. In the process of framing research it is necessary to be explicit about assumptions, and particularly about factors which have been excluded, so that researchers and the users of research output are made aware of the limitations and omissions of the research.

A theoretical framework is needed as a basis for the design of research instruments (such as questionnaires and interview schedules) because theory guides and structures the focus of observation of 'reality', and determines the priorities for data generation and collection. A good example of this issue would be the use of the sustainable livelihoods approach (which is outlined in Section 6.3c of Chapter 6) as a basis for an interview schedule which would have one section for each of the five forms of capital identified in this approach (human, social, natural, financial and productive). In this context theory provides the matrix defining the data needs of the research. Theory is also needed as a guide to the types of inter-relationships which will be explored in the process of analyzing data generated by the research study (an example of which is given by the Sustainable Livelihoods which is described in more detail in Chapter 6). In this way theory helps to generate research outcomes and conclusions through the provision of a basis for claims relating to causation and explanation. In this context theory provides a framework for the behavioural linkages between the data which have been collected.

4.2b. What exactly is theory?

There is an array of theories, conceptual and analytical frameworks and approaches within the constituent disciplines and subject areas of DS. Each has their own components, foci, emphases and limitations.

What is a theory? The word itself – theory – derives from the Greek word *theōría* meaning a 'viewing'. In short, a way of viewing the world. However, Preston (1996: 5) suggests that 'social theorizing' encompasses a 'wide variety of activities'. In her recent book on development theory and practice Willis (2005: 27) identifies 12 different main approaches to development which have been established since the 1950s. Approaches which feature strongly in her view of development theory include modernization, structuralist analysis, dependency theory, basic needs, neo-liberalism, and post-development (i.e. post-modernist theory). A critical view of Willis' useful classification would probably question the extent to which some of the 'approaches to development' (Willis, 2005: 27) are really theoretical in the sense used in our discussion in this chapter.

For example, the Lewis model of economic development with unlimited supplies of labour (which Willis includes quite legitimately as relating to structural change, but omitting the critical capital accumulation element – Willis, 2005: 42) is undoubtedly a development theory.[2] However, neo-liberalism and the debt crisis, which are discussed in the same chapter (Willis, 2005: 45–50), would not usually be regarded as part of the body of development theory. This raises the question of whether the development community, representing a number of constituent disciplines, has a coherent view of what represents 'development theory'.

There are development theories that have an unambiguously theoretical pedigree – such as Structuralism, Dependency and Modernization. These are theories which seek to be universal in application and are based on an understanding of a long-term development process (as we have discussed in Chapter 1 above). There are also 'approaches' which relate to specific aspects of development – such as grassroots development, social and cultural dimensions of development, but which many in the 'development community' would not regard as 'theories'. These tend to seek to be context specific in application and are based not on an overall conceptual framework of development but more on a prescriptive understanding of the processes of change and differentiation.

Neo-liberalism, for example, is one component of the (mainstream) economic theory of markets, but few would refer to it as a theory of development in the sense that it comprises an overall conceptualization of the development process. The differentiation between terms is something Martinussen (1997) has considered.

Martinussen (1997) identifies 21 substantive theoretical sub-groups in his wide-ranging discussion of development theories, but puts these into four categories covering theories that relate to:

- Economic development and underdevelopment
- Third World politics and the state
- The state and socio-economic development
- Civil society and the development process

Martinussen (1997: 14–15) differentiates between a development theory, a development concept and a development strategy. He argues that confusion between these three elements has hindered theoretical progress in DS. A *development theory* is a hypothesis about promoting and obstructing conditions to development.[3] A *development concept* is a development objective. A *development strategy* is a set of actions and interventions to promote development. According to Martinussen, a *development theory* typically has a *development concept* and a *development strategy* associated with it. In this approach Structuralism is a theory of development, as is the Lewis model of economic growth with unlimited supplies of labour, while neo-liberalism is a *strategy* rather than a *theory*.

Following Martinussen's approach, and adapting it to encompass both normative and positive views of development, it is possible to identify a simpler and more basic difference between two *types* of *theory* in DS. These consist of 'grand' theory (the big picture) and 'context-specific' theory (instrumental approaches to the study of the 'micro' picture). An example of the former is Structuralism.[4] An example of the latter is the Sustainable Livelihoods Approach. The purpose of grand theories of development such as Structuralism is to theorize about how societies change in the long term. In contrast, the purpose of context-specific theories of development is to guide empirical enquiry and policy analysis.

Development *theories* which can be referred to as 'grand' theories might also be called 'general' theories or 'meta-narratives'. These development theories relate to the 'big picture', which features in the title of this chapter, and they are concerned with major socio-economic changes such as changes in economic production systems, income distribution, demographic dynamics and social structure. There are also 'context-specific' theories, which might also be thought of as 'micro picture' theories, that guide empirical work and seek to understand the process of change and differentiation (such as the Sustainable Livelihoods Approach). These are development theories which guide, for example, the design, implementation and analysis of household surveys or of policy interventions (such as in the agricultural or education sectors). Following Martinussen's taxonomy of *development theory* these theoretical frameworks may contain a *development concept* within their specification and may or may not include a *development strategy*.

A grand or general theory (or 'meta-narrative') can be said to be a description and explanation which relates to a particular 'world view'. In contrast, a context-specific theory is a somewhat more humble specification of the object under study in any particular piece of research. For Miles and Huberman the context-specific framework

> explains... ... the main things to be studied – the key factors, constructs or variables – and the presumed relationships among them. (1994: 18)

Bevan (2004: 10) has a more sophisticated outline which is summarized in Box 4.1. She identifies four components of theories. These are 'anatomy', 'physiology', 'dynamics' and 'histories'. The former two, anatomy and physiology, are synchronic (meaning that time is abstract) and the latter two, dynamics and histories, are diachronic (meaning that time is taken account of explicitly). For Bevan there is the 'real' – the structure and powers of objects – which is captured in the 'anatomy', 'physiology' and 'dynamics' but there is also the 'actual' which is to be captured in the 'history' – what happens – if and when powers are activated. These issues are directly relevant to our later discussion regarding researchers constructing their own framework (see Section 4.4b).

Box 4.1   Bevan's 'Anatomy', 'Physiology', 'Dynamics' and 'Histories'

The anatomy
   What are the components of the phenomenon and the structural relationships between them?
The physiology
   What are the relationships, processes and activities, which, other things being equal, maintain this system?
The (social) dynamics
   What are the stability and change processes? What factors account for the equilibria, shocks, rhythms, spirals, vicious and virtuous circles, ratchets, bifurcations, etc.?
The histories
   What actually happened in this specific instance as a result of the context, the actions and interactions of protagonists, and the mechanisms and processes at work and their consequences?

Source: Bevan (2004: 10).

To summarize, in DS there are general theories of development which aim to provide a 'world view', and there are context-specific theories which aim to provide a deeper understanding of a small piece of the world that is the focus of specific research of a more 'micro' nature.

Different theoretical frameworks capture and miss different things. For example, different frameworks identify different people as 'poor' because they have differing perspectives and definitions of poverty and wellbeing. As Laderchi et al. (2003: 243) put it in this context, although it is agreed that poverty consists of deprivation, there is less agreement about the form of deprivation (deprived of what?), the extent of deprivation (how much?) and the differential impact of deprivation (who is deprived?). The important point is that all theory is an abstraction.[5] Theory is based on simplifying assumptions which make an understanding of the phenomena which are being studied possible within the complexities of the world. However, it is essential to be aware of the assumptions which have been adopted within theoretical approaches and what they exclude. There is, of course, a danger that in 'bad theory' assumptions might rule out characteristics which are central to the situation which is the subject of the research. A theory might include assumptions about:

- the nature, definition or objectives of development;
- ontology and the nature of reality;
- epistemology and what can be known;
- the processes or outcomes which affect the subject of the research;
- the appropriate level of analysis (research at the macro level might overlook crucial issues at the micro level, or vice versa – and there are also meso levels)[6];
- the nature of human beings and their behaviour;
- the level of applicability or universality of the theory.

Theory formation in DS has been criticized by Martinussen (amongst others) for not being sufficiently fully aware, or for not fully taking account, of the implications of assumptions (explicit or implicit) which have been made.

4.3. THEORY FORMATION IN DS

4.3a. The current state of theory in DS

From the 1950s to the 1980s there was, unequivocally, a body of development theory (Corbridge, 1995; Preston, 1996). Development was typically defined as long-run structural societal change with a significant interventionist role given to the state. Grand theories and meta-narratives (such as Structuralism) were thought to be useful to understand, explain and facilitate the transformations which were envisaged within the development process.

However, during the 1980s, there was a disputed impasse in development theory which has been described as a stalemate between modernization and underdevelopment theories (Schuurman, 1993: 1). The impasse was, and still is, seen as a 'landmark' in the teaching of DS but its existence is disputed and it is argued that discussion of an impasse has simply disguised the revival of modernization theories (Munck, 1999: 196).

The disputed impasse was partly triggered by critiques of DS. Booth's (1985) seminal critique of development theory was a damning attack on theory formation in DS with particular reference to Marxist and neo-Marxist theory. It centred on the proposition that development theory was out of touch with reality, lacking in usefulness and theoretically flawed. Booth called for a return to comparative empirical case studies. Edwards' (1989) later critique of the irrelevance of DS (which in many respects came to the same conclusions as Booth) was influential in terms of the shift within DS from an approach which emphasized grand or high theory to one driven by a more instrumental or context-specific approach.

Development theory was also undermined during the 1970s and 1980s by significant global changes. Not only did the rise of the Newly Industrialized Countries change the balance of global economic power but the end of the Cold War in 1989, with the addition of 'transition economies' in Central and Eastern Europe, and in Central, Eastern and South East Asia, challenged the coherence of the 'Third World' category and thus the subject matter of significant areas of development theory. Modernization theories were criticized for their overriding belief in a linear, common path to development through economic growth and industrialization, especially as the environmental impacts of industrialization became more evident. There were also criticisms of a perceived over-emphasis on the 'macro' to the neglect of the 'micro' (especially intra-household social and economic relations) and meso (intermediate levels of analysis) and for the lack of empiricism and rigour (particularly testability and refutability). A detailed discussion of these issues can be found in the edited collection of Schuurman (1993).

Box 4.2   Martinussen's 'Minimum Requirements of a Good Social Science Theory'

A good theory should:

- explicitly state its ontological and epistemological basis (the fundamental conceptions of reality, of the nature of society, and how this reality can be analyzed and
comprehended);
- explicitly state its normative premises and the political priorities embodied in the
theory;
- explicitly state its sphere of applicability, or the circumstances under which it is
assumed to be valid or invalid;
- be logical consistent – concepts and theoretical propositions elaborated within the
theoretical framework should be compatible with the basic assumptions;
- be able to survive falsification tests relative to 'reality', while at the same time main-
taining the integrity of the abstract theory elements.

Source: Martinussen (1997: 346)

As noted previously in this chapter, Martinussen has been particularly critical of
theory formation in DS. He identified a list of 'minimum requirements of a good
social science theory' (Box 4.2) and argued that theory has been too broad, too aggregate,
and has placed too much emphasis on macro-phenomena, economic conditions and
either external or internal relations, to the exclusion of analysis which bridges or
combines both external and internal relations. In essence the problem identified by
Martinussen amounts to one of insufficient reflection about the significance of
assumptions in development theory, as his 'minimum requirements' emphasize.

There have been numerous 'post-impasse' theoretical contributions covering sustainability, gender and culture dimensions in particular within the development
context. The edited collection of Munck and O'Hearn (1999) contains a number of
contributions relating to these issues, tending to emphasize not so much grand theory
but more context-specific theory leading Molteberg and Bergstrøm (2000: 6) to suggest that 'the objective of theory building is largely redefined from the promotion of
development and growth to understanding processes of change and differentiation'.

4.3b. Cross-disciplinarity and theory in DS

If development is a multi-dimensional phenomenon, with development analysis
requiring inputs from disciplines covering, for example, social, economic, political and
cultural dimensions, then the analysis entails drawing on social theory, economic
theory, political theory and cultural theory as well as on a broader, multi-disciplinary,
development theory which links or transcends (particularly in the case of the trans-
disciplinary approach) individual disciplines and context-specific (or 'micro') theory.

Different disciplines can throw light on different dimensions of the same socio-economic phenomena, but there is no guarantee that they will complement each other.
For example, economic theory can be used for analysis of the relationship between
economic growth and income inequality. Kuznets (1955, 1963, 1971, 1979) implied

that income inequality is good for growth because it encourages the movement of labour from low wage, low productivity agriculture to higher wage, higher productivity non-agricultural sectors. In contrast social and political theories have suggested the opposite: that income inequality creates socio-political instability and thus reduces investment and hence future economic growth (Alesina and Perotti, 1996), or that in unequal societies there is a high density of credit-constrained people and thus less investment and economic growth, or that unequal societies create redistributive pressures leading to distortionary fiscal policy that reduces future growth (Rehme, 2001).

Because each constituent discipline of DS has its own body of theory, each with distinctive assumptions, there is a possibility that the respective assumptions may be mutually inconsistent. This makes awareness of the assumptions associated with theories within different disciplines even more critical if potential inconsistencies are to be highlighted and adequately dealt with. This consistency exercise is an essential part of the understanding of how DS research can achieve rigour and high standards of quality. This requires more self-awareness than might be apparent at first.

How should we view assumptions? Musgrave (1981, 1993) identified three types: negligibility, domain and heuristic assumptions (Box 4.3). They relate, respectively, to i) factors thought to be of no importance in a certain situation such as the assumption that individual product and factor markets are homogeneous and non-segmented within Economics; ii) factors which are only relevant under certain conditions such as the assumptions of ceteris paribus or of a closed economy with no international transactions in Economics; and iii) factors which are 'stepping stones' to theories and which facilitate the development of further thought such as the assumption that producers and consumers are 'maximizers' in much of neo-classical Economic theory. Other assumptions might relate to ontological and epistemological issues related to the fundamental conceptions of reality, of the nature of society, and how this reality can be analyzed and comprehended.

Another important issue is represented by the fact that many development researchers work in languages or dialects which are not their native language so that received and intended meanings may differ. Much can be lost before, during or after translation, and some theoretical terms may not translate 'neatly' into other languages or

---

Box 4.3 Typology of Assumptions

Negligibility assumptions:
  Some factors are of no importance in certain situations.
Domain assumptions:
  A theory is only relevant under certain assumed conditions.
Heuristic assumptions:
  Assumptions known to be false but used as 'stepping stones' to a theory which aids understanding.

Source: Musgrave (1981: 377)

---

dialects. Some words and concepts may not even exist in other languages and cultures, or they may exist in a fuzzy or an ambiguous way in other languages (further discussion occurs in Section 5.4b of Chapter 5).[7]

Theoretical assumptions differ between disciplines, and it is necessary to be aware that these differences are central to disciplinary tensions within the multi-, inter- and trans-disciplinarity of DS. The dialogue *Conversations between Economists and Anthropologists*, which has been referred to in Chapter 3 above, is of interest because Economics and Anthropology are often seen as extremes on the social science continuum in terms of theorizing and assumptions (as well as in terms of methodology and methods). For example, in Economic theory building the stylized tendency is a search for simplicity/parsimony, universal laws and abstract models. In Social Anthropology the stylized tendency is a search for complexity, local or context specificity and plurality of motives/objectives.

In Economic theory there is a common assumption that individuals are rational and that they aim to maximize utility (which can be read as maximizing their happiness) and that their behaviour and preferences are shaped exogenously (i.e. from outside the system under analysis). This assumption is sometimes referred to as 'autonomous agency'. In Social Anthropology theory a common assumption is that an individual's behaviour is shaped by the context ('embedded agency') within which they are viewed so that a holistic approach which understands people's actions and relationships within their cultural context is needed.

As Booth et al. sum up:

> What distinguishes the anthropological approach is sustained attention to both subtleties of meaning and belief (the emic) and patterns of observed behaviour and events (the etic)... [and] interpreting the frequently contradictory relationship between these two dimensions of social experience... ... Emic and etic are roughly translated as the actor's as against the observer's perspective respectively. (2006: 2)

In mainstream Economics the basic assumptions about the nature of human beings' behaviour lead to theories which focus on the behaviour of, and interaction between, individuals with other variables being exogenous and independent of the individual and group interactions which are the focus of the analysis. Often the focus is on market mechanisms, and particularly those of competitive markets, to the exclusion of other institutional structures (which may be equally as common as competitive markets). In contrast, in Social Anthropology the focus is more likely to be on the behaviour of and interaction of groups with groups and other variables are determined endogenously by the context. The focus may well be on non-market mechanisms.

It would be possible to argue that Economics could benefit from the contextualization of Anthropology, and that Anthropology could benefit from the generalizability of Economics. Bardhan and Ray observe that 'while anthropologists are better at telling us how a variable mattered to the outcomes, economists are better at measuring how much it mattered' (2006: 7).

In short, these opposing views apply not only to the very building blocks of behavioural theory – the nature of human beings – but also to what theory can hope to be applied to in an empirical context – universal or local specific. In Chapter 5 we will return to the issue of securing 'negotiation' between the methodologies, theoretical assumptions, and research methods of constituent disciplines within DS (refer to Sections 5.3a and 5.3b of Chapter 5).

4.4. CONSTRUCTING FRAMEWORKS FOR DEVELOPMENT RESEARCH

4.4a. The role of frameworks

The discussion in this chapter is intended to explore the intellectual basis for theoretical approaches adopted in DS research and writing, rather than to outline and compare development theories themselves. In the process of exploring the foundations of theory, and of theory used in DS research in particular, we now need to set out the relationship between theory and the direction of logic or of causation – which amounts to discussing the nature of 'inference'. It should be borne in mind that in most cases DS researchers will use existing bodies of theory, largely borrowed and adapted from the disciplines associated with DS.

There are differing perspectives on 'inference'. For Socrates, Plato and Aristotle, as was outlined in Section 3.2a of Chapter 3, the foundation of knowledge was through inductive inference (drawing generalizations – i.e. making theory – from evidence). However, for Galileo, Hobbes and Descartes the foundation of knowledge was through deductive inference (using theory as a basis for making generalizations and as a basis for collecting evidence).

Box 4.4 explains the range of bases for logical inference which include induction and deduction as well as retroduction and abduction. One or more of these might be combined in a research study as a whole (which would be known as an interductive approach). The approach which is actually taken would usually depend upon the researcher's home

---

Box 4.4   Theory and the Direction or Logic of Enquiry

Induction: This approach 'begins with singular or particular statements and concludes with a general or universal statement'.

Deduction: This approach is that '(r)ather than scientists waiting for nature to reveal its regularities, they must impose regularities (deductive theories) on the world and, by a process of trial and error, use observation to try to reject false theories'.

Retroduction: This is 'the process of building models of structures and mechanisms'.

Abduction: This 'is the process used to produce social scientific accounts of social life by drawing on the concepts and meanings used by social actors, and the activities in which they engage'.

Source: Blaikie (1993: 132, 95, 176, 168).

---

discipline. Economics and Politics are – very generally – associated with deduction and induction, whilst Sociology is often – very generally – associated with retroduction and Social Anthropology is – very generally – associated with abduction.

How should one choose between these alternative approaches? One might ask, as Brannen does, the question:

> is the study primarily to be inductive aimed at discovery? Or is it to be deductive aimed at testing hypotheses? Many projects seek to combine inductive and deductive logics of enquiry. (2005: 13–14)

We might wish to be inductive, starting with data collection, with the analysis deriving universal statements about relationships in the form of theory. The research question might then ask what the data tells us about the nature of, and the internal interrelationships within, the subject of the research. Alternatively, one might wish to be deductive, taking an existing theory and using it to determine the data which need to be collected, and then for testing the theory on the basis of the data which have been collected. In the first approach – inductive – data collection precedes theory formation, and in the second approach – deductive – theory comes before data collection.

An alternative approach is that of abduction which is based on the Relativist tradition (refer to Section 3.2b of Chapter 3). This takes the data collected and interprets the significance of actors' (i.e. the subjects of the research) 'meaning' from the data in a new way, through the development of new conceptual frameworks. Further, one might adopt retroduction, which is theory building through the analysis of the data collected during research and asking what qualities must exist for the data which have been collected to exist in the first place.

In sum, there are several approaches to inference. The 'logic of enquiry' drives the study and implies how and when the research tackles theory. An interesting, and suggestive, approach to the significance of inference in research is given in an example presented by Easlea (1973: 13). He explains how it was possible to use the physical laws and mathematical logic of Newtonian theory to predict the location of unknown planets prior to visual verification. In other words the theory preceded and informed the observation.

4.4b. Constructing your own framework

Most researchers and writers working in DS are concerned with the use of theories (both grand – the big picture – and context specific) which are already well established in the literature. Examples of these might be the Lewis model of economic development with unlimited supplies of labour (within economics), modernization theory (within politics), or alternatively Sustainable Livelihoods or Human Development (more within DS in a cross-disciplinary context). However many researchers, and particularly those who are notably more adventurous, might wish to combine the insights of several theories (Preston's 'package deals' discussed in the introductory section to this chapter) or even to try to develop an innovatory theoretical framework as a basis for answering their research questions and achieving research objectives. Box 4.5 attempts to set out the basic issues associated with the building of a theoretical framework – in response to the question 'what does a theoretical framework consist of?' Perhaps it will aid clarity if the answer to the question is broken down into four areas:

- *The basic concepts* – what concepts need to be included in the theory?
- *The underlying assumptions* – what are the basic assumptions of the theory, for example regarding the nature of reality, what we can know and the behaviour of human beings?
- *The general characteristics of the theory* – what are the functions, purposes and foci of the theory?
- *The consistency of the theory* – what is the logical consistency of the theory and how is it to be tested?

Box 4.5 Checklist for Building a Theoretical Framework

Basic concepts

- What are the key factors, constructs or variables of the study?
- What are the presumed relationships between the key factors, constructs or variables of the study?

Underlying assumptions

- What are the fundamental assumptions about reality?
- What are the assumptions about the extent to which we can 'know' this reality?
- What are the assumptions about the nature of human beings and their behaviour?
- What is our 'positionality', our normative premises and our political priorities?*
- What is the overall conceptualization of development in the study?

General characteristics of the theory

- What exactly is to be observed in the study?
- How do we take account of the context?
- What is the theoretical logic – the inference – of the study?
- What unit of analysis or combination of units of analysis should be taken – country, regional, community, household or intra-household levels?
- What are the assumptions relating to the level of applicability or universality of the theory?

Consistency of the theory

- Is it possible to submit the propositions regarding reality to falsification tests?
- Is there a logical consistency between all of the assumptions within the framework?
- What are the limitations of the theory and are they significant with respect to the answering of the research questions?

* On positionality, ethics and normative premises see the discussion in Section 2.4 of Chapter 2.

The *basic concepts* relate to Bevan's anatomy and physiology and are discussed in Box 4.4. It would be possible to make a list of the phenomena associated with the research question. Then the relationships between these phenomena can be specified and represented systematically (for example in a diagram) for ease of understanding, reflection and analysis. As a result of this 'mapping' it will be possible to reflect on the *underlying assumptions* of the approach. These *underlying assumptions* might be understood by considering several questions relating to reality, knowledge, human beings' behaviour, 'positionality' and the framework within which development is conceptualized (refer to Box 4.5).

The general characteristics of the theory can then be elaborated through responses to a few more questions regarding what exactly is to be observed, the context, the theoretical logic, the units of analysis and the applicability/universality of validity of the theory.

Finally, *the consistency of the theory* can be evaluated by asking questions regarding the testing of the theory for its internal logical consistency and for an assessment of its limitations and omissions.

4.5. SUMMARY

In this chapter we have addressed three areas:

4.5a. The importance of the 'big picture'

All theory consists of abstractions which are an essential aid to systematic thought and for analysis of the phenomena which are being studied. Although there are disputes within and between intellectual disciplines about the nature of the theory which is most appropriate to the study of development there should be no dispute about the need for theory as part of a systematic approach to study. We need theories of development in order to gain a better understanding of the phenomenon of development overall and also as a guide for specific pieces of research.

4.5b. Theory formation in DS

There are – broadly – two *types* of *theory* in DS. The first are 'grand' theories or 'meta-narratives'. These are theories regarding development overall – i.e. the 'big picture'. The second are 'context-specific' theories which are relevant at levels below the meta-narrative and which are theories for the guidance of empirical research. Assumptions are a necessary part of the process of abstraction (simplification of 'reality') so that the essence of the issues being addressed can be understood more clearly, and which are needed as a basis for theoretical constructs. Awareness of these assumptions is central to an understanding of the extent to which research is rigorous, bias has been avoided, and an appreciation of the limitations of a piece of research.

4.5c. Frameworks for development research

If development includes social, economic, political and cultural elements it is necessary to draw upon social theory, economic theory, political theory and cultural theory. Theories exist within constituent disciplines of DS which can be 'imported' and used in standalone or cross-disciplinary research. For many researchers the insights from several disciplines and theories are likely to be combined (i.e. 'package deals') into innovatory theoretical frameworks appropriate to the research questions which are being addressed. This requires careful reflection about the underlying assumptions on which theories have been based.

NOTES

1 'Abstractions' are usually described as being 'from reality'. However, given the view of post-modernists or constructivists that no single reality exists, it is perhaps best to leave the word 'reality' unqualified in this context.

2 We should note that Krugman (1995) disputes the value of the Lewis model, although most development economists would probably not agree with his arguments (Ghosh, 2007).

3 If a development theory 'is a hypothesis about promoting and obstructing conditions to development' (Martinussen, 1997: 14–15) this implies a normative definition of development rather than a positive definition. The promotion or obstruction of development must be associated with a normative view of what development consists of (i.e. development objectives – such as the Millennium Development Goals). A more objective view of development would emphasize structural change but without the imposition of value judgements about what is 'good' development and what is 'bad' development.

4 In Sociology and in Anthropology 'structuralism' relates to theoretical approaches which emphasize the importance of the characteristics of socio-economic structures in determining the behaviour of individuals and of societies. In Economics 'structuralism' relates to a methodological approach which is not based principally on neo-classical theory. Neo-classical theory is mainly focused on micro-economics and depends largely on marginal analysis – i.e. small changes in variables based on an existing set of relative prices – and is essentially 'institution-free' and 'universalistic'. Structuralist analysis explicitly recognizes the significance of major changes in, and differences between the structures of, economies which are largely absent from neo-classical analysis. Examples of such changes, and differences, include sectoral balances, e.g. agriculture and industry; relationships with the international economy, e.g. higher or lower dependence in international trade; and major institutional features, e.g. higher or lower significance of transnational corporations. While neo-classical economics tends to neglect the significance of market failure and of external economies in particular, economic structuralism emphasizes them.

5 Footnote 1 refers to the issue of 'abstraction'.

6 The 'macro' is not necessarily the national level and the 'micro' is not necessarily the lowest level. In different countries, with diverse administrative structures state, and non-state actors may mediate between the macro and micro levels and also meso levels (intermediate levels such as gender).

7 As an example of this, one of the authors was recently undertaking a training assignment in Albania relating to policy formulation. The Albanian language is essentially in the Germanic group, and it appears that this group of languages does not include the subtle distinction between 'policy' and 'politics' which exists in Anglophone languages. In an Anglophone context 'policy' can be related to a set of objectives and the means for achievement of these objectives, while 'politics' consists of the process (interactions between politicians, interest groups and political institutions) through which policy objectives are achieved. The online Oxford dictionary defines 'policy' as 'a course or principle of action adopted or proposed by

an organization or individual' or 'prudent or expedient conduct or action', and 'politics' as 'the activities associated with governing a country or area, and with the political relations between states; or a particular set of political beliefs or principles; or activities aimed at gaining power within an organization; or the principles relating to or inherent in a sphere or activity, especially when concerned with power and status' (Oxford, 2007).

REFERENCES

Alesina, A. and Perotti, R. (1996) 'Income distribution, political instability and investment', *European Economic Review*, 40: 1203–1228.

Bardhan, P. and Ray, I. (2006) *Methodological Approaches in Economics and Anthropology*. Q-Squared Working Paper Number 17. Centre for International Studies, University of Toronto. Available from http://www.q-squared.ca (accessed 1 August 2006).

Bevan, P. (2004) *Studying Poverty and Inequality in Poor Countries: Getting to Grips with Structure. Mimeograph.* Department of Economics and International Development, University of Bath, UK.

Bevan, P. (2006) *Researching Wellbeing Across the Disciplines: Some Key Intellectual Problems and Ways Forward*. Wellbeing in Developing Countries (WeD) Research Group Working Paper 25. Bath, UK: WeD.

Blaikie, P. (1993) *Approaches to Social Enquiry*. Cambridge, UK: Polity Press.

Booth, D. (1985) 'Marxism and development sociology: interpreting the impasse', *World Development*, 13 (7): 761–787.

Booth, D., Leach, M. and Tierney, A. (2006) *Experiencing Poverty in Africa: Perspectives from Anthropology*. Q-Squared Working Paper Number 25. Centre for International Studies, University of Toronto. Available from http://www.q-squared.ca (accessed 1 August 2006).

Brannen, J. (2005) *Mixed Methods Research: a Discussion Paper*. ESRC National Centre for Research Methods Review Paper. Available from http://www.ncrm.ac.uk

Corbridge, S. (ed.) (1995) *Development Studies a Reader*. London: Arnold.

Easlea, B. (1973) *Liberation and the Aims of Science*. Brighton: Sussex University Press.

Edwards, M. (1989) 'The irrelevance of development studies', *Third World Quarterly*, 11 (1): 116–135.

Ghosh, D. (2007) 'The metamorphosis of Lewis's dual economy model', *Journal of Economic Methodology*, 14 (1): 5–25.

Kanbur, R. (2001) 'Economic policy, distribution and poverty: the nature of disagreements', *World Development*, 29 (6): 1083–1094.

Krugman, P. (1995) *Development, Geography and Economic Theory*. Cambridge, Mass: MIT Press.

Kuznets, S. (1955) 'Economic growth and income inequality', *American Economic Review*, 45 (1): 1–28.

Kuznets, S. (1963) 'Quantitative aspects of the economic growth of nations: VIII, Distribution and income by size', *Economic Development and Cultural Change*, 11 (2): 1–80.

Kuznets, S. (1971) *Economic Growth of Nations: Total Output and Production Structure*. Cambridge, Mass: The Belknap Press of Harvard University Press.

Kuznets, S. (1979) *Growth, Population and Income Distribution: Selected Essays*. New York: W.W. Norton.

Laderchi, C.R., Saith, R. and Stewart, F. (2003) 'Does it matter that we don't agree on the definition of poverty? A comparison of four approaches', *Oxford Development Studies* 31 (3): 243–274.

Martinussen, J. (1997) *Society, State and Market: A Guide to Competing Theories of Development*. London: Zed Books.

Miles, M. and Huberman, A. (1994) *Qualitative Data Analysis*. London: Sage.

Molteberg, E. and Bergstrøm, C. (2000) *Our Common Discourse: Diversity and Paradigms in Development Studies*. Centre for International Environment and Development Studies, Agricultural University of Norway (NORAGRIC) Working Paper Number 20. Ås, Norway: NORAGRIC.

Munck, R. (1999) 'Deconstructing development discourses: of impasses, alternatives and politics', in Munck, R. and O'Hearn, D. (eds), *Critical Development Theory: Contributions to a New Paradigm*. London: Zed Books.

Munck, R. and O'Hearn, D. (eds) (1999) *Critical Development Theory: Contributions to a New Paradigm.* London: Zed Books.

Musgrave, A. (1981) 'Unrealistic assumptions in economic theory: the F-twist untwisted', *Kyklos,* 34: 377–387.

Musgrave, A. (1993) *Common Sense, Science and Scepticism: A Historical Introduction to the Theory of Knowledge.* Cambridge.: Cambridge University Press.

Oxford. (2007) AskOxford.com – Online Dictionary. Available from http://www.askoxford.com/ concise_oed/ (accessed 18 May 2007).

Preston, P. (1996) *Development Theory: An Introduction.* Oxford: Blackwell.

Rehme, G. (2001) *Redistribution of Personal Income, Education and Economic Performance Across Countries.* Darmstadt, Germany: Mimeograph. Technische Universitat Darmstadt.

Schuurman, F. (ed.) (1993) *Beyond the Impasse: New Directions in Development Theory.* London: Zed Books.

Willis, K. (2005) *Theories and Practices of Development.* London: Routledge.

CHAPTER FIVE

WHAT IS 'RIGOUR' IN DEVELOPMENT STUDIES?

Looking at a mountain from the North or from the East may lead two painters to draw very different pictures. People watching their paintings side by side might believe they represent two different mountains. Yet, they will not be surprised to discover that the name of the mountain written below each frame is the same. What is more, they will even be able to figure out immediately the true shape of the mountain in a 3-D setting. (Bourguignon, 2003: 44)

The desirability and usefulness to combine qualitative and quantitative methods to analyze social realities is pretty much accepted in the literature today; voices of segregation – still quite powerful in the 1980s – have subsided notably. (Hentschel, 2003: 75)

Mixed methods research means adopting a research strategy employing more than one type of research *method*. The methods may be a mix of qualitative and quantitative methods, a mix of quantitative methods or a mix of qualitative methods... ... Mixed methods research also means working with different *types of data*. It may also involve using *different investigators* – sometimes different research teams working in different research paradigms. (Brannen, 2005: 4)

Most of the criteria developed for evaluating the quality of research are rooted in the quantitative tradition and focus on reliability, replicability and validity... ... their application [to qualitative research] involves some redefinition of the terms. (Boaz and Ashby, 2003: 7)

The real basis for 'rigour' is the proper application of techniques. Badly or misleadingly applied, both quantitative and qualitatively techniques give bad or misleading conclusions... ... different techniques are appropriate to different settings... ... combining quantitative and qualitative work can strengthen both. (White, 2002: 512)

5.1. INTRODUCTION

In this chapter we focus on the process of doing research. We consider methodology, methods and what constitutes a rigorous approach to development research. In terms of Bevan's (2006: 5) knowledge foundations, which have been referred to in previous chapters, the elements relevant for this chapter relate to the foundations of research strategies and to empirical conclusions. These are areas of particular complexity for

DS research because of the cross-disciplinary nature of DS and the fact that DS draws on methodologies, methods and techniques from a range of constituent disciplines. Further, because DS research is often in areas with a strong policy- and practice-related dimension, with associated layers of potential and actual value judgements, there are important issues relating to rigour, subjectivity and the demarcation of acceptable biases.

It is not the objective of this chapter to undertake an in-depth review of all methodologies, methods and techniques used in DS research. The recent publications by Laws et al. (2003) and Mikkelsen (2005), and the edited collections of Desai and Potter (2006) and Scheyvens and Storey (2003), have covered this ground well.[1] Our particular concerns in this chapter are to discuss issues relating to the mixing of methods and approaches from different disciplines and to the nature of 'rigour' in DS research.

DS research combines methods and methodologies derived from constituent disciplines, which makes Bourguignon's (2003: 44) observation of the mountain from both (or even all) sides very relevant, and which represents a strength of DS. The combination of a range of methodologies and methods is, as Hentschel (2003: 75) puts it, 'pretty much accepted'. However, this type of combination is, in practice, a complex affair, and it can lead to a bewildering number of combinations. Brannen (2005: 4) observes that 'employing more than one type of research method' as well as 'working with different types of data' with 'different investigators – sometimes different research teams working in different research paradigms' requires a special type of attention to potential inconsistencies and methodological clashes.

Although the desirability of mixed methods may be accepted, the same cannot be said of how to judge the rigour or quality of the combined approach. Different constituent disciplines of DS have differing conceptualizations of rigour and quality in research. Typically validity, reliability, replicability and generalizability are the principal means for the evaluation of social research. However, in considering these means Boaz and Ashby (2003: 7) – amongst others – argue that 'their application [to qualitative research] involves some redefinition of the terms' because of the differing nature of qualitative and quantitative approaches.

Furthermore, there is an unhelpful misperception based on the perceived objectivity of quantitative techniques that they are more rigorous than qualitative approaches. However, as White (2002: 512) notes, 'badly or misleadingly applied, both quantitative and qualitative techniques give bad or misleading conclusions'. Indeed, as White continues, the issue is rather the appropriateness of quantitative or qualitative approaches to different settings, and the way in which both are combined.

In this chapter we address these issues. In Section 2 we discuss the research process and research design in a general sense. In Section 3 we focus on the adoption of mixed research methods in DS. In Section 4 attention is focused on the issues of rigour and bias. In Section 5 we summarize the contents of the chapter.

5.2. DOING RESEARCH

5.2a. The research process and points of departure

Different kinds of research will have different research processes. It is possible to distinguish between different levels and types of research in terms of their complexity and sophistication. Basic fundamental research – i.e. abstract concepts and theory building – would be at one end of a continuum while more applied research such as routine surveys (perhaps undertaken for commercial or attitudinal reasons) would be at the other. This issue is reintroduced into the discussion in Section 6.2 of Chapter 6. Davies (2004) has identified seven research variants in a typology which is reproduced in Box 5.1. The stylized research cycle (Box 5.1) is likely to differ to a greater or lesser degree for each variant so that, for example, routine survey research is unlikely to be methodologically innovative or to lead to the identification of future research priorities.

Another distinction which certainly applies within published research results relating to DS is that between problem-oriented research and techniques-oriented research. Problem-oriented research is intended to identify and to address specific research problems while techniques-oriented research is often more concerned to demonstrate facility in research methods and techniques. It has been suggested that economists have been excessively focused on techniques-oriented research rather than on a problem orientation. However, DS research is usually more problem oriented than other areas of enquiry because of its preoccupation with the analysis of policy and practice (refer to the discussion in Chapter 2).

The research process itself (see Box 5.2) can be viewed as consisting of six linked stages. However, in practice the research process or cycle (like the policy cycle – a stylized representation of policy management which is presented in Chapter 6) is likely to be more iterative than the heuristic device set out in Box 5.2 might suggest. For example, there is likely to be no discrete literature review stage in the sense that for each stage of the research it is necessary to depend on and to refer to relevant literature and to adjust the research process accordingly.

Box 5.1 Davies' Seven Types of Research

- Attitudinal (surveys, qualitative).
- Statistical modelling (linear and logistic regression).
- Impact (experimental, quasi-experimental, counter factual).
- Economic and econometric (cost benefit, cost-effectiveness, cost utility, econometrics).
- Ethical (social ethics and public consultation).
- Implementation (experimental, quasi-experimental qualitative, theories of change).
- Descriptive analytical (surveys, administrative data, comparative and qualitative).

Source: Davies (2004: 7).

Box 5.2   The Stylized Research Cycle

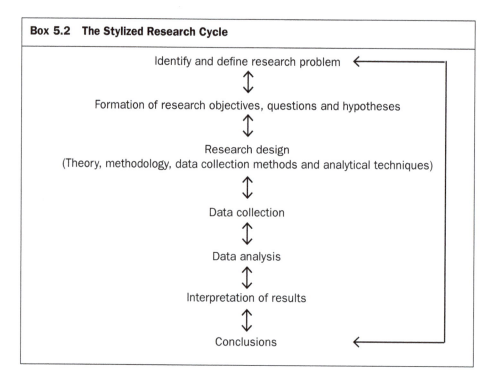

Identify and define research problem

Formation of research objectives, questions and hypotheses

Research design
(Theory, methodology, data collection methods and analytical techniques)

Data collection

Data analysis

Interpretation of results

Conclusions

Stage one of the research process or cycle is the identification and definition of a research problem. This would usually entail a literature review, and perhaps a process of consultation, leading to the identification of a problem area. Researchers are increasingly concerned about who sets the research agenda, and in certain approaches – such as participatory approaches – the participants (or subjects of the research) may be involved in setting the agenda for the research. Even in participatory approaches previous research relating to the relevant subject area will be reviewed for gaps or for new ways of looking at a problem area, perhaps with a view to challenging contemporary orthodoxy. Given that there are relatively few *totally* unresearched areas in DS this stage of the process or cycle often takes existing research and approaches and develops the current understanding further by reframing the research problem through the connection of hitherto unconnected phenomena, through collecting new up-to-date data (or reinterpreting old data), or through challenging orthodox beliefs with new or reinterpreted data and analysis. The definition of the research problem is often also affected by institutional factors, such as the priorities of a university department, of a research institute, or of a research funding body. Personal views about research priorities and research design are likely to be modified by an institutional matrix.

While a particular research problem will relate to the more general definition of a subject area, the objectives of the research are specific and the research questions or hypotheses which are established will specify a feasible research project that effectively addresses the problem identified.

The research objectives are generated from the identification and definition of a research problem. Objectives need to be specific, feasible and tangible. From the research objectives, research questions and/or research hypotheses are generated. Research questions and hypotheses might be said to mirror each other. Hypotheses can be expressed as a research question and vice versa. Research hypotheses will be stated explicitly when the researcher intends to test a proposition, particularly so if by statistical enquiry. Research questions are more likely to be used than a strict hypothesis testing approach if the researcher wishes to adopt a more broad, open and flexible method of enquiry. Mikkelsen (2005: 125) identifies different types of research question depending upon the type of study. At one level there are descriptive questions, explanatory questions and interpretative questions (see Box 5.3). At a second level there are action-oriented, empirical, normative and relativist-oriented studies for which Mikkelsen gives examples.[2] Thus the approach to research questions and hypotheses is informed by the research problem and by the type of study envisaged.[3]

5.2b. The research design and operationalization

After the research problem has been defined and research questions or hypotheses have been established, the next stage is the research design. This can be broken down into a series of sequential choices as follows:

i. The choice of theoretical/conceptual framework.
ii. The choice of methodology.
iii. The choice of (data collection) methods.
iv. The choice of (data) analysis techniques.

Although ethical and practical considerations will play a significant role in decisions, such choices (refer to the discussion in Chapter 2) should be led by the research problems and by the research questions or hypotheses. For example, the choice of

---

Box 5.3   Types of Research Questions

Descriptive studies: how does x vary with y?
Explanatory studies: which x causes y? Or which y are caused by x?
Interpretative studies: what is x? Or how does y interpret the phenomena x in a given context of z?
Action-oriented studies: how do people act in accordance with knowledge accumulated and disseminated in the course of the research process?
Positivist studies: how *is* power distributed in society and how can the distribution of power be explained and understood?
Normative studies: how *should* power be distributed in society, and how can the desired distribution be justified?
Relativist studies: how *can* power be distributed in society in a more equitable way, and how can the possible situation be reached?

Adapted from Mikkelsen (2005: 125–7)

the theoretical or conceptual framework is fundamental. If the research problem, questions or hypotheses relate to the livelihoods of poor households then the Sustainable Livelihoods Approach might be chosen. In most cases though the choice will not be as straightforward and may involve amending, blending or combining existing theories or, as noted in Chapter 4, the wholesale construction of a new theoretical framework as a basis for the conduct of the research.

The theory chosen will, to a large extent, shape the methodological choices. The methodology is the overall research strategy adopted in order to address the research questions or hypotheses. The methodology in turn informs not only the methods and techniques chosen for the collection of the data but also informs the choice of techniques for data analysis. The methodology is the strategy, the broad issue, while the methods and techniques are the detailed means for undertaking the research. Sometimes methodological choices in some areas may narrow options in the selection of methods and techniques so that earlier choices will restrict later options. For methodology there are at least five important questions to consider:

- Should the methodology be multidisciplinary, interdisciplinary or transdisciplinary, and what particular range of disciplines should be within the selected approach?
- Should the methodology be quantitative or qualitative or a combination of quantitative and qualitative?
- Should the methodology be participatory or non-participatory or a mixture (some aspects of participatory approaches incorporated)?[4]
- Should the methodology be related to a survey, case study or a combination of survey and case study approach?
- What level of complexity is required? (In terms of sample size, whether a comparative study is involved, whether it can be handled by a single person or whether the approach needs somebody more experienced, or whether a research team of whatever make-up is really needed.)

There are then further questions to be considered that lead on from choices in the above questions. For example, there is a variety of qualitative, quantitative and participatory methodologies available, and some of these may be mixed (this issue is discussed further below). In qualitative methodologies alone there is a wide variety of choice between, for example, ethnography, phenomenology, grounded theory, structural ethnography and symbolic interactionism (for a detailed discussion see Olsen, 2004).

If we consider the 'survey' and 'case study' options further it can be seen how methodological choices are highly deterministic. Surveys have the capacity to generate data which are statistically significant but which may be limited in 'depth' of meaning. Surveys typically have larger numbers of respondents with carefully structured interviewer- or self-administered questionnaires so that the number of questions and the depth of responses to individual questions are limited. Case studies involve smaller numbers of observations which may not be statistically significant, but can involve carefully structured samples. They typically have significant depth in the data created but limited breadth or generalizability. Descriptive and explanatory research questions might tend towards the surveys approach and in contrast, a more interpretive research question might tend towards case studies.

Both the choice of methods and choice of analytical techniques will be informed by the theoretical framework and methodological choices made previously. On the issue of data collection, one of the significant decisions is between the use of primary and secondary data. The collection (or generation) of primary data is resource intensive and can be expensive, utilizing a high proportion of the available research resources. However, particularly in developing countries, it is possible that relevant secondary data is either not available or is not sufficiently reliable as a basis for answering the research questions which have been set up (see Box 5.8 and the related discussion on rigour). In some cases it may be necessary to compromise in the formulation of research questions in order that secondary data can be used. We have previously (Section 5.2a) distinguished between different levels of research, and the suitability of primary and secondary data to particular levels and to particular research objectives is an important consideration.[5]

It is then necessary to select specific research methods which are consistent with the theoretical or conceptual framework, and with the methodology, which have been adopted.[6] In the case of methods and techniques, as with methodology, one can make a distinction between quantitative and qualitative approaches.

The terms 'quantitative' and 'qualitative' refer not only to methodologies but also to the:

- types of data collection – i.e. the specific methods;
- types of data collected – i.e. the raw data;
- types of data analysis – i.e. the techniques of analysis;
- types of data output – i.e. the data in the final report or study.

To illustrate, we compare quantitative and qualitative approaches to poverty measurement and analysis. Carvalho and White characterize the quantitative and the qualitative approaches as follows:

> The quantitative approach to poverty measurement and analysis ... typically uses random sample surveys and structured interviews to collect the data – mainly, quantifiable data – and analyzes it using statistical techniques. By contrast, the qualitative approach ... typically uses purposive sampling and semi-structured or interactive interviews to collect the data – mainly, data relating to people's judgment, preferences, priorities, and/or perceptions about a subject – and analyzes it usually through sociological or anthropological research techniques. (1997: 1)

Although quantitative and qualitative have been described as distinctly different approaches to methods of data collection and to types of data, qualitative methods can be used to produce quantitative data. However, the opposite is not true – quantitative methods cannot produce qualitative data.[7]

The data collection stage can be seen as an operational stage – the methods chosen are used to generate the data that will be analyzed. The data, whether primary or secondary, must relate directly to the research question or hypotheses if they are to directly and unambiguously address the objectives of the research. There are several important issues which need to be considered at this stage, with particular dimensions relating to DS research.

The first issue is that of how access to the data is to be secured. For primary research this means access to the actual target population itself (i.e. the subjects of the research), and for secondary research it means access to existing data and documentation. Both raise ethical questions (refer to the discussion in Section 2.3 of Chapter 2). To recap, there is a list of technical but important issues relating to the research process itself – such as reciprocity, anonymity, confidentiality, informed consent, and safety and there are several sets of ethical guidelines from which DS can draw upon.

Sampling is usually adopted for the generation of primary data from a target population because limitations of cost and time make collection of data from all members of the target population impossible. In addition, statistical inference means that it is 'scientifically' unnecessary to obtain data from all members of the population in order to generate data which are representative of the relevant population characteristics. Box 5.4 illustrates two of the most common approaches to sampling.[8]

Choice of a sampling approach depends not only on the level of claims to generalization (i.e. statistical significance) required but on practical considerations as well. The important issue is that there is an underlying logic to systematic sampling based on the extent to which it will be claimed that the characteristics of the sample are representative of the characteristics of the population from which the sample has been drawn. Sampling is a major issue for DS research based on primary data as well as for assessment of the statistical validity of secondary data. A fundamental issue is that a properly designed sample is based on a sampling frame (i.e. a full listing of the members of the target population). In many developing countries official records such as the electoral register, population census or telephone directory – which are often used as a basis for the sampling frame in industrialized countries – may be inaccurate, incomplete, inaccessible or non-existent. Researchers often find that they have to construct their own sampling frame.[9]

Data analysis is the stage when the researcher takes all data collected and examines, considers, categorizes and processes. Data can then be tabulated systematically and trends, regularities and patterns are identified in order to address the research questions and/or to test the hypotheses. For quantitative data the analysis can take the

---

Box 5.4   Common Types of Sampling

Random or probability sampling
  This is when 'each unit of the population has an equal probability of inclusion in the sample'.
Purposive or non-probability convenience sampling
  This is when 'a sample that is selected because of its availability to the researcher... some units of the populations are more likely to be selected than others'.

Source: Bryman (2004: 538, 541).

---

form of presentation of descriptive statistics and, more elaborately, processing using statistical or mathematical methods such as regression analysis. Computer software such as SPSS or more advanced packages allow survey data to be 'inputted', to be presented in tables, and to be 'processed'.[10] Economists, for example, have specialist software for macroeconomic analysis such as PC-GIVE, although microeconomic analysis can often use more standard social science and generic computer software. For qualitative data a choice can be made between content analysis (which can lead to the generation of quantitative data from qualitative data) or various forms of discourse analysis (both are discussed in David and Sutton, 2004). Both content and discourse analysis involve coding the data using themes or 'codes' that are either 'top down' (where the codes are decided before the data collection) or 'bottom up' (where the codes emerge from the data after collection). Software packages (such as NUD*IST, Nvivo or ATLAS) have the capacity to code research data at word, line, sentence and/or paragraph level for concepts, patterns, regularities, systems and themes.[11]

After the data have been 'organized' (presented) and 'processed' (analyzed) the results need to be interpreted and contextualized, which is arguably the most difficult part of the research exercise, before being written up in reports of various types. These stages and processes, of course, become more complex if methods and methodologies are 'mixed' in DS research.

5.3. DOING RESEARCH IN DS

5.3a. Combining methods and cross-disciplinarity

Mixing methodologies and methods (also know as 'qual-quant' or 'q-squared' or 'q-integrated' to reflect the mix of qualitative and quantitative methods) has become popular in DS in order to see the shape of Bourguignon's (2003) 'mountain'. Such 'mixing' is widely accepted in the social sciences, as noted by Hentschel (2003) in another of the opening quotations to this chapter.

When Bourguignon (2003: 44) writes of two painters viewing a mountain from different directions and thus painting two different pictures, we are referring to the combination of breadth (quantitative) and depth (qualitative).[12] However, there is no guarantee that different approaches, methods or data will be comparable, and they might enrich or explain rather than confirm or refute, perhaps even telling 'different stories' about the same subject because quantitative methods are good for specifying relationships (i.e. describing) and qualitative methods for explaining and understanding relationships (Thomas and Johnson, 2002: 1).[13]

There is also the prospect of antagonistic dialogue between researchers using different approaches. In short,

> [q]uantitative researchers have seen qualitative researchers as too context specific, their samples as unrepresentative and their claims about their work as unwarranted – that is judged from the vantage point of statistical generalisation. For their part qualitative researchers view quantitative research as overly simplistic, decontextualised,

> reductionist in terms of its generalisations, and failing to capture the meanings that
> actors attach to their lives and circumstances. (Brannen, 2005: 7)

Because DS seeks to be cross-disciplinary there are also tensions between different disciplinary methodologies, methods and insights. Sharp (2005: 3) argues that discussion about research methods in DS divides into four research elements rather than into the 'broad (discipline-based) categories of "qualitative" and "quantitative"'. Sharp believes that distinction between the *sampling approach* (random or purposive); *data collection methods* (structured or interactive); *types of data collected* (quantifiable or perceptual); and *analytical techniques* (statistical or sociological/anthropological) categorization gives greater clarity in discussion about alternative approaches to DS research than to focus on disciplines. In this context the 'traditional dichotomy' of Economics versus Social Anthropology (see Chapter 4) is again worth revisiting.[14]

For Economics, the aim is to choose methods and methodologies in order – broadly speaking – to explain, to focus on outcomes, to seek objectivity and to find general laws that will provide empirical observations of what is seen and heard. Perhaps most significantly Economics has long had links to policy analysis, particularly in the context of macroeconomics, so that prediction of future levels of national income, of tax revenues, of imports, exports and capital flows are of the utmost importance in the management of the economy both for industrialized or developing countries.[15] In contrast, for Social Anthropology the aim is to choose methods and methodologies in order to translate – in a metaphorical (and often literal) sense – and that look for 'voices' excluded from the dominant discourse (i.e. marginalised populations). This element of prediction of future events is, of course, also very significant for other constituent disciplines of DS, particularly in the context of policy analysis.

Although it might appear that there is an association between Economics and quantitative approaches and Social Anthropology and qualitative approaches this has been questioned as a limiting intellectual stereotyping that is itself part of the problem as Hulme and Toye suggest in a recent paper:

> [T]o label economics as a quantitative discipline and other social sciences as qualita-
> tive disciplines lacks any fundamental justification. It seems plausible only because
> people confuse 'quantitative' with 'mathematical'... ... Economics is not intrinsically
> more amenable (or less, as many famous economists have argued!) to statistical
> treatment than politics or sociology or even history. (2006: 1091)

Indeed, Hulme and Toye argue that simplistic associations of Economics with quantitative analysis on the one hand and other social sciences with qualitative analysis on the other are unjustified and unhelpful because such dichotomies are not justified by reality. Hulme has further developed issues associated with qualitative and quantitative analysis in another paper (2006).

The underlying rationale for combining approaches is summed up by the concept of triangulation. In a recent paper Olsen has outlined a number of different dimensions of triangulation (Olsen, 2004). The basic idea of triangulation is that more than one approach to a particular research problem can be used and that, if the same conclusion is reached from each of the approaches greater confidence exists that conclusion is valid. If different conclusions are reached from different approaches then doubt is cast on the validity of the conclusions. In her paper Olsen reviews the use of both qualitative and quantitative approaches to researching a specific problem in this context, but extends this to include the use of methods and approaches from different research paradigms in the context of triangulation. Further extension is possible to the use of alternative sets of data, alternative data analysis techniques, and alternative disciplinary (or cross-disciplinary) perspectives. The origin of the word triangulation is from the use of trigonometry in mapping the Earth's surface, so that the accurate measurement of distance and of physical features can be determined through this method. The significance of triangulation cannot be over-emphasized within the context of this discussion of rigour in DS research.

5.3b. Mixing methods in practice

Combining methodologies and methods is complicated in practice. It is possible to mix qualitative and quantitative methods, or to mix different types of quantitative methods, or to mix different types of qualitative methods. A further, and common,

---

Box 5.5   Specific Combinations of Data Collection Methods

Simultaneous designs of data collection methods:
1. QUALITATIVE + quantitative or
2. QUALITATIVE + QUANTITATIVE
3. QUANTITATIVE + quantitative or
4. QUANTITATIVE + QUANTITATIVE
5. QUALITATIVE + qualitative or
6. QUALITATIVE + QUALITATIVE

Sequential designs of data collection methods:
1. QUALITATIVE > qualitative or
2. qualitative > QUALITATIVE or
3. QUALITATIVE > QUALITATIVE
4. QUANTITATIVE > quantitative or
5. quantitative > QUANTITATIVE or
6. QUANTITATIVE > QUANTITATIVE
7. QUALITATIVE > quantitative or
8. qualitative > QUANTITATIVE or
9. QUALITATIVE > QUANTITATIVE
10. QUANTITATIVE > qualitative or
11. quantitative > QUALITATIVE or
12. QUANTITATIVE > QUALITATIVE

Key
CAPITALS denote the dominant method (covering the majority of primary data collected);
+ denotes simultaneously occurring methods;
> denotes temporal sequencing of methods.

Source: Brannen (2005: 14).

complication arises for both quantitative and qualitative methods when different types of data, data from different (and potentially inconsistent) sources, or data from different types of investigators are combined.

Brannen (2005: 14) identifies 18 specific conceivable combinations of mixed methods which are set out in Box 5.5. In each combination there is a 'dominant method' (i.e. the method that covers the majority of the data) and a 'non-dominant' method (i.e. the method that covers the minority of the data). If the proportion of data covered by both is approximately similar, then both are 'dominant' methods in Brannen's categorization. Combination can be simultaneous (denoted by a + in Box 5.5) or temporally sequential (denoted by a > in Box 5.5). The researcher thus needs to consider two questions. First, which is their dominant method – that which relates to most of the data? Second, are methods to be mixed sequentially or simultaneously?

How should the researcher decide which to use? Resources, practical considerations and the function of the combination are significant factors. Brannen (2005: 12) identifies four functions of combinations which are:

- Elaboration or expansion ('the use of one type of data analysis adds to the understanding being gained by another').
- Initiation ('the use of a first method sparks new hypotheses or research questions that can be pursued using a different method').
- Complementarity ('together the data analyses from the two methods are juxtaposed and generate complementary insights that together create a bigger picture').
- Contradictions ('simply juxtapose the contradictions for others to explore in further research').

One illustration of mixed methods may be taken from poverty researchers who have sought to combine quantitative approaches (in order to identify the level and location of poverty) and qualitative approaches (in order to identify the causes and dynamics of poverty). These combined methods seek to combine household surveys (perhaps more associated with Economics) and participatory poverty assessment (PPA) case studies (perhaps more associated with Social Anthropology). Household surveys are characterized as involving statistical sampling, closed questions, numerical data and statistical analysis. PPAs typically involve purposive sampling, open interviews, participant observation or focus group discussions and yield non-numerical qualitative data which are not easily subject to statistical analysis. However, although this discussion suggests that surveys are more likely to be associated with quantitative methods and PPAs are more likely to be associated with qualitative methods, the association need not arise – as has been emphasized by Hulme and Toye (2006: 1091) in the quotation included above.

Table 5.1 below sets out the generic strengths and weaknesses of surveys and of PPAs. The contents of the table have been summarized from the identified sources.

It is possible to combine or integrate quantitative and qualitative methods at either (or both) the data collection or data analysis stages as has been outlined in Table 5.2. For data collection this could involve conducting a simultaneous survey and PPA with

Table 5.1 Selected Possible Generic Strengths and Weaknesses of PPAs and Surveys

	Strengths	Weaknesses
PPAs	Richer definition of poverty; more insights into causal processes; holistic – a set of relationships as a whole, not pre-selected attributes; scope for attention to processes as well as snap shots of the situation; feedback loop – new/more interviews for interrogating data; focus on context and people's experiences	Lack of generalizability (but the sample can be made more or less representative of the population); difficulties in verifying information; limited systematic disaggregation; possibly unrepresentative participation; agenda framing by facilitators; pitfalls in attitudinal data – arrival of a PPA team changes people's behaviour
Household surveys	Aggregation and comparisons possible across time and with other datasets; reliability of results is measurable; credibility of numbers with policymakers; credibility of national statistics with policymakers; allows simulation of different policy options; correlations identify associations raising questions of causality	Misses what is not easily quantifiable; sampling frame may miss significant members of the population; may fail to capture intra-household allocation; assumes that numbers are objective and conclusive; assumes that the same question means the same thing in different cultural contexts

Source: Appleton and Booth (2001), Carvalho and White (1997), Chambers (2001).

the same sample, using surveys to identify subgroups for PPAs, or using PPAs to identify survey questions. For data analysis, this could involve synthesizing findings into one set of results, merging outcomes from mixed teams of qualitative and quantitative researchers, using PPAs to confirm or refute the validity of surveys (or vice versa), or using PPAs to enrich or to explain information on processes in survey variables.

Bourguignon comments on the combination of methods, suggesting that:

> The distinction between qualitative and quantitative approaches to poverty analysis, or the analysis of any other social or economic phenomenon, is of the same nature: two different types of perspectives, the reunion of which is the only

Table 5.2 Combining Qualitative and Quantitative Data Collection and Analysis

		Function	
		Combining	Integrating
Stage of research process	Data collection	Conduct a simultaneous survey and PPA in the same sample (ideally nationally representative)	Use surveys to identify subgroups for PPAs or use PPAs to identify survey questions
	Data analysis	Synthesize findings into one set of results or merge outcomes from mixed teams of qualitative and quantitative researchers	Use PPAs to confirm or refute the validity of surveys (or vice versa); use PPAs to enrich or to explain information on processes in survey variables (or vice versa)

Source: Constructed and expanded from text in Carvalho and White (1997) and Thorbecke (2003).

way to get some idea of the reality. The only thing is that this reunion, as well as the drawing of each perspective may be more complicated than taking the picture of an object under different angles. (2003: 44)

While combining methods may be complicated by the array of choices faced by researchers, the adoption of this approach has the capacity to provide a greater degree of rigour within many DS research situations.

5.4. DOING RIGOROUS RESEARCH IN DS

5.4a. What is 'rigour'?

In the Social Sciences there has been increased interest in recent years in the quality of research and the question of 'rigour'.[16] We have attempted to give a clear definition of our personal understanding of 'rigour' in our introduction. Quality is often judged by whether the results of the research are published in a peer-reviewed (refereed) journal and whether the research has been funded through a process including peer review. However, publication is a 'post-process' activity and it has been questioned whether it is any guarantee of high-quality research (Grayson, 2002). When Becker et al. (2006: 7–8) asked over 250 social policy researchers and users of research how they conceptualized 'quality' in social policy research they placed research publication at the bottom of the list. Box 5.6 shows the criteria identified as very important in determining research quality in this exercise. The top five included accessibility, addressing research questions, transparency in methods and analysis and the contribution of the research.

Box 5.6   Quality in Social Policy Research

Respondents classifying criteria as 'very important'
Top 5
1. The research is written in ways that are accessible to the appropriate audiences – 82.9%.
2. The research design adopted clearly addresses the research question(s) – 82.5%.
3. The ways in which data were collected and analyzed are transparent – 78.8%.
4. An explicit account of the research process and analysis of data is provided – 76.5%.
5. The research makes a contribution to knowledge – 68.9%.

Bottom 5
30. The research is published in a prestigious refereed academic journal – 13.2%.
31. The research provides good value for money – 12.8%.

32. A randomized controlled design was used – 12.8%.
33. A publication deriving from the research is cited in prestigious refereed academic journals – 11.6%.
34. The research is published in a professional journal/magazine – 7.6%.
35. The research is published as a chapter in a book – 2.4%.

Source: Becker et al. (2006: 5).

Box 5.7   Criteria for Assessment of Qualitative Research

The four guiding principles for research are that it should be:

- contributory (in advancing wider knowledge or understanding);
- defensible in design (by providing a research strategy to address questions posed);
- rigorous in conduct (through the systematic and transparent collection, analysis and interpretation of data);
- credible in claim (through well-founded, plausible arguments based on data generated).

The 12 tenets of robust research are that it:

- sets aims and purpose in context;
- gives logic of enquiry design;
- shows openness to emergent issues;
- offers transparency about conduct;
- provides understanding of subjective meanings;
- provides understanding of context;
- provides faithful representation of data;
- conveys depth, diversity, subtlety and complexity;
- shows sound interrogation of evidence;
- presents well-founded argument;
- offers reflection on research process;
- has utility or relevance.

Eighteen appraisal questions for assessment of research are:

- How credible are the findings?
- How has knowledge or understanding been extended by the research?
- How well does the evaluation address its original aims and purpose?
- How well is the scope for drawing wider inference explained?
- How clear is the basis of evaluative appraisal?
- How defensible is the research design?
- How well defended are the sample design/target selection of cases/documents?
- How well is the eventual sample composition and coverage described?
- How well was the data collection carried out?
- How well has the approach to, and formulation of, analysis been conveyed?
- How well are the contexts of data sources retained and portrayed?
- How well has diversity of perspective and content been explored?
- How well has detail, depth and complexity of the data been conveyed?
- How clear are the links between data, interpretation and conclusions?
- How clear and coherent is the reporting?
- How clear are the assumptions/theoretical perspectives/values?
- What evidence is there of attention to ethical issues?
- How adequately has the research process been documented?

Source: Spencer et al. (2003: 6, 7, 22–8, 71–2, 105).

There have been a number of attempts to establish a system of research standards in bio-medical research and some of these have been incorporated into evaluation of Social Science research in recent years (Long and Godfrey, 2004; Marsland et al., 2001). One example is the wide-ranging discussion by Spencer et al. (2003) of the assessment of qualitative research. Although intended to apply only to qualitative methods it provides a helpful basis for the evaluation of quantitative approaches as well. Spencer's study identifies four guiding principles, 12 principles of robust research and 18 questions to assess which are summarized in Box 5.7.

The survey by Becker et al. (2006: 7–8), which was referred to above, also includes a stimulating discussion about research standards arguing that qualitative and quantitative approaches in the Social Sciences need to be judged by alternative definitions, as set out in Table 5.3. It has also been suggested that the word 'rigour' is problematic because it is biased towards a perception of precision and with an association with objectivity and quantitative methods (David and Dodd, 2002: 281). As Boaz and Ashby (2003: 7) note in one of the quotations at the beginning of this chapter, while criteria such as validity, reliability, replicability, and generalizability are the prominent criteria used to judge quantitative research these may not be entirely appropriate for qualitative research. For example, although replicability is often regarded as a key issue in determining socio-economic (and DS) research quality it might be argued that no research is replicable because not only will the research context have changed from the exact point in time when the research was conducted but in addition a different researcher conducting the research would inevitably interact differently with the researched. Thus replicability in socio-economic, including DS, research involves different issues to those which apply in the physical and purely mathematical sciences.

In short, as Becker et al. (2006: 7–8) argue, because traditional criteria are biased towards quantitative approaches, alternative assessment criteria should seek to be more inclusive (refer to Table 5.3). Thus, rather than thinking of 'truth' we could think of 'trustworthiness'; rather than thinking of 'validity' we could think of 'credibility'; rather than thinking of 'generalizability' we could think of the 'transferability' of context; rather than thinking of 'reliability' we could think of 'dependability'; and rather than thinking of 'objectivity' we could think of 'confirmability'.

Table 5.3 Quality Criteria and Definitions

Traditional criteria	Alternative criteria
Validity: the extent to which there is a correspondence between data and conceptualization	Credibility: the extent to which a set of findings are believable
Reliability: the extent to which observations are consistent when instruments are administered on more than one occasion	Transferability: the extent to which a set of findings are relevant to settings other than the one or ones from which they are derived
Replicability: the extent to which it is possible to reproduce an investigation	Dependability: the extent to which a set of findings are likely to be relevant to a different time than the one in which it was conducted
Generalizability: the extent to which it is possible to generalize findings to similar cases which have not been studied	Confirmability: the extent to which the researcher has not allowed personal values to intrude to an excessive degree

Source: Becker et al. (2006: 7–8).

Patton (2002) goes further and proposes lists of alternative quality criteria by type (see Table 5.4), including traditional scientific criteria, social constructivist criteria, artistic and evocative criteria, critical change criteria and evaluation standards and principles. Potentially all of these could appeal to parts of the DS research community. Traditional scientific criteria are often associated with research rigour from a positivist perspective – i.e. referring to objectivity and to the validity of the data. In contrast, social constructivist criteria might be more associated with research rigour from a relativist perspective – i.e. subjectivity is acknowledged and embraced together with other researchers' perspectives. There are also artistic and evocative research criteria such as creativity and aesthetic quality which are regarded as being important, together with stimulating and provocative qualities. Patton also lists critical change criteria, noting their neo-Marxist and feminist roots which relate to critical perspectives, increasing consciousness about injustice, sources of inequalities and injustice and representations of the perspectives of the less powerful. Finally, criteria for evaluation standards and principles are included, together with instrumental criteria.

The debates about rigour within DS research are complex partially because they revolve to a significant extent around the combination of quantitative and qualitative methods. A further complicating factor is that different disciplines which co-exist under the DS 'umbrella' regard research quality in different ways. For example, there is a perception (not least in the economics profession) that research in Economics is quantitative and objective and is therefore hard or rigorous while other Social Sciences are generally qualitative and subjective and thus soft or non-rigorous. As Harriss notes:

> I recognize that in terms of rigor and of parsimony it [economics] is exemplary in the social sciences... ... My point is that the economics discipline does not have a monopoly on... ... 'hardness' or rigor... ... and economics has its own kind of softness, as for example when analytical rigor involves such oversimplification as to misrepresent reality, or (even more crassly) when analysis is allowed to be dictated by the availability of data. (2002: 487)

Kanbur has remarked on this issue:

> [O]ther social sciences disciplines [other than economics] and social scientists... ... feel looked down upon by economists, as being 'soft' or 'unrigorous'. But increasingly... ... criticism is coming from economists themselves, who are finding their tools and techniques, strong as they are, to be inadequate. (Kanbur, 2002: 477)

White has also commented on this issue:

> There is a perception among economists that quantitative techniques provide more 'rigor' than qualitative techniques. Hence it is often felt that economics, with its more rigorous footing, is a sounder basis from which to formulate policy advice. (White, 2002: 512)

Thus Harriss, Kanbur and White all conclude that the distinction between on the one hand hard, rigorous and quantitative Economics versus, on the other hand, soft,

Table 5.4   Alternative Quality Criteria

Traditional scientific criteria i.e. positivist	Social constructivist criteria i.e. relativist	Artistic and evocative criteria	Critical change criteria (neo-Marxist, some feminist)	Evaluation standards and principles
Objectivity (attempts to minimize bias); validity of the data; systematic rigour of fieldwork practices; triangulation (for consistency of findings); reliability of coding and pattern analysis (multiple coders); correspondence of findings to reality; strength of evidence supporting causal hypotheses; generalizability; contributions to theory	Subjectivity acknowledged and embraced; trustworthiness and authenticity – fairness and coverage of others' perspectives; triangulation (for capturing multiple perspectives); reflexivity and praxis – understanding one's own background and how to act in the world; particularity – doing justice to unique cases; contributions to dialogue – encouraging multiple perspectives	Opens the world to us in some way; creativity; aesthetic quality; interpretive vitality; flows from self-embedded in lived experience; stimulating; provocative; connects and moves the audience; voice is distinct and expressive; feels 'true', 'authentic' and real': case studies become literary works, blurring of boundaries	Critical perspectives – increases consciousness about injustice; identifies nature and sources of inequalities and injustice; represents the perspective of the less powerful; makes visible the ways in which those with more power exercise and benefit from this power; engages those with less power respectfully and collaboratively; builds capacity of those involved to take action; identifies potential change – making strategies; clear historical and values context; consequential or catalytic validity	Utility – if not going to be useful to some audience, then no point doing it; propriety – fair and ethical; accuracy; systematic inquiry; integrity/honesty and respect for people; responsibility to general public welfare

Adapted from Patton (2002: 544).

non-rigorous and qualitative non-Economics represents a false dichotomy. White (2002) comments that research in economics can be soft (i.e. non-rigorous) and can use qualitative methods and that research in non-Economics can be hard (i.e. rigorous) and can use quantitative methods.

Although the choice of criteria may differ, we would argue that rigour is essentially about taking a systematic approach. By this we mean that the research problem is properly defined; that the research question(s) is articulated clearly; that research questions and hypotheses are closely aligned with the research problem; and that the scope of the research questions is not so broad as to make meaningful research difficult. Furthermore, a systematic approach means that the data collection is in close alignment with the research question; and that there is consistency in the analysis through the use of accepted and standardized techniques. In short, the entire research process is systematically linked to the research questions and the entire research process is transparent. This amounts to the systematic application of the research cycle which was discussed in Section 5.2a and the findings are consistent with criteria set out in Table 5.3 from the Becker et al. study.

5.4b. Subjectivity and acceptable/unacceptable bias

The instrumental, policy-oriented or normative point of departure of many researches in DS raises the issues of subjectivity and bias. Table 5.5 illustrates how intentional and unintentional bias can arise at various stages in the research process. The important subjectivity-objectivity issue amounts to acknowledging that DS research is often concerned with normative issues so that subjective bias may be introduced, some of which may be acceptable and some of which is certainly not. As far as is possible, subjective or normative positionality should be made explicit, and allowance should be made for this in data collection, analysis and interpretation. The evaluation of rigour in DS research involves distinguishing between deliberate misinterpretation or omission which bias the outcomes in a direction which coincides with the bias of the researcher (this being unacceptable), and acknowledged bias in values (such as recognizing that poverty is a multi-dimensional concept) or in data (these being acceptable).

Table 5.5 Possible Types of Bias in Development Studies Research

	Unintentional bias	Intentional or deliberate bias
Bias introduced by researcher	Personal values and positionality	Design of research – specification of research problem Rejecting evidence that does not support the researcher's position
Bias introduced by the researched	Mis-reporting and imperfect recall	Responding on behalf of others
Bias introduced by the research process	Availability of accurate sample frame Imperfect access to data	Interviewer influence – (the 'Hawthorne effect')

In short, bias can be introduced by the research process, by the researched or by the researcher. To illustrate this point White describes two researchers: the 'data-analyst' and the 'data-miner':

> The data analyst is looking for the interpretation most consistent with the data, i.e. letting the data tell the story. The data miner knows what she is looking for and keeps digging until she finds it. Then she stops and that is the story she tells. Data miners are equally at home using either quantitative or qualitative data. (White, 2002: 513)

White is referring to the fact that 'data-mining', according to his definition, is essentially subjective – or biased – in that the conclusions have been predetermined and that the researcher looks for evidence to support them. On the other hand research that seeks to be unbiased starts with the research problem, and gathers evidence in order to lead the investigators to conclusions. Table 5.6 illustrates that there are different views about what data mining consists of.

Complementing White's conceptualization of data mining is the unselective assembly of large quantities of data without any clear notion of what the data represent or their relation to a research problem or questions. While this approach cannot necessarily be associated with allegations of bias, in an extreme form it is certainly unsystematic and lacking in rigour. Another form of 'research' which lacks a systematic approach and rigour is the unselective – and unfocused – running of large numbers of regressions without any direct relationship to research questions and hypotheses, and often looking for a good statistical fit without any notion of behavioural relationships (refer to the discussion in Kenny and Williams, 2001; Sala-I-Martin, 1997). Another problem is represented by visiting researchers who visit a country for a few weeks (or even a few days) and gather large quantities of (mostly secondary) data without due acknowledgement to the efforts of local statisticians and researchers who have been wholly or partially responsible for assembling and collecting the data, without due understanding of or regard to the limitations of the data, and without a clear set of research questions or hypotheses to which the data might relate. Yet, another category might be the researchers who only use databanks (increasingly available from internet websites, 'plugging in' unselectively) without due regard to what the data represent or how they were collected.[17]

Table 5.6 Examples of 'Data Mining'

Data mining in primary methods	Data mining in secondary methods
Sample chosen to support the researcher's position	Data source is chosen to support the research question and hypotheses
Research instruments written to support the researcher's position	Data is rejected if they are inconsistent with the research questions and hypotheses
Data interpreted to support the researcher's position	Data cleaning – data unacceptable to the researcher's position are rejected

There are further limitations which need to be considered in the context of method-specific bias issues within DS research. Some of these apply to research in industrialized countries as well as developing countries but not necessarily to the same extent or in the same way. For example, an interviewer with an upper class English accent may get an unsympathetic response from a working class respondent.

In developing country settings primary methods such as interviews, focus group discussions, questionnaires and observation may lack reliability and validity due to under-reporting and recall difficulties or to concern over the use of the information collected from respondents. 'Interviewer influence' may be exacerbated by inhibitions and perceptions created by the interviewer-researcher such as the questioner's accent, dialect, sex, age, class, education, or appearance. Local socio-cultural factors may also influence responses: household heads or village leaders may answer on behalf of the respondents who are actually being targeted. Responses may be influenced by culture, by who is present at the interview, or what the respondent thinks the interviewer wishes to hear.

Research undertaken in languages which are unfamiliar to the researcher or to the researched also create a set of issues. Received and intended meanings may differ, and there may be much meaning which is 'hidden' or lost in translation. It is impossible for researchers to learn all relevant local dialects, implying that the social dynamics of translation are important considerations together with hidden meanings and the 'unspoken'.

There are no easy answers. Bujra (2006) notes that research in 'other cultures' involves a process of translation not only in data collection but also in analysis and dissemination. She proposes that researchers aim for a working knowledge of the local language, or where this is impossible local research partners double up as translators and as members of the research team. Using this approach it is possible to discuss the research process and the modalities of translating prior to fieldwork with someone who has an appreciation of the issues raised by research methods and rigour. Additionally, there is the dynamic relationship between researcher, translator and researched to be considered. Bujra asks what is more important to the study – a technically superb translation or an imperfect but insider interpretation?

Cassette or digital voice recorders can be used in interviews but raise the problem of whether respondents may answer differently if recorded in this way (with permission of course) as compared with written notes. Cameron (2004: 9) also offers advice, suggesting that local languages should be transcribed and included parallel to any translation in order to remind the researcher of the process of translation and to aid transparency for the reader.

Secondary data, and official documents, are major sources for much DS research, and they raise a number of issues relating to bias which are summarized in Box 5.8. Governments and the major international agencies (such as the International Labour Office (ILO), International Monetary Fund (IMF), the World Bank, United Nations Development Programme (UNDP) and United Nations Conference on Trade and Development (UNCTAD)) release regular annual reports which contain large appendices of social and economic data.[18] Much research in Economics is typically based on

---

Box 5.8   Secondary Data and Rigour

Secondary data is the end product of a (lengthy) social process, which at every stage is shaped by the bias of agents involved. Errors are virtually certain to occur in both the sampling and non-sampling aspects of research. In the early stages, bias appears in the choice of survey questions and the interviewer may influence respondents' answers. There may be inaccurate reporting of consumption or expenditure due to recall difficulties or concern over the use of the information. Under-representing of some groups in socioeconomic surveys will happen because sample frames are often based on incomplete official records (such as national identity card or electoral register) that 'hide' those without full 'legal status' such as the homeless or slum-dwellers. It is also likely that a disproportionate number of the 'hidden' households will be poor and thus there will be a downward bias in the absolute number of the poor as calculated. Further, in the later stages, when the data are collated, processed and interpreted, bias (and more errors) are introduced in the stages of inputting and defining how the raw data fit the definition of a specific indicator.

With this in mind, a non-exhaustive list of salient questions for reflection when utilizing data might include the following: how are these indicators created? Who collects them and for what purpose? How is the sample frame created? Who is omitted? What definitions are used? How are these indicators used? What are they used for?

Thus official data may be problematic not only in terms of whether they conceptually capture the phenomenon in question (take for example adult literacy – what does it mean to be 'literate'?) but also empirically, in terms of the quality and accuracy of what is captured.

---

secondary data from these sources, including macro-data from national income accounts or micro-data from household surveys which are electronically accessible. These published sources are used because of the cost, time and practicability of collecting original data. However, this practice raises the issue of 'rigour' on a number of grounds, including comparability between years and statistical series, and between countries. The organizations assembling and publishing this data (such as the World Bank) take great efforts to resolve many such issues, but the processes involved cannot all be published.

In most developing countries secondary data are cheap and readily available, and raw data tapes can often be purchased. The quality of secondary data within any one country may be suspect on the grounds of consistency across time and across changing definitions. Combining data from different sources is highly problematic. For cross-country comparative studies all data would need to be standardized across all countries and between all data series if complete consistency was to be achieved. As an example, it can be noted that the data presented for maternal mortality in the UNDP *Human Development Report* and World Bank *World Development Report* are not always consistent.[19]

However, the situation is improving (take for evidence initiatives such as the OECD's Paris 21 'Partnerships in Statistics for Development in the 21st Century', the World Bank's 'Demographic and Health Surveys' and UNICEF's Multi-indicator Cluster surveys).[20]

While the limitations which have been discussed in this section are important there is a danger that they may be regarded as being somewhat 'academic' by practitioner researchers when data availability is limited and policymakers are impatient for research results based on statistics which are already in existence but which may be questionable.[21]

DS research draws heavily on secondary documents. Much development research is undertaken in-house or is commissioned by organizations with the direct aim of informing specific policy options. Such in-house or commissioned research can be viewed alongside more academic research relating to similar policy-relevant topics, some of which may be funded by the same organizations which undertake in-house research or commission external bodies to undertake specific research projects. These organizations inevitably have specific policy agendas even when they might aim to fund research on purely academic criteria. The results of commissioned research are sometimes subject to intellectual property restrictions because the results may be regarded as being 'owned' by the commissioning agency. To the extent that knowledge is itself becoming a crucial basis of development, the monopolization of knowledge on development by agencies such as the World Bank is highly contentious and this is outlined in Box 5.9.[22]

Woolcock (2007: 64–5) has recently discussed the question of what Masters degree students should be taught in DS, arguing that

> an enduring feature of working in developing countries (or, for that matter, on development issues more generally) is paucity of quality – or sometimes any – data ....most of the data needed to make informed decisions... are highly imperfect, incomplete, or simply not available. Students armed with only a narrow arsenal of data analysis tools, even (or especially) highly sophisticated ones, are going to be less than fully equipped to handle situations where they will be routinely required to work with fragmented, dated and flawed data originally col-

---

Box 5.9 Whose Reality Counts? The World Bank as a 'Knowledge Bank'

In recent years the World Bank has shifted from its conventional role as a loan provider to focus on its development expertise and knowledge. This would assume that knowledge is a public good to be transferred to the ignorant; that knowledge is not contested and once accessed the poor will benefit. In October 1999, at the Bank's annual meeting, the President's speech launched the idea of the Bank as a storehouse of knowledge or a 'knowledge bank'. This was followed by the 1998 *World Development Report* on Knowledge for Development and later by the Global Development Network – a huge internet portal established by the Bank to contribute to the Bank's aim 'to be the first port of call for development expertise'. The gateway was controversial both inside and outside the bank. Further, the resignation of Ravi Kanbur as lead author on the *World Development Report* 2000/1 following what he felt was unreasonable pressure to tone down sections on globalization, or the fact that the *Voices of the Poor* report had a predetermined message, provided evidence for the critical positions taken in post-development thinking.

Source: Mehta (2001).

---

lected for other purposes… [Students need to be] a data entrepreneur, able to make connections across disparate sources and forms of evidence to build or refute a case. Is what I am doing as a practitioner making a difference? How do I know? How would I know if I was wrong? How do I distinguish between the effects my project is having and the impact of other events happening simultaneously? How do I go about assembling the data (qualitative and quantitative) I need to answer these questions?

These are questions for researchers at all career stages, not just master students, to reflect upon. Perhaps the most significant of these question is 'how would I know if I were wrong?'

5.5. SUMMARY

In this chapter we have been concerned with three areas:

5.5a. Doing research

It is helpful to view the research process as a process but bearing in mind that there are different types of research. The research process may differ depending on the level or type of research.

5.5b. Doing research in DS

Mixing methodologies and methods has become popular in DS in order to 'see every angle' of the 'mountain'. However, there is no guarantee that different approaches, methods or data will be combinable or comparable. There is often antagonistic dialogue between researchers and there are different disciplinary approaches within DS. Although there is an association between Economics and quantitative approaches and Social Anthropology and qualitative approaches, this has been questioned as a limiting and 'intellectual stereotyping' that is itself part of the problem of securing a uniform view of research design and priorities between disciplines. Combining methodologies and methods is complicated in practice by the range of possible ways in which quantitative and qualitative methods can be combined.

5.5c. Doing rigorous research in DS

The most common research quality criteria are often whether the research results are published in a peer-reviewed (refereed) journal and whether the research has been funded through a process which includes peer review. However, publication is post-process and has recently been questioned. One issue has been the question of what kind of 'criteria' might be used to judge 'quality' and 'rigour'. Typically we think of the validity, reliability, replicability and generalizability to evaluate social research.

However, some have argued that quantitative and qualitative approaches in the Social Sciences (and specifically in DS) need to be judged by different or 'alternative' criteria. There are rigour issues raised by the implications of the policy-related nature of much DS research and by the question of positionality. Development researchers are part of a process they want to influence. The discussion raises the issue of distinguishing between acceptable and unacceptable bias.

NOTES

1 In addition there are publications which represent summaries of generic social science research methods, notably by Blaikie (1993), Bryman (2004), David and Sutton (2004) and Denscombe (2003) which are very relevant for DS research.

2 Action-oriented studies and normative studies differ in that the former intends the study itself to be a catalyst for change among the participants of the study. In contrast a normative study seeks to recommend change beyond the participants.

3 A research problem would identify an issue such as clarification of the impact of policy on poverty reduction. A research problem would be operationalized through the generation of a number of research questions and/or hypotheses. A research question would take the more specific form of: how is poverty reduction affected by gender-oriented policy? The equivalent research hypothesis would take the form of: gender-oriented policy has an effect on poverty reduction. The question raises the issue in a broad but researchable manner, while the hypothesis creates a testable or refutable proposition.

4 As noted in Chapter 6 (Section 6.3c), there is a family of approaches to participatory methodology which are increasingly used in DS. It is necessary to distinguish between participatory methods used in a research context, and those which are used in a policy and practice context. In a research and planning context methods such as Rapid Rural Appraisal (RRAs) and Participatory Poverty Assessments (PPAs) are 'a family of approaches and methods to enable local (rural and urban) people to express, enhance, share and analyze their knowledge of life and conditions, to plan and to act' (Chambers, 1994: 1253). They are used as techniques to elicit poor households' perspectives about wellbeing and development. Chambers is widely recognized as one of the main 'driving forces' in this change. Indeed, Chamber's new paradigm has become an orthodoxy for many development researchers. The increased use of the participatory approach is at least in part a response to critics who have argued that western knowledge has come to dominate DS at the expense of indigenous knowledge. The most renowned such study is the World Bank's 'Voices of the Poor' study (Narayan et al., 2002). Participatory methods and techniques have faced criticism due to a perceived obsession with the local as opposed to wider structures of injustice and oppression, an insufficiently sophisticated understanding of how power operates and is constituted, and thus of how empowerment may occur. The participatory approach has also been accused of including a bias towards the civic and the social as opposed to the political, and towards a tendency for certain proponents of participatory development to treat participation as a technical method of project work rather than as a political methodology of empowerment (Hickey and Mohan, 2003: 5, 6).

5 For economic research in developing countries it is often the case that only secondary data can be used, unless a very large amount of resources is made available for the creation of an entirely new database. We have in mind research relating to macroeconomic issues such as economic growth, public finance and international trade and payments – and also where international cross-country and comparative research is involved. However, for economic research relating to the household level, for example on poverty research, questions about primary data collection strategies are just as relevant to economics as to other disciplines.

6 A very good overall review of many research methods used in the social sciences has been provided by Denscombe (2003) and by David and Sutton (2004) but there are, of course, other such reviews.

7   A recent special issue of the journal World Development has been devoted to 'Experiences of Combining Qualitative and Quantitative Approaches in Poverty Analysis' (Kanbur and Shaffer, 2007).

8   Bryman's (2004) discussion of sampling methods is particularly clear, but there are many other sources in the literature which cover sampling principles and practices, and several of these focus especially on data collection in developing countries.

9   During the process of rapid urbanisation many new urban (or peri-urban) residents may not be officially registered and would therefore be unlikely to be represented in the sampling frame, in sample data or in survey findings (for discussion of an Indonesian case see Suryahadi and Sumarto, 2001). There are examples of researchers studiously constructing their own sample frames, rather than relying on previously available frames (e.g. Edusah, 1999; Mensah, 2000).

10   For an informative introductory discussion of both qualitative and quantitative data analysis and its use in computer packages see in particular David and Sutton (2004).

11   Further information about each of the software packages mentioned in this paragraph are readily available using an online search facility.

12   An alternative analogy relates particularly to the impressionist painters. Monet, for example, painted a number of canvasses from precisely the same point, but in different light, at different times of the day, or in different weather conditions – which gave different dimensions to the same observed object.

13   There is also, of course, the possibility of disputes over alternative interpretations of the outcomes from research studies.

14   This stylized dichotomy is a useful heuristic device because it demonstrates the contrast of approaches and the extremes which we seek to combine.

15   It is significant that modern macroeconomic analysis dates from the mid-1930s when Keynes and his associates were particularly concerned with the avoidance of high levels of unemployment. Later developments of macroeconomic analysis, including that related to the prediction and control of economic cycles in industrialized economies, were concerned with the political implications of mass unemployment in the light of the rise of the National Socialists in Germany during the 1920s and 1930s. The perceived link between the post-1945 Marshall Plan and the role of the World Bank (International Bank for Reconstruction and Development – IBRD) reminds us of these dimensions.

16   Although reference has been made to the Social Sciences here it needs to be borne in mind that DS covers a range of disciplines wider than this. Study of rural and agricultural development and of environmental aspects of development, to give two examples, require knowledge beyond social sciences. This point has been made in Chapter 3 above (Section 3.3b). Further, by rigour we also include fundamentals such as specification of all sources of data and documents in a full standardized referencing style such as Harvard referencing (including page numbers).

17   A distinction should be drawn between carefully assembled 'databanks' (such as the Deininger–Squire and UNU WIDER data on which the Dollar and Kraay work relating to the relationship between economic growth and poverty was based (Deininger and Squire, 1996; Dollar and Kraay, 2000, 2001, 2002, 2004; UNU WIDER, 2000) and more generic statistical databanks for which detailed sources and methods for the data are difficult to access (such as the much used *World Development Indicators* produced by the World Bank (2007)).

18   More recently non-traditional data such as political data (for example the World Bank's 'governance' indicators including the CPIA – Country Policy and Institutional Assessment) and environmental data (such as US$ estimates for resource depletion) have also been made available. In the case of the World Bank the amount of data now published in the annual *World Development Report* has been reduced as their *World Development Indicators* become more readily available in printed and electronic forms.

19   Loup and Naudet (2000: 11) cite a comparison of maternal mortality rates in the Human Development Report (HDR) and World Development Report (WDR) in the mid 1990s. The WDR listed 56 countries with data and the HDR listed the same countries (minus one) together with a further 48. Of the 55 listed in the WDR (and in the HDR) only a quarter

were within a similar range – half were significantly higher and a quarter significantly lower as compared with the data in the HDR.

20 For further details refer to http://www.paris21.org/ and http://www.measuredhs.com and http://www.childinfo.org/

21 For example, the UNDP (2003: 35) noted that even for some of the main Millennium Development Goals – the UN poverty targets for 2015 – 50–100 countries have no reliable trend data (two observations separated by three years in the 1990s) and 20–50 countries had no data at all. For the dollar-a-day measure 100 countries had no trend data for the 1990s and 55 countries had no data at all.

22 For example, the World Bank is the only source – producer – of consistent global income poverty data – data upon which the activities of the World Bank itself is evaluated (see discussion in Redde and Pogge, 2002). For discussion of the impact of the World Bank on approaches to research in development economics refer to Broad (2006) and for further discussion of the Kanbur resignation see Wade (2001).

REFERENCES

Appleton, S. and Booth, D. (2001) *Combining Participatory and Survey-based Approaches to Poverty Monitoring and Analysis*. Q-Squared Working Paper Number 14. Centre for International Studies, University of Toronto. Available from http://www.q-squared.ca (accessed 1 August 2006).

Becker, S., Bryman, A. and Sempik, J. (2006) *Defining 'Quality' in Social Policy Research: Views, Perceptions and a Framework for Discussion*. Suffolk, UK: Social Policy Association.

Bevan, P. (2006) *Researching Wellbeing Across the Disciplines: Some Key Intellectual Problems and Ways Forward*. Wellbeing in Developing Countries (WeD) Research Group Working Paper 25. Bath, UK: WeD.

Blaikie, P. (1993) *Approaches to Social Enquiry*. Cambridge, UK: Polity Press.

Boaz, A. and Ashby, D. (2003) *Fit For Purpose: Assessing Research Quality For Evidence Based Policy and Practice*. ESRC UK Centre for Evidence Based Policy and Practice Working Paper Number 11. London: Queen Mary, University of London.

Bourguignon, F. (2003) 'Qualitative and quantitative approaches to poverty analysis: two pictures of the same mountain?', in Kanbur, R. (ed.), *Q-Squared: Qualitative and Quantitative Methods of Poverty Appraisal*. Washington, DC: Permanent Black.

Brannen, J. (2005) *Mixed Methods Research: a Discussion Paper*. ESRC National Centre for Research Methods Review Paper. Available from http://www.ncrm.ac.uk

Broad, R. (2006) 'Research, knowledge, and the art of 'paradigm maintenance': The World Bank's Development Economics Vice-Presidency (DEC)', *Review of International Political Economy*, 13 (3): 387–419.

Bryman, A. (2004) *Social Research Methods*. London: Oxford University Press.

Bujra, J. (2006) 'Lost in translation? The use of interpreters in fieldwork', in Desai, V. and Potter, R. (eds), *Doing Development Research*. London: Sage.

Cameron, J. (2004) *The Epistemology of Post-Modernism and Post-Structuralism*. Paper prepared for Development Studies Association Annual Conference. Church House, London, 6 November. Available from http://www.devstud.org.uk

Carvalho, S. and White, H. (1997) *Combining the Quantitative and Qualitative Approaches to Poverty Measurement and Analysis*. World Bank Technical Paper Number 366. Washington, DC: World Bank.

Chambers, R. (1994) 'Participatory rural appraisal: challenges, potentials, and paradigm', *World Development*, 22 (10): 1437–1451.

Chambers, R. (2001) 'The best of both worlds?', in Kanbur, R. (ed.), *Q-Squared: Qualitative and Quantitative Methods of Poverty Appraisal*. Washington, DC: Permanent Black.

David D. and Dodd J. (2002) 'Qualitative research and the question of rigour', *Qualitative Health Research*, 12 (2): 279–289.

David, M. and Sutton, C. (2004) *Social Research: The Basics*. London: Sage.

Davies, P. (2004) *Is Evidence Based Government Possible?* Paper presented at the 4th Annual Campbell Collaboration Colloquium, Washington, DC, 19 February.

Deininger, K. and Squire, L. (1996) 'A new data set measuring income inequality', *The World Bank Economic Review*, 10 (3): 565–591.

Denscombe, M. (2003) *The Good Research Guide*, 2nd ed. Maidenhead: Open University Press.

Desai, V. and Potter, R. (2006) *Doing Development Research*. London: Sage.

Dollar, D. and Kraay, A. (2000) *Growth is Good for the Poor*. World Bank Policy Research Working Paper Number 2587. Washington: World Bank.

Dollar, D. and Kraay, A. (2001) Growth is Good for the Poor. World Bank Policy Research Working Paper Number 2587 (revised). Washington: World Bank.

Dollar, D. and Kraay, A. (2002) 'Growth is good for the poor', *Journal of Economic Growth*, 7: 195–225.

Dollar, D. and Kraay, A. (2004) 'Growth is good for the poor', in Shorrocks, A. and Van Der Hoeven, R. (eds.), Growth, Inequality, and Poverty: Prospects for Pro-poor Economic Development. Oxford: Oxford University Press. pp. 62–80.

Edusah, S. (1999) *The Socio-Economic Significance of Rural Small-Scale Industries in Ghana*. PhD Thesis, University of Bradford, Development and Project Planning Centre.

Grayson, L. (2002) *Evidence Based Policy and the Quality Of Evidence: Rethinking Peer Review*. ESRC UK Centre for Evidence Based Policy and Practice Working Paper Number 7. London: Queen Mary, University of London.

Harriss, J. (2002) 'The case for cross-disciplinary approaches in international development', *World Development*, 30 (12): 487–496.

Hentschel, J. (2003) 'Integrating the Qual and the Quan: when and why?', in Kanbur, R. (ed.), *Q-Squared: Qualitative and Quantitative Methods of Poverty Appraisal*. Washington, DC: Permanent Black.

Hickey, S. and Mohan, G. (2003) *Relocating Participation within a Radical Politics of Development: Citizenship and Critical Modernism*. Draft working paper prepared for conference on 'Participation: From Tyranny to Transformation? Exploring New Approaches to Participation in Development', 27–28 February 2003, University of Manchester.

Hulme, D. (2006) *Integrating Quantitative and Qualitative Research for Country Case Studies of Development*. Brooks World Poverty Institute, University of Manchester, and ESRC Global Poverty Research Group. Manchester: Universities of Manchester and Oxford. Available from http://www.sed.manchester.ac.uk/idpm/staff/documents/DH_GDNPaper.pdf (accessed 2 July 2007).

Hulme, D. and Toye, J. (2006) 'The case for cross-disciplinary social science research on poverty, inequality and wellbeing', *Journal of Development Studies*, 42 (7): 1085–1107.

Kanbur, R. (2002) 'Economics, social science and development', *World Development*, 30 (3): 477–486.

Kanbur, R. and Shaffer, P. (eds) (2007) 'Experiences of combining qualitative and quantitative approaches in poverty analysis', *Special Issue of World Development*, 35 (2): 183–354.

Kenny, C. and Williams, D. (2001) 'What do we know about economic growth? Or, why don't we know very much?' *World Development*, 29 (1): 1–22.

Laws, S., Harper, C. and Marcus, R. (2003) *Research for Development: A Practical Guide*. London: Sage.

Long, A. and Godfrey, M. (2004) 'An evaluation tool to test the quality of qualitative research studies', *International Journal of Social Research Methodology*, 7 (2): 181–196.

Loup, J. and Naudet, D. (2000) *The State Of Human Development Data And Statistical Capacity Building In Developing Countries*. Human Development Report Office Occasional Papers, March. Geneva: UNDP.

Marsland, N., Wilson, I., Abeyasekera, S. and Kleih, U. (2001) *A Methodological Framework for Combining Quantitative and Qualitative Survey Methods*. Socio-Economic Methodologies Best Practice Guidelines 10. Chatham: Natural Resources Institute.

Mehta, L. (2001) 'The World Bank and its emerging knowledge empire', *Human Organization*, 60 (2): 189–196.

Mensah, J.V. (2000) *Small-Scale Industries in Ghana's Economic Development: Comparative Economic Efficiency of Rural and Urban Small-Scale Industries in the Central Region*. PhD Thesis, University of Bradford. Development and Project Planning Centre.

Mikkelsen, B. (2005) *Methods for Development Work and Research: A Guide for Practitioners*. London: Sage.

Narayan, N., Patel, R., Schafft, K., Rachemacher, A. and Koch-Schulte, S. (2002) *Voices of the Poor: Can Anyone Hear Us?* Washington, DC: World Bank.

Olsen, W. (2004) 'Triangulation in social research: qualitative and quantitative methods can really be mixed', in Holborn, M. (ed.), *Developments in Sociology 20*. London: Pearson Education. pp. 103–118. (This publication is based on an invitation to write a chapter for a book for schoolteachers at A-Level in Sociology. Available from http://www.ccsr.ac.uk/methods/festival2004/programme/Sat/pm/MSTheatre/documents/Olsen_000.doc (accessed 18 June 2007).

Patton, M. (2002) *Qualitative Research and Evaluation Methods*. London: Sage.

Redde, S. and Pogge, T. (2002) *How Not to Count the Poor*. Department of Economics Working Paper. Colombia University, New York.

Sala-I-Martin, X. (1997) 'I just ran two million regressions', *The American Economic Review*, 87 (2): 178–183.

Scheyvens, R. and Storey, D. (2003) *Development Fieldwork: A Practical Guide*. London: Sage.

Sharp, K. (2005) *Squaring the 'Q's? Methodological Reflections on a Study of Destitution in Ethiopia*. Working Paper No. 7. Q-Squared, Toronto.

Spencer, L., Ritchie, J., Lewis, J. and Dillon, J. (2003) *Quality in Qualitative Evaluation: A Framework For Assessing Research Evidence*. London: Government Chief Social Researcher's Office.

Suryahadi, A. and Sumarto, S. (2001) *The Chronic Poor, the Transient Poor and the Vulnerable in Indonesia, Before and After the Crisis*. Social Monitoring and Early and Early Response Unit (SMERU) Working Paper. Jakarta: SMERU.

Thomas, A. and Johnson, H. (2002) *Not Only Reinforcing but also Different Stories: Combining Case Studies and Survey to Investigate how Postgraduate Programmes can Build Capacity for Development Policy and Management*. Paper for 'Combined Methods' conference, Centre for Development Studies, Swansea, 1–2 July 2002.

Thorbecke, E. (2003) 'Tensions, complementarities and possible convergence between the qualitative and quantitative approaches to poverty assessment', in Kanbur, R. (ed.), *Q-Squared: Qualitative and Quantitative Methods of Poverty Appraisal*. Washington, DC: Permanent Black.

UNDP. (2003) *Human Development Report 2003*. New York: Oxford University Press.

United Nations University: World Institute for Development Economics (UNU WIDER) Research. (2000) *World Income Inequality Database*. Available from http://www.wider.unu.edu/wiid/wiid.htm

Wade, R. (2001) 'Making the World Development Report 2000: attacking poverty', *World Development*, 29 (8): 1435–1441.

White, H. (2002) 'Combining quantitative and qualitative approaches in poverty analysis', *World Development*, 30 (12): 511–522.

Woolcock, M. (2007) 'Higher education, policy schools, and development studies: what should Masters degree students be taught?' *Journal of International Development*, 19 (1): 55–73.

World Bank. (2007) *World Development Indicators 2007*. Washington: World Bank.

CHAPTER SIX

HOW ARE RESEARCH AND PRACTICE LINKED IN DEVELOPMENT STUDIES?

Euclid is supposed to have told Ptolemy: "There is no 'royal road' to Geometry". It is not clear that there is any royal road to evaluation of economic or social policies either. A variety of considerations that call for attention are involved, and evaluations have to be done with sensitivity to these concerns. Much of the debate on the alternative approaches to evaluation relates to the priorities in deciding on what should be at the core of our normative concern. (Sen, 1999: 85)

We therefore conclude that greater attention to ESW [Economic and Sector Work] in the form of elaborating the broader context, clarifying the rational for a specific type of intervention, and assessing its feasibility and economic desirability against a broader set of potential alternatives could result in the design of better projects and thus less need for spending time on preparation or supervision. (Deininger et al., 1998: 415)

6.1. INTRODUCTION

This chapter is intended to explore the relationship between DS research and writing on the one hand, and development policy and practice on the other. The need for innovatory methods and approaches for the management of policy, of programme and project design, and of monitoring and evaluation has associated DS researchers closely with development practice and practitioners for many years.

The main objective of this chapter is not to provide an overview of development issues and controversies, but rather to focus on a range of methodologies and methodological issues relevant to 'development practice', on their evolution, and on their employment. Some criticism of the DS literature, and of 'development practice' has referred to a lack of rigour. Much of this criticism has been based on the view that too much of the development literature has been excessively descriptive and insufficiently analytical, and in particular that it has lacked a robust theoretical and methodological basis. It is hoped that the chapter will demonstrate that there is a wealth

of analytical methods and techniques which can be used to make development practice rigorous and systematic.

The quotation from Amartya Sen at the beginning of this chapter has been selected
with a view to emphasizing that no single approach to evaluation studies (which are
perhaps the main policy-related activity in DS which has a significant research content) can be recommended above all others. Diversity of practice is common and
acceptable. The quotation from Deininger et al. is intended to emphasize that a systematic approach to project, sector and policy-related DS work is likely to lead to
more cost-effective and better quality outcomes. Both imply that 'development practice' can benefit from systematic, rigorous and high-quality inputs from DS practitioners.

Following this brief introduction Section 2 of the chapter will discuss aspects of the
relationship between more academic dimensions of DS and DS practice (as exercised
by practitioners) which is summarized in Table I.1 in the Introduction to this book.
Section 3 focuses on what might be thought of as the more 'micro' aspects of development policy management and practice. It first reviews the relationship between
policy management and project management including a policy hierarchy and a
policy cycle. Then the logical framework is presented and discussed in the context of
results-based management (RBM). Participatory approaches to development management and the sustainable livelihoods approach are then discussed. The section ends
with an explanation and illustrations of the very important 'incremental analysis'
approach to the appraisal and evaluation of development interventions. Section 4
relates to the 'broad picture' and explores experience with evaluation of structural
adjustment programmes and policy reform more generically in the context of the
search for an effective methodological approach.[1] The critical issue of the use of
'shadow prices' in economic analysis is explained and discussed in this context.
Finally, Section 5 provides some overall conclusions relating to the issues raised in
the chapter.

6.2. DS PRACTITIONERS AND DEVELOPMENT PRACTICE

Development practitioners need to be just as systematic and rigorous in their pre-
paratory and evaluation studies and reports as academic and independent researchers
are in their research.[2] However, it has to be recognized that the objectives of
practitioners and researchers, and the time scales within which they work for their
respective research and associated activities, differ. This means that development
practitioners need to be as aware of the need for a systematic approach as development researchers and writers, implying that appropriate approaches, theories, methods and techniques should be used. Two comparatively recent and interesting books
illustrate the methodological problem. Kirkpatrick et al. (2002) provide an edited
selection of invaluable contributions covering many aspects of development policy
and management for developing countries, however the book as a whole has very
little reference to methodology, methods or techniques. Wollman (2003) aims to

provide a comprehensive evaluation of public sector reform in Europe, but this is in an edited collection of country studies which does not contain any significant use of recognized evaluation methods and techniques. Both of these edited collections would have been of considerably more value if they had systematically used established methods and techniques. A major objective of this chapter is to outline a number of methods and approaches which significantly contribute to more systematic understanding of development issues and experience.

One approach to an understanding of the contemporary DS community would focus on a distinction between the discourse and practice tendencies which has been outlined in summary form in our Introduction to this book and in more detail in Chapter 3.[3] The first emphasizes intellectual discourses, with a concentration on broad concepts of development within a long time perspective but sometimes with limited practical application to current development problems and their resolution (Apthorpe and Gasper, 1996; Escobar, 1995). The second might be described as 'empiricists', with a concentration on theory, methods and techniques which can be applied through empirical analysis to increased understanding of development problems and to the design of 'solutions' (Chambers, 1994a, 1994b, 1994c; Oakley, 1991, 1995; Potts, 2002). To some extent the two tendencies overlap, with 'discourse' people also contributing as 'empiricists' – a good example of which is provided by Apthorpe who has contributed significantly to the 'discourse' literature as well as to practical, policy-related, empirical studies (Apthorpe, 1972, 1999; Apthorpe and Atkinson, 1999; Wood et al., 2001).

It is perhaps self-evident, but needs emphasizing, that a considerable amount of activity associated with the analysis of policy and practice in both industrialized and developing countries involves a research-related approach. This includes the generation of primary data, the critical assembly of secondary data, and the application of analytical methods in interpreting data, in the process of designing and evaluating policy, programmes and projects. Many developing countries do not have a comparable wealth of readily available secondary data (including data banks) to that which exists in industrialized countries, making the need for the gathering of primary data more pressing. The fact that development practitioners (i.e. those who work directly on development policy and practice) often perceive a need to achieve 'results' very quickly increases the significance of reliable data gathering and analysis. Longer-term academic and other independent research include traditional concerns for a critical view of both data and of analytical methods and techniques – concerns which are often not found in the work of practitioners. The distinction between the time scale of the activities of independent researchers (with a tendency towards the long term) and of practitioners (with a tendency towards the short term) will be a concern of much of this chapter.

An attempt has been made to identify the position of research theory and methods in the design of policy, programmes and projects in Figure 6.1. On the left-hand side of the diagram there is a two-way relationship between Independent Research and Research Methods and Techniques – indicating that independent research both uses and creates/modifies methods and techniques. In the middle of the diagram the

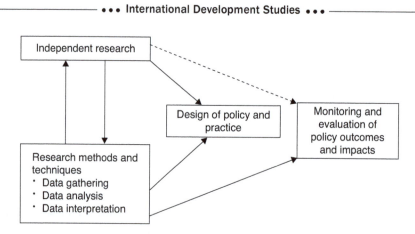

Figure 6.1 **'Development Research': Activities, Policy and Practice**

Design of Policy and Practice is largely based on findings from independent research using established research methods and techniques but not creating or modifying these methods and techniques. On the right-hand side of the diagram the Monitoring and Evaluation of Policy Outcomes and Impacts uses the results of independent research as part of its secondary data and also generates primary data using established research methods and techniques but not usually creating or modifying these methods and techniques. This said, it needs to be recognized that some of the development of research methods and techniques has been instigated by international aid agencies, but not usually in the course of the direct undertaking of policy design or its monitoring and evaluation.

The distinction which is being made between basic, applied and routine research in Figure 6.1 is analogous to points made in a discussion about research in science and technology subjects by Stewart (1977: Chap. 5) in the context of development. We have already developed this distinction in Section 5.2a of Chapter 5 in this book. Basic research relates to fundamental work on methodology (for example the development of qualitative research methods), applied research relates to the application of these principles to practical uses (for example analysis of factors affecting levels of poverty) and routine research relates to regular activities (for example collection of statistics for cost of living indices). Quite a few methods and techniques are shared between these three levels of research, and the three levels can complement each other iteratively, as routine monitoring and evaluation studies of policies, programmes and projects can inform more fundamental development-related research findings.

──────── **6.3. SYSTEMATIC APPROACHES TO DEVELOPMENT POLICY** ────────

Over the last few decades there has been a focus amongst empiricists, as well as amongst those who concentrate mainly on discourse, on appropriate overall approaches to development. These issues have been discussed in Chapter 1 of this book.

Many contributions to the literature have taken the view that development occurs as the result of government policy interventions. Others have an opposing view: that development occurs as a result of complex interactions between many influences, only some of which are the result of government action, and that the achievement of community-related development objectives will sometimes require resistance to government interventions. Between these two bi-polar extremes there lies a range of views within a continuum or spectrum. Many development practitioners, particularly those associated with the international aid community, necessarily work through government agencies, and so many development strategies have been public sector-, and international aid-, oriented. Approaches which have been heavily criticized in more recent years, such as integrated rural development policies, infant industry protection, and the provision of major economic and social infrastructure services through public corporations, largely originated during a pre-independence period of colonial rule. The continuity represented by the adaptation of these development strategies by post-colonial independent governments – even if conceptualized within a different political philosophy or ideology – was only broken during the period of 'structural adjustment' in the 1980s and 1990s which had the institutional support of, and enforcement by, the International Financial Institutions (IFIs) and, more broadly, of the international aid community.[4]

One clarification which we should perhaps make at this juncture concerns the relationship between research, policy-related research, systematic policy management, and the political process. It is inevitable that politicians involved in development policy and practice will wish to determine priorities and to approve policy design. It is not the function of DS researchers to establish development priorities or to approve policy interventions. It is therefore necessary to distinguish between the role of DS researchers (including practitioners and consultants) and the role of decision-makers. It is impossible to entirely isolate policy-related research from the political process, but we take the view that despite the practice-related orientation of much DS research it should be viewed separately from the directly political decision-making process.

The discussion in this chapter ranges over a number of analytical methods and techniques – some well established and others innovatory. There is a constant and healthy evolution of the methods and techniques which are used in DS research and practice. However, the discussion is necessarily selective, and the objective has been to focus on some of the major approaches. In the process some valuable contributions are likely to have been omitted – and apparently overlooked. We hope that readers will understand our selectivity.

6.3a. Broad Issues – Development Planning and Policy

In recent years as a result of dissatisfaction with the project-based approach to international aid, development policy and expenditure management there has been an implicit move towards what can be termed a policy hierarchy. Such an hierarchy is explicit within analytical methods such as the Logical Framework and its derivatives through to RBM (Results Based Management, see for example UNDP, 2002) which will be outlined in more detail later in this chapter. Development agencies (see for example DFID, 2005: 53) and developing countries (see for example Republic of Uganda, 2000: Section 3.5) have been critical of project-based development management, principally because it leads to a fragmented and incoherent approach to public policy and public expenditure management.[5]

In the 1960s, 1970s and early 1980s there was considerable emphasis within the international aid community, including the IFIs (mainly the World Bank and the International Monetary Fund), on the project level management of development programmes (Baum and Tolbert, 1985; Gittinger, 1982). Some early national development plans consisted of little more than lists or catalogues of public sector development projects (e.g. Uganda, 1961) without any overall perspective within the context of national or sectoral development experience or of the institutional framework. However, over time, there were more serious attempts to achieve greater emphasis within development planning on: a) macroeconomic projections for the testing of internal consistency and for estimation of the resource envelope (i.e. the resources available to government through tax revenue, aid disbursements and other receipts); b) a more comprehensive discussion of sectoral, regional and institutional factors, including greater attention to prioritization (e.g. Government of Malaysia, 1991; Government of Pakistan, 1988; Republic of Kenya, 1986; Republic of Uganda, 1966, 1972; Waterston, 1979); and c) inclusion of non-economic (or indirectly economic) issues such as the institutional framework, public administration and social development.

However, in the 1970s and 1980s several events impinged on the type of development planning which had been widely practiced in developing countries in the previous two to three decades. First, there was a change in the political complexion of governments in the United States and the United Kingdom (Reaganomics and Thatcherism specifically) which led to an increased emphasis on market-based solutions to long-term development issues and to a shunning of planning in what has been described as the neo-liberal counter revolution (Toye, 2003: 30–32). Second, major changes in international financial markets led to significant re-alignments of foreign exchange rates, with the – at least temporary – effect of making the international economy less predictable. Third, a number of the major developed economies experienced higher rates of inflation than had been the norm over the previous two to three decades, adding a further dimension to the unpredictability of international financial markets. Fourth, political instability, particularly in the Middle East, led to significant fluctuations in international crude oil prices. Fifth, international interest rates increased in both nominal and real terms making the cost of borrowing significantly greater, and putting increased pressure on public finances and the balance of payments of increasingly indebted developing countries. These factors, when combined, had the effects of making: a) development planning politically suspect amongst major Western powers (on ideological grounds – planning being associated in the mind of key political leaders with Soviet-style command-and-control management systems and on the grounds that development objectives were not being achieved); and b) the prediction of the course of international and national economic events much more difficult (with the effects that planning became more difficult to undertake, and that objectives were less likely to be achieved).[6]

The factors outlined above tended to destabilize the environment within which development planning was intended to operate. This destabilization created additional arguments for concentrating on the project (or micro-) level management of government development interventions with a relatively short-term focus. Project level development management has much to recommend it (see Box 6.1) but it also has major disadvantages which are discussed fully by Mosley and Eeckhout (2000).[7] To the extent that individual developing countries experienced fragmented project-based management of public sector development interventions there was an increased tendency for development policy as a whole to be more uncoordinated and lacking in cohesion, and to have high transactions costs for recipient countries (DFID, 2005).

Note that the level of sophistication of project management will vary depending upon the size and complexity of the project – the smaller and simpler the project the lighter the project management touch.

A basic reference for many of these issues is provided by Baum and Tolbert (1985), and more recently by Potts (2002).

In response to criticisms that interventions by the IFIs (and more broadly by the international aid community) the World Bank initiated a Comprehensive Development Framework[8] (CDF) approach in 1999. Although the CDF had a low profile outside the IFIs and the international aid community, it represented an 'umbrella' incorporating the Poverty Reduction Strategy Papers (PRSPs), the Millennium Development Goals (MDGs – originally International Development Targets – IDTs) (United Nations, 2007), and the Heavily Indebted Poor Country (HIPC – World Bank, 2006) debt write-off programme. This change in emphasis followed about 20 years of Structural Adjustment Programmes (SAPs) which had been severely criticized by many development specialists (see for example Mohan et al., 2000; Mosley et al., 1995). The change of approach by the World Bank, and by its directly and indirectly associated multilateral and bilateral agencies, came about for two reasons. First, the basic objectives of the SAPs in changing the economic management and control systems of many countries had largely been achieved by the mid 1990s. Second, the World Bank and other bodies wished to respond to the criticisms which

---

Box 6.1   Components of Project Management

1. Examination of the relationship between the individual project and broader national and sector goals
2. Careful quantitative specification of project objectives, outcomes and impacts
3. Use of objectively verifiable indicators of performance
4. Projections of financial expenditure requirements for medium-term project sustainability and of income generation
5. Consideration of technical, economic, financial, social, environmental, and institutional implications
6. Analysis of the major areas of risk and uncertainty associated with the project
7. Incorporation of monitoring and evaluation into the project management scheme

had been directed at the SAPs – particularly in terms of the failure of the SAPs to be perceived as under the ownership of the developing countries, and their failure to address poverty reduction adequately (Killick, 1995). Of course, even the new approach has not satisfied many of the critics, however it cannot be denied that there was a sea-change in Washington and other international centres in the late 1990s.

The 'thinking-through' represented by the Comprehensive Development Framework is consistent with the switch from a project-based approach to development management to a broader policy-based approach. As has been explained, this policy-based approach does not mean that project management has been abandoned, but simply means that projects should now be more effectively placed within their macro socio-economic context, implying the need for an overall policy hierarchy.

Figure 6.2 sets out a policy hierarchy, with Strategy (the broad overview – poverty reduction or industrialization for example) at the top, Policy below this (the approach to a particular area of the economy or society applying the elements of the strategical overview), Programmes below again (usually applying at a sector or sub-sector level and comprising a number of inter-linked projects), Projects below programmes (involving specific time-bound interventions), and Activities at the bottom (activities being individual actions – as within Network Analysis for example where each activity is a necessary but not sufficient element of a project).

Figure 6.3 places the basic policy hierarchy (to the left of the table) in the context of a sectoral decomposition of the policy framework (middle column) and of a regional/decentralized approach to policy management which has become increasingly significant since the early 1980s (for example Aryeetey and Goldstein, 2000: 294–5; Kokor and Kroes, 2000; Republic of Kenya, 1984).[9]

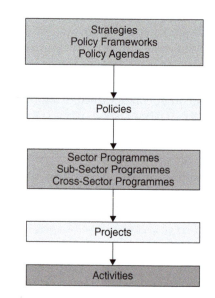

Figure 6.2 A Policy Management Hierarchy

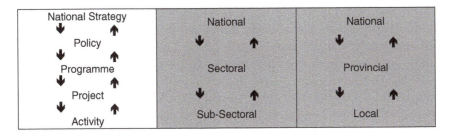

Figure 6.3   Hierarchies within the Policy Management System

An example from primary education might clarify the concept of the policy hierarchy in a practical developing country context. The Strategy is 'Poverty Reduction', the Policy is 'Educational Development' as a means of achieving poverty reduction, the Programme is 'Primary Education' as a major aspect of educational development (there are also sub-programmes such as primary teacher training development), the Project is the building of an individual school, and the Activity is something such as the building of the foundations of the school. Another example might be improvement of potable water supply. The Strategy is 'Improvement of Public Health', the Policy is 'Improvement of Public Water Supply', the Programme is 'Development of Piped Water Supply', the Project is the 'Extension of Water Purification Works', and the Activity is 'Enhancement of Water Pumping'.

It is evident that a project-based approach to development policy management within this type of policy hierarchy is hardly likely to be very successful. Prior questions about strategies, policies and programmes are likely to be overlooked if the basic entry point for international aid interventions are at the level of the project. Even with a focus on sectors a number of very significant cross-cutting issues such as poverty reduction, gender, the environment, decentralization and financial sustainability are likely to be neglected (refer to the PRSP Sourcebook – Klugman 2002: 235–401).[10] However, to suggest that aid agencies have actually been managing their country programmes on a project-oriented approach would be to misjudge their sophistication. Many of the aid agencies have had country strategies, but in recent years there have been greater efforts to coordinate the activities of international aid agencies in recipient developing countries setting out jointly agreed overall approaches to development assistance which include consultation and agreement with recipient countries (e.g. DFID et al., 2005). Without these efforts to make country strategies consistent with the development strategies and priorities of recipient country governments the international aid community would be open to the charge of relying on 'donor-driven' strategies and priorities, detracting from the country ownership principle of the Comprehensive Development Framework (CDF).

One aspect of the overall picture presented in this chapter is the Policy Cycle. In many respects this has been derived and developed from the Project Cycle which was so ubiquitous in handbooks and manuals dealing with project cycle management in the 1970s, 1980s and 1990s (Baum and Tolbert, 1985: 334–5; MacArthur, 1994;

Picciotto and Weaving, 1994; Potts, 2002: 12–17). With the change in emphasis within international aid management from a project-based to a policy- and sector-based approach it was necessary to establish a 'Policy Cycle' to complement the 'Project Cycle', and one approach to this can be found in the OECD's SIGMA series (2001). The United Kingdom's Green Book (on Appraisal and Evaluation in Central Government – HM Treasury, 1997) contains a ROAMEF (Rationale, Objectives, Appraisal, Monitoring, Evaluation, Feedback) cycle which is directly analogous to the type of policy cycle which is being sought.

Figure 6.4 provides an example of a comprehensive Policy Cycle, and its derivation from the Project Cycle will be clear from the literature which has been referred to above. In many respects it does not matter where discussion about the elements of the policy cycle begins simply because it is an integrated cycle which we are dealing with. In addition much policy-related work will be iterative, with planning activity moving back and forth between the various stages of the cycle. It is easiest to start at the top left-hand corner of the diagram with the determination of a problem or of a policy agenda.[11] This may consist of an entirely new policy issue coming from outside the system or it may be internally defined through analysis within the existing policy cycle. The next set of activities in the policy cycle consists of careful definition of the problem, identification of alternative means of achieving the defined objectives, data collection and data/policy analysis. There follows decision-making, including – not least – the definition of the areas where policy decisions are needed. For example, which alternative should be selected, how big should the intervention be, or what type of phasing and timing should be involved in policy implementation. The next set of activities includes the preparation of an implementation plan and the undertaking of the implementation, together with the monitoring and evaluation of the implementation. A distinctly separate set of activities is the monitoring and evaluation of the policy outcomes and impacts. Then on the basis of this evaluation modification of the policy problem or policy agenda may be necessary, following which the cycle starts again. This brief tour of the diagram has necessarily been sketchy and suggestive rather than comprehensive, and the reader may wish to refer to more specialized literature on the subject which has been outlined in the previous paragraph.

Many readers who are familiar with the realities of policy formulation and management might view the apparent determinism of this policy cycle with disbelief. They might regard the degree of discipline required in order to follow the logical steps set out in the cycle to be impossible to achieve given the complexity of institutional frameworks in the real world. Indeed, within the political process it might even be found that high-level policymakers would regard the discipline imposed by such a policy cycle as being inconsistent with their exercise of political control – the external discipline would be seen as reducing their scope for political bargaining. A first response to such a reaction is that the policy cycle represents a heuristic device, conceptualizing the various stages involved in the management of policy interventions. Like any other theory, or heuristic device, the model is an abstraction which

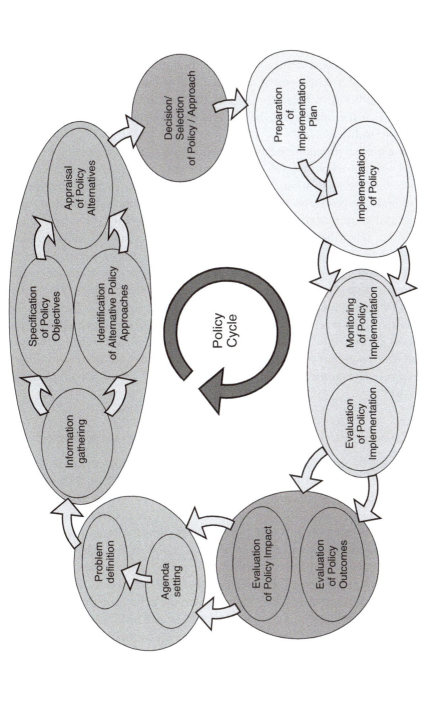

Figure 6.4 – A Suggested 'Policy Cycle' for Policy Management

Note: The contributions of Shkelzen Marku (Centre for Rural Studies, Tirana) to the production of this diagram are gratefully acknowledged.

establishes the important elements and issues. A second response is that in the contemporary world there is considerable emphasis on the need for improved standards of governance and of transparency in public policy (and in private sector) management as a means of achieving policy objectives more effectively and of reducing the extent of corruption. Any improvement in the effectiveness of policy management is likely to involve a reduction in the extent of political discretion. However, there is a need in realistic policy management to distinguish between, on the one hand the systematic specification of objectives and of the instruments for achieving those objectives, and on the other hand the political measures needed to convert policy aspirations into reality.[12]

Efforts to achieve a programme-based approach to government development initiatives had not been very successful. Integrated Rural Development Projects which attempted to link together various aspects of rural communities (including, for example, agricultural extension advice, agricultural credit, water supply, health and medical services and education (Livingstone, 1979) into programme-type interventions experienced considerable coordination problems. In this sense all three levels of development management have been seriously questioned: a) national development planning; b) programme level interventions; and c) project-based management – over the last three decades. Decentralization has also experienced difficulties, and did not really offer an alternative approach which could circumvent the problems experienced with the three levels of development management. The decentralized local dimension of government in many developing countries suffered particularly from manpower deficiencies (in terms of both numbers and skills) and from serious revenue generation constraints (Aryeetey and Goldstein, 2000: 294–5; Charlton, 2005; Robinson, 2007).

6.3b. Development 'micro-management' – techniques, methods and approaches

The use of logical frameworks in project analysis began in 1971 based on a request by the United States Agency for International Development (USAID) to a consultancy organization called Practical Concepts Inc. to develop such a method (MacArthur, 1993: 4). The Logical Framework emphasizes the logical connection between broad goals, narrower objectives, inputs and outputs on its vertical axis, and between narrative description, the use of objective indicators, data sources, and assumptions/risks on its horizontal axis.[13] Continuous development of the 'Logframe' has emphasized the importance of means/instruments for achieving objectives, and the distinction between inputs, outputs, outcomes and impacts. On the latter issue the ZOPP (objectives-oriented project planning) approach of the German aid agency (GTZ, 1992, 1997) has led to the development of RBM which extends the four horizontal elements of the Logical Framework to six, adding outcomes and impacts.[14]

Figure 6.5 illustrates these issues, with the lighter shaded area being the original 4 x 4 matrix of the Logical Framework and the more heavily shaded area representing the addition of the outcomes and impacts of the RBM approach to the vertical logic.[15] Excellent discussions of the RBM approach are readily available from the Canadian

	NARRATIVE SUMMARY	OBJECTIVELY VERIFIABLE INDICATORS	MEANS OF VERIFICATION	IMPORTANT ASSUMPTIONS
Vertical Logic ↑	Programme or Sector Goal:	Measures of Goal Achievement:		Assumptions for achieving programme goal targets:
	Project Purpose:	Conditions that will indicate purpose has been achieved:		Assumptions for achieving project purposes:
	Project Outputs:	Magnitude of Outputs:		Assumptions for achieving outputs:
	Project Inputs:	Implementation Target (Type and Quantity):		Assumptions for providing inputs:
	Project Outcomes			
↓	Project Impact			
	Horizontal Logic ←—————————————————————————————→			

Figure 6.5   The Logical Framework and Results-Based Management

International Development Agency (CIDA, 1999), the Organization for Economic Cooperation and Development (OECD, 2000), the United Nations Development Programme (UNDP, 2002) and the World Bank (Kusek and Rist, 2004).

The convincing arguments for the use of the RBM approach are that projects (or policies) are not implemented for the sake of the outputs themselves but for the outcomes which arise from the outputs, and even these outcomes are not intrinsically functional unless they lead to desirable impacts. An example will make these arguments clearer in a development context.

The RBM approach implies that the success of a policy should not be judged by the disbursement of money, but rather by the achievements of the project, programme or policy. The expenditure of money is a means of achieving objectives through the purchase of inputs which lead to the outputs which follow. Outcomes and impacts are results which flow from these outputs. In the context of developed market economies in recent years the British Government, for example, has introduced a number of innovations into the management of public expenditure including Public Service Agreements (PSAs) and Resource Accounts Budgeting (RAB) recognizing that outcomes from public expenditure do not fit neatly into financial years, that the outcomes and impacts are of greater policy significance than expenditures (inputs), and that ministerial programming does not fit neatly into the conventional budgetary straitjacket (Balls and O'Donnell, 2002: 240–2).

For example, in a developing country context a policy may have the objective of enhancing the quality of life and the productivity for low-income groups in urban areas through better health standards arising from better quality water supply. The objective may be achieved either by the direct supply of water by the public sector, or through government interventions facilitating improved water supply by the private sector (which includes civil society and private households). The success of the policy should be judged on the basis of whether it results in an improved quality of life and productivity, not on whether it results in a better quality water supply, and least of all whether it results in the expenditure of more money on water supply systems. It is even possible to envisage a situation where the improved quality of life and productivity arising from better water supply does not even involve considerable public sector investment in water supply systems but is more concerned with public health education and with changing regulation and environmental enforcement systems. It also needs to be borne in mind that the long-term achievement of policy objectives, not least in the water supply sub-sector, may depend critically on the financial sustainability of institutions.

Considerable disquiet, fuelled by research, over the project-based approach to development policy management has led to broader perspectives including policy orientation, a focus on sustainable livelihoods and on wellbeing, identification of cross-cutting issues,[16] and the sector-wide approach (the latter being referred to as SWAPs – see notes 5,9 and 10 to this chapter). Much of recent thinking about development planning relies considerably on an indicators-led approach at project, programme, policy, strategy and international levels.[17] At the same time, parallel work has concentrated on the importance of market liberalization (both domestic and international) and of decentralization (including considerably increased emphasis on the role of non-governmental organizations (NGOs) and of civil society in general).

6.3c. Participatory approaches and sustainable livelihoods

One of the issues which has been central for many development specialists over the last 10 to 15 years is that of the participatory approach to managing projects, programmes and policies (Harper, 1997; Mikkelsen, 2005; Oakley, 1991; OXFAM, 1995: Pt 3). Many would take the view that participation involves a democratic principle, and that a lack of participation by the relevant communities in policy interventions is unacceptable. However in the context of this chapter we are more concerned about the technical issues associated with the nature and utilization of participation, which can be applied at a number of stages of the policy cycle (refer to Figure 6.4) – particularly the data gathering, preparation, implementation and monitoring/evaluation stages.

Consultation with groups who are likely to be principally affected (either positively or negatively) by a project, programme or policy can provide a basis for an enhanced positive impact, and/or a reduced negative impact. Through a process of consultation, or participation, the acceptability of projects, programmes or policies to those who are most affected can be significantly improved. The groups which are likely to be principally affected can be regarded as 'stakeholders' (MacArthur, 1997). The process of consultation – or participation – can be used as a basis for the modification of the design of a project, programme or policy in order to make it more acceptable and more effective in achieving the objectives and priorities of communities. At later stages in the project or policy cycle the process can be extended to implementation and operations improving the chances of the entire cycle achieving smooth and effective implementation within cost and time schedules, and also enhancing the chances of effective achievement of outcomes and impacts. Thus participation of those who have a direct interest in the outcomes of policy in the design, decision-making, implementation and operations of an 'intervention' can, in principle, make a positive contribution to success and to positive impacts on the economy and society.

Perhaps naturally, the proponents of participatory methods have had less to say about the possibility that some stakeholders are likely to perceive both government and non-government interventions as being against their interests. In some cases this may relate to communities rejecting 'interventions' which are against their interests and, for example, this may arise in circumstances where governments act on behalf of powerful economic interests, such as transnational corporations. Stakeholders may take great pains to frustrate the adoption and implementation of a planned intervention. They may even refuse to engage effectively in the process of participation, or they may try to disrupt this process. A converse possible scenario could be where a transnational corporation perceives a particular government intervention as being against its interests, and itself acts as a non-cooperative stakeholder. The range of potential circumstances are too numerous to categorize here. However it should be clear that, within the context of the participatory approach, forward thinking by those responsible for interventions is always likely to lead to better and more acceptable outcomes and impacts than situations where there has been inadequate forward planning (Fritzen, 2007).

The Rapid Rural Appraisal (RRA) approach has been applied to rural development projects in developing countries in cases which were not easily amenable to regular economic appraisal, and where a 'full-blown' feasibility study would probably be regarded as a misallocation of scarce resources. This approach has been modified, and re-named, as Participatory Rural Appraisal (PRA) and one of the principal initiators of this has been Chambers (1994a, 1994b, 1994c). A significant resource is the Resource Centres for Participatory Research and Action network, which is an 'alliance of seventeen different organizations from around the world, that strives to promote the empowerment of the disadvantaged through participation in their own development' (RCPLA Network, 2007). The principles of this approach are transferable to many projects in areas which are far from being rural, and are also transferable to developed countries as well as being used in the developing countries for which they were originally conceived.

The participatory approach can take a variety of forms. It might consist of a series of high-level meetings with influential community leaders, or the process of consultation might extend to the grassroots. Surveys might be organized with questionnaires, and based on sampling techniques rather than involving all of those

potentially affected. Alternatively, focus-group meetings might be arranged for discussion between the planners and the stakeholders. The range of possible methods of
consultation in a participatory spirit may be almost endless, and are reviewed in the
sources which have been cited above. What is certain is that the more sensitive a
project, programme or policy is to stakeholder interests, particularly at a community
level, the more likely is the participatory approach to reap dividends in the form of
more effective design, implementation and operation.

A World Bank Review of *Participation in Practice* published in 1996 contained the findings reproduced in Box 6.2 taken from three major studies of the costs and benefits of
participation providing fairly robust evidence for the overall benefits of the approach.[18]

Another comparatively recently developed approach to the analysis of development interventions, particularly larger interventions by government agencies, is that
of Sustainable Livelihoods. This is an approach which has been espoused by the UK
Department for International Development (DFID) and has been mainly related to
rural development. Figure 6.6 reproduces the basic sustainable livelihoods diagram
from the comprehensive DFID guide to development planning entitled *Bridging the
Gap* (DFID, 2001: 43–7).[19] The sustainable livelihoods approach recognizes that development interventions take place within a socio-techno-economic context which is

---

Box 6.2   Benefits Arising from the Participatory Approach

- Participatory projects cost the World Bank 10 per cent to 15 per cent more, on average, than non-participatory projects in terms of staff time spent during preparation
  and appraisal.
- Participatory projects require more staff time during the early stages of supervision,
  to help establish the participatory processes.
- Overall the elapsed time from identification to the start of disbursements, was *not*
  significantly longer for participatory projects compared to non-participatory ones. In
  some cases, the participatory projects were actually quicker to disburse due to
  increased stakeholder commitment and better project performance.
- Beneficiary participation is the single most important factor in determining overall
  quality of project implementation.
- To be effective, beneficiary participation needs to be incorporated in all stages of the
  project cycle, not injected after the main decisions on local-level project activities
  have been taken by other stakeholders.
- Beneficiary participation was not found to be a significant factor in determining the
  quality of *macro*-project design: the involvement of other stakeholders and institutional and technical factors are the more important determining factors.
- The participation costs incurred by beneficiaries and borrowers can be considerable
  and can severely hamper the successful implementation of the participatory initiative,
  if not adequately addressed.
- There are clear examples of participation in Bank-financed operations leading to
  increased project effectiveness, increased efficiency, strengthened capacity of com-
  munity-level groups, and empowerment of beneficiaries.

Source: Rietbergen-McCracken (1996: 3).

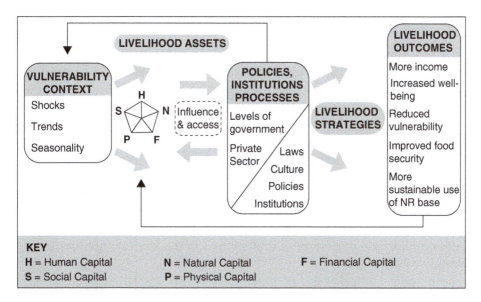

Figure 6.6   DFID's Sustainable Livelihoods Diagram
Source: DFID (2001: 44)

much wider than conventional project analysis. However, unlike the Integrated Rural Development Projects of the 1970s it does not aim to provide the framework for a tightly co-ordinated range of connected development interventions, but provides a framework for analysis and 'joined up thinking'. As such it does not substitute for more conventional economic and social analysis, but complements such analysis. Many of the elements of Figure 6.6 are to be found in contributions to development planning techniques and methods such as that by Baum and Tolbert (1985: 391–538) which emphasized the separated but closely related technical, environmental, institutional, social, financial and economic dimensions of project analysis. The sustainable livelihoods approach represents a similar form of the continuity and evolution of techniques and methods as that exhibited in the logical framework and the RBM approaches.

Figure 6.6 can be seen to have development interventions at its centre, outcomes to the right-hand side, inputs (assets) to the left of the policies, institutions and processes box, and a vulnerability context to the left-hand side. An overall context is provided by livelihood strategies and by influences and access. The strengths of this approach are mainly associated with the fact that it places individual development interventions into a directly relevant framework. This framework explicitly includes shocks, which can be interpreted as risks, and which are closely related to the important assumptions column of the logical framework. The weaknesses of the approach are largely concerned with a certain lack of clarity about how it interrelates with financial and economic analysis of projects, programmes and policies in particular. However, the same criticism could be made of the logical framework and of RBM.

6.3d. The contribution of research methods to development policy and practice – incremental analysis

The discussion in this chapter has ranged widely over broad issues, with reference to evidence which is intended to make the logic of the argument sustainable and plausible. An important question is 'how do we know all this'? The answer is that the evidence has largely been provided through a) evaluation studies undertaken directly by government agencies or by consultants hired and funded by these agencies; b) through independent research, much of it by universities but also by research institutions outside the university sector, funded by public or private research foundations or directly by governments (often by bilateral aid agencies) or by multilateral aid agencies. Evaluation studies have also provided significant inputs into comparative international studies and academic writing, some of which is externally funded but with a considerable proportion of contributions to the literature not having been institutionally funded.[20]

Good-quality evaluation studies employ social science research techniques and are similar to research project reports, and the personnel who undertake them need to be well qualified and experienced. The principal data and information sources on which evaluation studies are based are mainly provided through the systematic monitoring of the outcomes and impacts of development interventions.[21] Data generated by the monitoring process is effectively primary in nature, and in addition there will be secondary data available from other sources which complement the primary data.

The questions to which evaluation studies wish to provide answers are largely related to the incremental, or with/without, analytical approach. This approach addresses the issue of 'what difference has the specific intervention which is being analyzed made to the target variables?' Gittinger was one of the first to set out this approach systematically (Gittinger, 1982: 47–50). The main issue is that in the absence of the 'intervention' the target variables might have improved spontaneously, or they might have deteriorated spontaneously. Comparing observations 'before' and 'after' the implementation of the intervention does not give a proper view of its impact. If the situation would have improved anyway even in the absence of the intervention the difference between the 'before' case and the 'after' case overstates the impact of the intervention. If the situation would have deteriorated in the absence of the intervention then the difference between the 'before' and 'after' cases understates the impact of the intervention. Using a 'before' and 'after' approach to the analysis of the impact of policy, programme or project interventions is therefore not sufficiently rigorous or systematic, although in the absence of reliable data for the 'with' and 'without' approach it may give an impressionistic 'rough and ready' answer to the questions which have been posed.

Further elaboration of this incremental approach can be given through two empirical examples illustrated with diagrams. In order to make these examples relevant to the exposition of the chapter, the first will focus on the micro-level and the second on the macro-level. Later in the chapter discussion of SAPs will extend incremental analysis to economic policy reform.

Gittinger uses the First Livestock Development Project in Syria for one of his illustrations. When this project was appraised

> production in the national sheep flock was projected to grow at about 1 percent a year without the project. The project was to increase and stabilize sheep production and the incomes of seminomadic flock owners and sheep fatteners by stabilizing the availability of feed and improving veterinary services. With the project, national flock production was projected to grow at the rate of 3 percent a year. In this case, if the project analyst had simply compared the output before and after the project, he would have erroneously attributed the total increase in sheep production to the project investment. Actually, what can be attributed to the project investment is only the 2 percent incremental increase in production in excess of the 1 per cent that would have occurred anyway. (Gittinger, 1982: 47)

Figure 6.7 is taken from Gittinger's book, and it shows the net benefits associated with both the 'with project' case and the 'without project' case. The net benefits are simply the revenues minus the costs for each year of operation of the activity being analyzed discounted at an appropriate discount rate. Figure 6.7 shows that the 'without' project case has slowly increasing net benefits associated with the 1 per cent growth rate of output from the flock. The 'with' project case shows that during the investment phase project total costs exceed total benefits and that net benefits are significantly lower than they would have been without the project. However, after the cross-over point is reached (after the investment phase has been completed) revenues rise strongly associated with a 3 per cent growth of output from the flock, and net benefits grow significantly faster than they would have done in the absence of

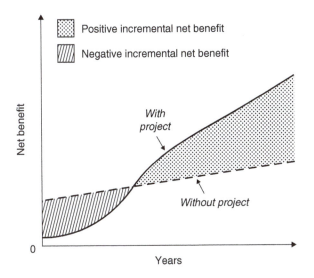

Figure 6.7   National Sheep Flock, First Livestock Development Project, Syria
Source: Gittinger (1982: 48)

the project. The incremental net benefits to the project are simply the net benefits with the project minus the net benefits without the project. Overall, using a discounted cash flow (DCF) approach to benefit appraisal, the economic value of the national flock is much greater with the project than it is without the project.[22]

The second example focuses on government policy towards the control of inflation (see Figure 6.8). Suppose that the rate of inflation in an economy is running at 25 per cent per annum, that the government states that it wishes to bring it down to 5 per cent per annum within a five-year period, and that policy measures are introduced aiming to achieve this objective. In the event, the rate of inflation actually falls to 10 per cent per annum over this five-year period, but because of factors outside the control of government the rate of inflation would have fallen to 20 per cent anyway.[23] In this case the government can take credit for the reduction of inflation by 10 per cent as a result of its policy measures, while the objective was to reduce inflation by 20 per cent. Government has failed to achieve its objective of a 5 per cent rate of inflation after 5 years, so that the actual rate of inflation is twice as high as had been hoped. Without the policy measures the rate of inflation would have been 20 per cent (this is known as the 'counterfactual'[24]). Government policy has achieved a measure of success – it cannot be said to have completely failed – but it has been much less successful than had been hoped. This type of analysis can easily be applied to situations where, for example, inflation has increased rather than decreased – with a counterfactual rate of inflation which is even higher than that which occurs in actuality – so that government can take the credit for keeping the rate of inflation lower than it would otherwise have been. The notes to Figure 6.8 make it clear that evaluation of the degree of success of the policy measures might be made on three

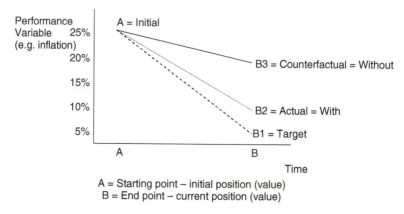

Figure 6.8 Evaluation of With Policy/Without Policy
Notes: a) Target v Actual is B1 – B2 = shortfall of 5%: an actual improvement of 15% compared with the target improvement of 20%
b) Before and After is A – B2 = fall of 15% and
c) With v Without is B2 – B3 = fall of 10%: an actual improvement of 15% 'with' the programme compared with an improvement of 5% 'without' the programme

bases – target versus actual, before versus after, and with versus without. Of these the first and third are valid approaches, but the before versus after approach is to be avoided wherever possible.

6.4. THE BROAD PICTURE – MACRO-ANALYSIS

6.4a. Structural Adjustment Programmes – A methodological case study

SAPs and the associated policy conditionality, represented a very controversial approach to development management in the 1980s and 1990s. The intellectual underpinnings of the SAPs were provided by the neo-liberal school of thought represented by Reaganomics and Thatcherism (mentioned in Section 6.3a of this chapter). The Washington Consensus, as expounded by Williamson (1982, 1993, 1994),[25] summarized the arguments for the adoption of the SAPs. There is no intention to discuss the political philosophy which lay behind the SAPs in this chapter, and the focus is rather on an exploration of the objectives behind them and on evaluation of their outcomes and impacts. It should be recalled that the SAPs were first designed and implemented before the issue of poverty reduction had been moved higher up the international development agenda through the World Bank's Comprehensive Development Framework. The prime concern of the SAPs was nominally to improve the economic governance of the developing countries through an enabling of the market mechanism. The justification for this 'marketization' was provided to a considerable degree by the view that many of the market failures which had justified corrective government policy measures were actually themselves caused by inappropriate public policies (or government failure). In theory, the removal of the inappropriate policies would reduce the extent of market failures, and would in turn reduce the need for corrective public policy, reducing public sector and private sector transactions costs. The logic behind this chain of reasoning is difficult to fault, although it is clear that the preoccupation of the SAPs with trade and other international economic issues, and with purely economic performance, could be said to have placed distributional, welfare and poverty reduction issues too low on the policy agenda.

A major criticism of the SAPs arose due to the circumstances surrounding their adoption in many developing countries. In many cases national sovereignty, recently secured following long periods of colonial rule, was challenged by the policy conditionality approach adopted by the IFIs. Receipt of international aid, and other forms of financial support, were conditional upon developing countries adopting the policies outlined by the IFIs in the SAPs. However, in some cases it was convenient for the governments of developing countries to make the IFIs the scapegoats for unpopular policies which they themselves wished to introduce but which domestic political opinion found to be largely unacceptable. The question of ownership was therefore understandably central to the Comprehensive Development Framework when it was formulated in the late 1990s. Another key controversial issue associated with the SAPs was the 'one size fits all' philosophy which tended to be adopted.

This discounted the significance of individual country's historical circumstances and socio-economic characteristics. The fictional image of reports and recommendations of SAP missions being written not so much in the departure lounges of international airports following all-to-brief assignments but in the departure lounges *before* the mission had even started gives a graphic impression of the fears behind this criticism.

A key research question is whether, within their own terms of reference, the SAPs actually achieved their objectives, and particularly whether they led to improved economic performance and to higher economic growth. This is an evaluation question, and centres on whether a) the effects of the economic policy measures of the SAPs can be distinguished from the effects arising from non-SAP events, and b) the economic statistics are sufficient in number and quality to permit the type of sophisticated analysis implied by the research question. These are issues associated with rigorous research and analysis, a central theme of this book. It has been emphasized that evaluation of the impact of policy should be based on the incremental, or 'with/without', approach involving the establishment of a counterfactual. This implies that rigorous analysis of the economic impact would need to compare the likely economic performance with and without the policy shifts and measures introduced by the SAPs.

One of most systematic of the major research studies on the impact of the SAPs was reported in a two-volume study entitled *Aid and Power* (Mosley et al., 1995: particularly Chapter 6). A central issue was how to define the counterfactual, and two alternatives were selected: a) based on individual country domestic circumstances; and b) based on international comparison. For the b) case it was possible for the 'with' scenario to be represented by a country or countries which had adopted an SAP (or a number of SAPs), and the 'without' scenario by a country or countries which had not adopted SAPs. In experimental terms the 'without' case represents a 'control group', but because of the nature of economic and social sciences it is not possible to set up such a counterfactual situation in advance because the laboratory conditions never exist.

One of the first round findings of the Mosley et al. study was that the economic performance of non-SAP countries (the counterfactual or 'without' group) was better than that of the SAP group (the 'with' group) (1995: 199). What might explain this apparent paradox? One possibility is that the SAPs were poorly conceived, and that their impact had been negative – a reassuring conclusion for the trenchant critics of the SAPs. Another possibility is that the SAPs were adopted in poorly performing countries in order to try to improve economic performance, and were not adopted in better performing countries so that the results using the international comparison counterfactual could lead to misleading conclusions. This second possibility could have arisen as a result of the selection of countries for the 'with' and 'without' comparator groups – a selection which would inevitably have been influenced by the availability and accuracy of available economic statistics. It should be borne in mind that the type of economic research undertaken in order to evaluate the impact of SAPs has to be based largely on the use of readily available secondary data, and that primary data collection which might be expected to generate more appropriate and reliable data is usually impractical.[26]

One remaining question, which affects much policy-oriented research, relates to the time dimension – shown on the horizontal axis of Figure 6.8. The discussion which follows will be better understood by referring to the Policy Cycle established in Figure 6.4. Policy changes are generally introduced due to the perception of a problem which needs to be addressed, and which may relate to observations of dysfunctional performance within a current policy context, or in response to a desire to introduce a new policy initiative. 'Good' policy interventions need a period for the assembly and analysis of information which defines the nature of the problem and the policy options which are feasible. Following the design of the basic features of a policy intervention it is necessary to establish an implementation plan and then to undertake the implementation itself. After implementation is complete, which may occur in stages over a fairly lengthy period, the outcomes and impacts will themselves arise only after a further delay. An example from Ghana should illustrate this point.

The Ghana Investments Centre (GIC) was established to facilitate participation of international investors in the Ghanaian economy. One of the objectives of the Ghanaian 1983 Economic Recovery Programme, and of the SAPs which followed, was to stimulate international investment, much of it in the form of collaborative arrangements (joint ventures) between domestic and foreign investors. The reform of the GIC was undertaken in order to address this objective. The nature of the economic decline which Ghana experienced over the period between about 1972 and 1982 had a severely negative impact on the confidence of international investors. The re-establishment of business confidence was necessary to underpin significant inflows of foreign private capital and was expected to take some years. Following the re-establishment of international business confidence there would then be a further period during which potential ventures were identified, appraised, negotiated and investment plans prepared, after which implementation could take place. After the completion of implementation and commissioning the operation phase could start, with production building up – possibly gradually as initial problems were resolved and markets were established or re-established. These outcomes and impacts then need to be observed on the basis of reliable data, which would have to be assembled and made available to analysts. In the case of the GIC the expectation might be that a time-lag of about 10 years could elapse between policy reform and evaluation of outcomes and impacts (Acheampong and Tribe, 1998: 69–71 and fn 3 and 4; Huq, 1989: 74, 260–2). This description has been somewhat laboured, but is intended to demonstrate that policy reform does not necessarily lead to quick results. It should be clear that, because of the nature of the socio-economic systems to which the policy reforms have been applied, there is likely to be a significant delay before the outcomes and impacts arising from reforms become apparent, and an even longer delay before the outcomes and impacts show up in statistics which can be used in evaluative analysis.

This discussion of research issues associated with SAPs has been less concerned with the intrinsic nature of, and controversies surrounding, these important features of international development over the last quarter century, and has been more concerned with the establishment of some of the dilemmas which have been encountered in disinterested study and analysis.

6.4b. Management of the economy and the use of shadow prices

Some of the more technical economic questions which are associated with discourse around economic policy reform have often been omitted from analysis of a more political nature (which is more likely to be often biased by subjective judgements of one sort or another). Where this occurs the value of the conclusions arising from the discourse will inevitably be limited. The same judgement applies where economic analysis has been undertaken in the absence of any consideration of political issues. Those more concerned with political analysis may not have a lot of sympathy with some of the arguments which are set out here, but non-economists are often viewed by economists as being insufficiently rigorous in their approach to policy analysis and this is a good example of the arena of dispute between the disciplines.

In the 1960s a number of country studies (Brazil, India, Mexico, Pakistan, the Philippines and Taiwan) of industrial development were undertaken under the auspices of the OECD by leading economists, and these studies were summarized and synthesized by Little et al. (1970). Broadly speaking, the studies concluded that government policy (significantly not including any African countries due to their limited manufacturing development at that time) relating to industrial development included significantly higher effective trade protection than most analysts had been aware of, inflexible licensing arrangements, and other dysfunctional policy measures. A parallel study undertaken by the OECD (Little and Mirrlees, 1969) concluded that the combined effect of government policies and market structures in many developing countries justified the use of 'shadow prices' or 'accounting prices' in the economic appraisal of manufacturing investments (refer for example to Potts, 2002: Chapter 11). The use of shadow prices is justified where market prices differ significantly from 'economic opportunity costs', which is generally explained by 'market failure'. The concept of 'market failure' is well established in the economic literature and includes conditions where a) the market does not function properly – the case of market imperfections; b) the market result is incorrect – the case of external economies; c) no market exists for the relevant activity – the case of public goods; and d) the market yields undesirable results in terms of objectives other than resource allocation (see Meier, 1995: 540). Market imperfections include situations where there is monopoly power in markets, significant incidence of government taxes and subsidies, and significant government controls for example. The outcomes from appraisals based on the use of 'shadow' or 'economic accounting' prices rather than on market prices would implicitly lead to a different set of investment priorities. However, in order to operationalize these 'corrections' for market distortions it would logically be necessary for the government to introduce further taxes, subsidies or market controls in order to make private profitability consistent with 'public' or 'social' profitability. Thus, a holistic approach would be required in order to modify private sector market behaviour to make it consistent with the outcomes of the shadow-priced appraisal. This was no easy task, and it was always going to be unlikely that private (both domestic and international) investors would be persuaded to make decisions consistent with this modified system.

Two further complications can be added in order to explain the frustrated nature of shadow-priced investment appraisal in developing countries. First, although the use of shadow prices (on the basis of long-established economic concepts and theories) was conceived in the context of manufacturing investment (Little and Mirrlees, 1969) their most enthusiastic adoption was actually in public sector investment analysis particularly related to projects largely funded through international aid, for example in the agricultural and infrastructure sectors. There was never any significant adoption of shadow prices for the analysis of private, or joint venture, investments in the manufacturing sector. Second, very few countries actually developed sets of shadow prices which could be used consistently by investment analysts, meaning that where shadow pricing was attempted in appraisals it was often ad hoc and internally inconsistent depending upon the uncoordinated hunches of consultants (for Ghana's experience see Huq, 1989: 260–5).

Given the unsuccessful nature of the attempt to make investment priorities more consistent with economic realities some alternative 'corrective' measures were seen as necessary in order to compensate for the dysfunctional nature of 'economic control systems' in many developing countries as identified in the OECD studies summarized by Little et al. (1970). Thus, because the use of 'shadow prices' (which can be perceived as one arm of a 'getting prices right' approach) was adopted patchily with negligible and delayed effects, the alternative was to 'correct' the types of 'market failures' identified in the OECD studies through 'marketization' – the liberalization of internal and external markets which was the cornerstone of the structural adjustment programmes.

This line of discussion provides a form of support for the basic elements of structural adjustment based not on neo-liberal and neo-classical arguments but on 'market failure' or 'structuralist' arguments. The controls, taxes and subsidies which were identified in the OECD studies were simply failing to achieve their nominal economic objectives, and so an alternative approach was needed if the consensual policy objectives were to be achieved.

6.5. SUMMARY

This chapter has attempted to demonstrate that there is considerable range of methods and techniques available to development analysts – academic researchers and practitioners alike. Some of these methods and techniques have been initiated within analytical work in developing countries, and have then been used in industrialized countries later. Other methods and techniques have been 'borrowed' from industrialized country contexts as a basis for analysis in developing countries, often with adaptations in order to make them more relevant to different socio-economic contexts. One thing is clear from the discussion in this chapter – there is no shortage of theory, methods and techniques which can be employed to make contributions to the DS literature lively, relevant and rigorous. The remainder of these conclusions will consist of a very brief summary of some of the main points to emerge from the chapter.

6.5a. DS practitioners and development practice

It is possible to distinguish between two 'camps' of DS researchers and writers who can be represented as those concerned with discourse and with empiricism. There is limited overlap between the two camps.

The need for policy-relevant results from research undertaken within a limited timeframe does not reduce the need for a rigorous and systematic approach.

6.5b. Systematic approaches to development policy

There is a critical need to contextualize policy- and practice-related research and study within a policy hierarchy and a policy cycle within which established methodologies and methods are used.

DS research and writing has been innovatory in developing new and adapted methodologies and methods, some of which are transferable from the developing country contexts in which they first appeared to the context of industrialized countries.

6.5c. The broad picture – macro-analysis

A distinction is necessary between policy objectives (e.g. better governance) and policy frameworks (e.g. conditionality), especially where subjective judgements and bias can readily intervene (e.g. the analysis of the impact of structural adjustment programmes in developing countries).

NOTES

1 It has to be acknowledged that 'structural adjustment' and the associated 'policy reform' approaches to development policy by the international financial institutions has been superseded by the more recent poverty reduction strategy papers (PRSPs), by Country Policy and Institutional Assessment (CPIA), and by Policy and Social Impact Analysis (PSIA) (for example DFID and GTZ, 2005). The discussion here is focused on evaluation methods and techniques rather than on the nature and experience of structural adjustment.

2 The 'independence' of research is a relative, rather than absolute, issue. Independent research is conceived as research undertaken by bodies (particularly universities, research institutions and think tanks) independently from the institutions which are responsible for determining, influencing and implementing policy. However, there is an issue over the extent to which, where research by these institutions is funded by policy-oriented bodies (such as a government ministry or aid agency), research priorities, the research agenda, and research problems and questions may be significantly influenced by the funding body

(beyond basic concern for the quality of funding applications). It is conceivable that research undertaken by an 'independent' body but funded by a policy-oriented body may be indistinguishable from research undertaken directly by the policy-oriented body itself. Therefore, where reference has been made to 'independent research' in this chapter it should be clear that the authors are aware of these complex issues of 'ownership' of the research and of the 'influence' of funding bodies. In this context the concerns of the UK Higher Education Funding Councils during the 2001 Research Assessment Exercise that the development research agenda in the university sector was too heavily influenced by public bodies is very relevant.

3 In referring to 'discourse and practice tendencies' the intention is to distinguish between, on the one hand, members of the DS community who are more concerned with intellectual discourse around more conceptual and methodological issues ('discourse') and, on the other hand, those who are more directly concerned with policy and practice ('practice'). Both tendencies will have a concern with empirical observations ('empiricism') but from differing standpoints. The discussion in the text of Chapter 6, and elsewhere in the book, makes it clear that there is overlap between the two tendencies, and that they should be regarded as parts of a continuum rather than as two 'absolutes'.

4 One example of this continuity is represented by the distinction made in the World Bank report on the economic development of Tanganyika at the point of independence (which, of course, was soon to become the United Republic of Tanzania) between the 'improvement' and 'transformation' approaches to agricultural development (Government of Tanganyika, 1961: Chap. 6). The 'transformation' approach was later referred to as 'villagisation' and developed into the 'Ujamaa villages' strategy of the Tanzanian government (refer to Belshaw, 2003; Collier et al., 1986; Ghai et al., 1979; Hyden, 1975, 1980: Chaps. 3 and 5; Newiger, 1967; Ruthenberg, 1964). Another example of this continuity relates to African industrial development strategies of the late 1950s and 1960s which were considerably influenced by Arthur Lewis through his 'Report on Industrialization and the Gold Coast' (later Ghana) (1953) published by the UK Colonial Office.

5 The basic version of the project-based approach to aid management involves international aid institutions approving the release of aid funds on a project-by-project basis. Alternatives, which involve fewer direct administrative interventions by aid institutions, are programme-based aid management (each programme including several projects), the sector-wide approach (each sector plan including a number of programmes), and general budget support (which involves aid institutions releasing funds to supplement developing country government receipts (with approval based on the level of 'effectiveness' achieved in managing development expenditure). Recipient management of international aid is, of course, one element of public expenditure management in developing countries (World Bank, 1998).

6 Many of these issues are reviewed in some detail in the World Bank's *World Development Report* for 1983 (World Bank, 1983).

7 Paradoxically Mosley and Eeckhout's broadly consensual criticism of the project-based approach to development management extends to Integrated Rural Development Projects (IRDPs). However, the IRDP approach to rural development experienced difficulties largely due to the problems associated with the coordination of its tightly integrated 'programme' nature, rather than to any 'project-based' characteristics. The IRDP cannot therefore be used as an example of the failure of the project-based approach – rather it is an example of the failure of one variant of the 'programme approach'. See also Livingstone (1979).

8 The Comprehensive Development Framework (CDF) is only rarely referred to in the middle of the first decade of the twenty-first century. This is symptomatic of a tendency to adopt new 'initiatives' in order to achieve specific objectives which may be essentially political. However, the CDF provided a welcome holistic approach to development which effectively addressed a large number of the shortcomings of the structural adjustment programmes, but which was associated with the World Bank Presidency of James Wolfensohn (1998). Another example of this type of initiative is the New International Economic Order (NIEO) of the 1970s (see for example Wälde, 1995) which was overtaken by the disruptive international economic events which have been referred to in this chapter in the explanation of the decline of development planning.

9 This policy hierarchy can be integrated with the SWAP (Sector Wide Approach) which was recently advocated by a number of writers (e.g. Brown et al., 2001). In many respects the SWAP is not new, so that – for example – the sector-based chapters in many national development plans prepared in the 1970s in particular were often the outcome of sector working parties (e.g. Government of Pakistan, 1988; Republic of Uganda, 1972). The World Bank's PRSP Sourcebook also, of course, is based largely on a sectoral approach to socio-economic planning (Klugman, 2002).

10 This is, of course, essentially recognition of the limitations of the sector-wide approach (SWAP – refer to footnote 9 above) which has been widely supported by some international aid institutions in recent years.

11 Examples of policy agendas are poverty reduction, decentralization, regional integration, better governance, market liberalization.

12 Systematic approaches employing models related to this type of project cycle are not new, and several specialists have ventured into the area. One valuable discussion is provided by Thomas and Grindle (1990), and another holistic discussion can be found in Sutton (1999). At the Institute of Development Studies at Sussex University the Knowledge, Technology and Society Team have recently produced a review of their research on policy processes relating to the environment (see for example, KNOTS, 2006).

13 Following its initial adoption by the USAID the Logical Framework has been used by many international aid organizations, and several produced their own variations (such as the UK Overseas Development Administration (Cracknell, 1989; McCulloch, 1986) and the European Union (Directorate General for Development, 1993) which added little to the original version but which added considerably to the complexity of aid management in recipient countries. For clear discussions of the Logical Framework and its derivatives see MacArthur (1993, 1995, 1998), NORAD (1996) and Potts (2002: 31–6).

14 An invaluable recent publication relating to methods and techniques for policy analysis has been the Overseas Development Institute's *Toolkit for Progressive Policymakers in Developing Countries* (Sutcliffe and Court, 2006).

15 It could be argued that, logically, inputs should come above outputs in the vertical logic, but the difference would not be significant for the original version. For the extended version, including the results-based aspects, there is a better argument for placing inputs above outputs.

16 One of the major issues incorporated into the World Bank's 'Poverty Reduction Strategy Paper' (PRSP) approach was that of cross-cutting issues, identified as: Participation, Governance, Community-Driven Development, Gender, Environment. It is unlikely that anybody would differ from the view that these issues are of great importance (Klugman, 2002: Vol. 1, iii).

17 The technical notes included as annexes to most of the chapters of the World Bank's PRSP Sourcebook include, inter alia, guidance on the use of sector- and issue-specific indicators and several of the chapters relate particularly to measurement and to indicators (Klugman, 2002: Vols. 1 and 2, iii).

18 There is a potential problem associated with using a source from about a decade ago in this context, and with relying on a World Bank source in relation to an issue where the World Bank may not be perceived as the most obvious authority. However, the detailed nature of the conclusions which have been included in Box 6.2 seems to us to be of particular interest.

19 This publication was originally conceived as a guide for DFID employees and consultants working on the preparation and evaluation of development projects, programmes and policies in developing countries. Like many other such publications from international aid agencies *Bridging the Gap* is also an invaluable resource for development researchers, practitioners and teachers/lecturers in a much wider context than the original target readership. An earlier version of the Sustainable Livelihoods approach can be found in an IDS Discussion Paper by Scoones (1998).

20 Some evaluation studies are, inevitably, confidential and inaccessible. However the international aid institutions make a considerable amount of their evaluation work available through their websites. The UK's DFID has a section of their website devoted to evaluation studies (http://www.dfid.gov.uk/aboutdfid/evaluation.asp), and the World Bank has an

Operations and Evaluation Department (OED) with an internet presence (http://www.worldbank.org/oed/).

21 Basically monitoring consists of the generation of data and information and evaluation consists of analysis of this data and information. For a discussion of outcomes and impacts refer to Section 6.3b of this chapter.

22 For an approach to project rehabilitation using these methods refer to Yaffey and Tribe (1992: Chap. 5).

23 Factors such as better rainfall, lower prices for strategic imports (such as fuel oil) and higher productivity growth that had been anticipated in key areas of the economy could account for this order of magnitude of the fall in the rate of inflation.

24 The 'counterfactual' is what would have happened in the absence of the project – or of the policy. The counterfactual is 'speculative' on both *ex ante* and *ex post* bases because it is what *might* have happened. However, it is no more speculative than the *ex ante* targets for the objectives of project or policy interventions. This approach can, of course, be applied to the analysis of both public and private sector activities.

25 Williamson's (1982, 1993, 1994) expositions of the Washington Consensus are the most authoritative references outlining its main features. For one critical view of the neo-liberal approach see Tribe (2006). Stiglitz (1998) is one of the leading economists who has provided an explanation of the thesis-antithesis-synthesis process which led to the Post-Washington Consensus although even this has been criticized more recently.

26 A similar analytical problem is represented by the conclusion of Husain and Faruquee that international aid to six sub-Saharan African countries had not compensated for losses arising from the reduction in international income through adverse movements in the terms of trade, which was not – of course – the objective of the aid programmes (Husain and Faruquee, 1994: 7).

REFERENCES

Acheampong, I. and Tribe, M. (1998) 'The response of Ghana's manufacturing sector to structural adjustment', in Cook, P., Kirkpatrick, C. and Nixson, F. (eds), *Privatization, Enterprise Development and Economic Reform*. Cheltenham: Edward Elgar. pp. 63–85.

Apthorpe, R. (1972) Rural Cooperatives and Planned Change in Africa: An Analytical Overview. Geneva: UNRISD (United Nations Research Institute for Social Development).

Apthorpe, R. (1999) 'Development studies and policy studies: in the short run we are all dead', *Journal of International Development*, 11 (4): 535–546.

Apthorpe, R. and Atkinson, P. (1999) *Towards Shared Social Learning for Humanitarian Programmes*. London: ALNAP (Active Learning Network for Accountability and Performance in Humanitarian Action). Available from http://www.reliefweb.int/rw/lib.nsf/db900SID/LGEL-5JHM5L/$FILE/alnap-shared-jul99.pdf?OpenElement (accessed 7 June 2007).

Apthorpe, R. and Gasper, D. (eds) (1996) *Arguing Development Policy: Frames and Discourses*. London: Frank Cass.

Aryeetey, E. and Goldstein, M. (2000) 'The evolution of social policy', in Aryeetey, E., Harrigan, J. and Nissanke, M. (eds.), *Economic Reforms in Ghana: The Miracle and the Mirage*. London: James Currey. pp. 284–303.

Balls, E. and O'Donnell, G. (eds) (2002) *Reforming Britain's Economic and Financial Policy: Towards Greater Economic Stability*. London: Palgrave Macmillan for HM Treasury.

Baum, W.C. and Tolbert, S.M. (1985) *Investing in Development: Lessons of World Bank Experience*. New York: Oxford University Press for the World Bank.

Belshaw, D.G.R. (2003) 'Sustainable agricultural and rural development in Sub-Saharan Africa', in Tribe, M., Thoburn, J. and Palmer-Jones, R. (eds.), *Development Economics and Social Justice: Essays in Honour of Ian Livingstone*. Aldershot: Ashgate. pp. 159–181.

Brown, A., Foster, M., Norton, A. and Naschold, F. (2001) *The Status of Sector Wide Approaches*. Working Paper 142, Centre for Aid and Public Expenditure, Overseas Development Institute, London. Available from http://www.odi.org.uk/publications/working_papers/index.html

Canadian International Development Agency. (1999) *Results-Based Management in CIDA: An Introductory Guide to the Concepts and Principles*. Results-Based Management Division, Performance Review Branch, January. Available from http://www.acdi-cida.gc.ca/CIDAWEB/ acdicida.nsf/En/EMA-218132656-PPK (accessed 9 October 2006).

Chambers, R. (1994a) 'The origins and practice of participatory rural appraisal', *World Development*, 22 (7): 953–969.

Chambers, R. (1994b) 'Participatory rural appraisal (PRA): analysis of experience', *World Development*, 22 (9): 1253–1268.

Chambers, R. (1994c) Participatory rural appraisal (PRA): challenges, potentials and paradigm. *World Development*, 22 (10): 1437–1454.

Charlton, R. (2005) 'Deconcentration, devolution and donors: explaining centralisation – decentralization cycles in developing countries', in Tribe, M., Thoburn, J. and Palmer-Jones, R. (eds), *Development Economics and Social Justice: Essays in Honour of Ian Livingstone*. Ashgate: Aldershot. pp. 84–96.

Collier, P., Radwan, S., Wangwe, S. and Wagner, A. (1986) *Labour and Poverty in Rural Tanzania. Ujamaa and Rural Development in the United Republic of Tanzania*. Oxford: Clarendon Press.

Cracknell, B. (1989) 'Evaluating the effectiveness of the logical framework in practice', *Project Appraisal*, 4 (3): 163–167.

Deininger, K., Squire, L. and Basu, S. (1998) 'Does economic analysis improve the quality of foreign assistance?' *World Bank Economic Review*, 12 (3): 385–418.

Department for International Development. (2001) *Poverty: Bridging the Gap – Guidance Notes*. London: HMSO. Available from http://www.dfid.gov.uk/Pubs/files/poverty_bridgegap_ guidance.pdf

DFID. (2005) *Evaluation of General Budget Support: Inception Report June: Joint Evaluation of GBS*. Available from http://www.dfid.gov.uk/aboutdfid/performance/files/evd2-inception-report. pdf (15 August 2006).

DFID and GTZ (2005) *Principles for PSIA Process in Policy Cycles and Stakeholder Participation*. Available from http://www.dfid.gov.uk/mdg/aid-effectiveness/newsletters/psia-policy-cycles. pdf (accessed 30 May 2007).

DFID et al. (2005) *Joint Assistance Strategy Paper for Uganda 2005-2009*. Available from http:// www.dfid.gov.uk/pubs/files/joint-assistance-strat-uganda.pdf (accessed 16 August 2006).

Directorate General for Development (1993) *Project Cycle Management: Integrated Approach and Logical Framework*. Brussels: Commission of the European Communities.

Escobar, A. (1995) *Encountering Development: The Making and Unmaking of the Third World*. Princeton NJ: Princeton University Press.

Fritzen, S.A. (2007) 'Can the design of community-driven development reduce the risk of elite capture? Evidence from Indonesia', *World Development*, 35 (8): 1359–1375.

Ghai, D. and Green, R.H. (1979) 'Ujamaa and Villagisation in Tanzania', in Ghai, D., Khan, A.R., Lee, E. and Radwan, S. (eds), *Agrarian Systems and Rural Development*. London: Macmillan for the International Labour Organization. pp. 232–256.

Gittinger, J.P. (1982) *Economic Analysis of Agricultural Projects*, 2nd ed. Baltimore: Johns Hopkins University Press for the Economic Development Institute of the World Bank.

Government of Malaysia. (1991) *Sixth Malaysia Plan 1991-1995*. Kuala Lumpur: National Printing Department.

Government of Pakistan. (1988) *Seventh Five Year Plan 1988-93 and Perspective Plan 1988-2003*. Islamabad: Planning Commission.

Government of Tanganyika. (1961) *The Economic Development of Tanganyika*. Baltimore: Johns Hopkins Press for the International Bank for Reconstruction and Development.

Government of Uganda. (1961) *This is Your Plan: Uganda's First Five Year Development Plan*. Entebbe: Government Printer.

GTZ (Deutsche Gesellschaft fur Technische Zusammenarbeit). (1992) *Guidelines for Project Progress Review*. May.

GTZ (Deutsche Gesellschaft fur Technische Zusammenarbeit). (1997) *ZOPP: Objectives-Oriented Project Planning*.

Harper, C. (1997) *The Power in Participatory Practice: Strengthening Participation in Donor Assisted Projects and Policy*. London: Save the Children Fund.

HM Treasury. (1997) *Appraisal and Evaluation in Central Government: Treasury Guidance*, 2nd ed. London: HMSO.

Huq, M.M. (1989) *The Economy of Ghana: The First Twenty-five Years since Independence*. Basingstoke: Macmillan.

Husain, I. and Faruquee, R. (1994) 'Adjustment in Seven African Countries. Introduction', I. Husain and R. Faruquee (eds), *Adjustment in Africa: Lessons from Country Case Studies*. Washington: World Bank. pp. 1–10.

Hyden, G. (1975) 'Ujamaa, villagisation and rural development in Tanzania', *ODI Review*, 1: 53–72.

Hyden, G. (1980) *Beyond Ujamaa in Tanzania: Underdevelopment and an Uncaptured Peasantry*. London: Heinemann.

Killick, T. (1995) *IMF Programmes in Developing Countries: Design and Impact*. London: Routledge.

Kirkpatrick, C., Polidano, C. and Clarke, R. (2002) *Handbook on Development Policy and Management*. Cheltenham: Edward Elgar.

Klugman, J. (2002) *A Sourcebook for Poverty Reduction Strategies*, 2 Vols. Washington: World Bank.

KNOTS (Knowledge, Technology and Society Team). (2006) *Understanding Policy Processes: A Review of IDS Research on the Environment*. Brighton: Institute of Development Studies, University of Sussex.

Kokor, J. and Kroes, G. (2000) *Central Grants for Local Development in a Decentralised Planning System, Ghana*. Dortmund: SPRING Centre, University of Dortmund.

Kusek, J.Z. and Rist, R.C. (2004) *Ten Steps to a Results-Based Monitoring and Evaluation System: A Handbook for Development Practitioners*. Washington: World Bank.

Lewis, W.A. (1953) *Report on Industrialization and the Gold Coast*. Accra: Government of the Gold Coast.

Little, I.M.D. and Mirrlees, J.A. (1969) *Manual of Industrial Project Analysis in Developing Countries: Vol. 2. Social Cost Benefit Analysis*. Paris: Organization for Economic Co-operation and Development.

Little, I.M.D., Scitovsky, T. and Scott, M.Fg. (1970) *Industry and Trade in Some Developing Countries: A Comparative Study*. London: Oxford University Press for the OECD.

Livingstone, I. (1979) 'On the concept of integrated rural development planning', *Journal of Agricultural Economics*, 30 (1): 49–54.

MacArthur, J.D. (1993) *The Logical Framework: A Tool for the Management of Project Planning and Evaluation*. Discussion Paper 42, Development and Project Planning Centre, University of Bradford. A version of this paper is reprinted in Analoui, F. (ed.) (1994) *The Realities of Managing Development Projects*. Aldershot: Avebury. pp. 87–113.

MacArthur, J.D. (1994) 'The project sequence: a composite view of the project cycle', in MacArthur, J. and Weiss, J. (eds), *Agriculture, Projects and Development*. Aldershot: Avebury. pp. 127–154.

MacArthur, J.D. (1995) *The Evaluation of Development Projects: A Review of the Approaches and Experiences of Donor Agencies*. New Series Discussion Papers No 61, July, Development and Project Planning Centre, University of Bradford, Bradford.

MacArthur, J.D. (1997) 'Stakeholder analysis in project planning: origins, application and refinements', *Project Appraisal*, 12 (4): 251–265.

MacArthur, J.D. (1998) *Project Failure: Causes and Rehabilitation: A Review of International Evidence*. Discussion Paper Series 2 No 10, February. Development and Project Planning Centre, University of Bradford, Bradford.

McCulloch, M. (1986) 'Project frameworks – a logical development for more effective aid', in *Overseas Development Administration: British Overseas Aid in 1985*. London: HMSO. pp. 52–55.

Meier, G.M. (1995) *Leading Issues in Economic Development*, 6th ed. New York: Oxford University Press.

Mikkelsen, B. (2005) *Methods for Development Work and Research: A Guide for Practitioners*, 2nd ed. London: Sage Publications.

Mohan, G., Brown, E., Milward, R. and Zack-Williams, A.B. (2000) *Structural Adjustment: Theory, Practice and Impacts*. London: Routledge.

Mosley, P. and Eeckhout, M.J. (2000) 'From project aid to programme assistance', in Tarp, F. and Hjertholm, P. (eds.), *Foreign Aid and Development: Lessons Learnt and Directions for the Future*. London: Routledge. pp. 131–153.

Mosley, P., Subasat, T. and Weeks, J. (1995) 'Assessing adjustment in Africa', *World Development*, 23 (9): 1459–1473.

Mosley, P., Toye, J. and Harrigan, J. (1995) *Aid and Power: The World Bank and Policy-based Lending – Volume 1: Analysis and Policy Proposals*, 2nd ed. London: Routledge.

Newiger, N. (1967) 'Village settlement schemes: the problems of cooperative farming', in Ruthenberg, H. (ed.), *Smallholder Farming and Smallholder Development in Tanzania*. Munich: Weltforum Verlag. pp. 249–274.

NORAD. (1996) *The Logical Framework Approach (LFA)*, 3rd ed. Oslo: Norwegian Agency for Development Cooperation.

Oakley, P. (1995) *People's Participation in Development Projects: A Critical Review of Current Theory and Practice*. INTRAC Occasional Papers series, No. 7. Oxford: INTRAC.

Oakley, P. et al. (1991) *Projects with People: The Practice of Participation in Rural Development*. Geneva: World Employment Programme, International Labour Office.

Organization for Economic Cooperation and Development. (2000) *Results Based Management in the Development Co-operation Agencies: A Review of Experience. DAC Working Party on Aid Evaluation*. Paris: OECD. Available from http://www.oecd.org/dataoecd/16/25/1886519.pdf

Organization for Economic Cooperation and Development. (2001) *Improving Policy Instruments through Impact Assessment*. SIGMA Paper No 31. Paris: OECD. Avalable from http://www.oecd.org/puma/sigmaweb

OXFAM. (1995) *The Field Director's Handbook: An OXFAM Manual for Development Workers*. Oxford: Oxford University Press for OXFAM.

Picciotto, R. and Weaving, R. (1994) 'A new project cycle for the World Bank', *Finance and Development*, 31 (4): 42–43.

Potts, D. (2002) *Project Planning and Analysis for Development*. London: Lynne Rienner.

RCPLA Network. (2007) *Resource Centres for Participatory Learning and Action Network*. Available from http://www.rcpla.org/about.htm (accessed 9 June 2007).

Republic of Kenya. (1984) *District Focus for Rural Development (rev June 1984)*. Nairobi: Office of the President.

Republic of Kenya. (1986) *Economic Management for Renewed Growth*. Nairobi: Government Printer.

Republic of Uganda. (1966) *Work for Progress: Uganda's Second five-Year Plan 1966-1971*. Entebbe: Government Printer.

Republic of Uganda. (1972) *Uganda's Third Five-Year Development Plan 1971/2-1975/6*. Entebbe: Government Printer.

Republic of Uganda. (2000) *Revised Volume I of the Poverty Eradication Action Plan (PEAP): Final Draft*. Kampala: Ministry of Finance, Planning and Economic Development.

Rietbergen-McCracken, J. (ed.) (1996) *Participation in Practice: The Experience of the World Bank and other Stakeholders*. World Bank Discussion Paper No 333. Washington: World Bank.

Robinson, M. (ed.) (2007) 'Decentralising service delivery?', *Special Issue – IDS Bulletin*, 38 (1): 1–90.

Ruthenberg, H. (1964) *Agricultural Development in Tanganyika. Ifo-Institut fur Wirtschaftsforschung, Afrika-Studienstelle – Afrika-Studien Nr. 2*. Berlin: Springer.

Scoones, I. (1998) *Sustainable Rural Livelihoods: A Framework for Analysis*. Working Paper 72, Institute of Development Studies, University of Sussex, Brighton.

Sen, A. (1999) *Development as Freedom*. Oxford: Oxford University Press.

Stewart, F. (1977) *Technology and Underdevelopment*. London: Macmillan.

Stiglitz, J.E. (1998). *More Instruments and Broader Goals: Moving toward the Post-Washington Consensus*. WIDER Annual Lectures 2, United Nations University World Institute for Development Economics Research: Helsinki. Available from http://www.wider.unu.edu/

Sutcliffe, S. and Court, J. (2006) *A Toolkit for Progressive Policymakers in Developing Countries*. London: Overseas Development Institute.

Sutton, R. (1999) *The Policy Process: An Overview*. Working Paper 118 August. London: Overseas Development Institute.

Tarp, F. and Hjertholm, P. (eds.) (2000) *Foreign Aid and Development: Lessons Learnt and Directions for the Future*. London: Routledge.

Thomas, J.W. and Grindle, M.S. (1990) 'After the decision: implementing policy reforms in developing countries', *World Development*, 18 (8): 1163–1181.

Toye, J. (2003) 'Changing perspectives in development economics', in Chang, H.-J. (ed.), *Rethinking Development Economics*. London: Anthem Press. pp. 21–40.

Tribe, M. (2006) 'Globalization, free trade and market asymmetry', in Carling, A. (ed.), *Globalization and Identity: Development and Integration in a Changing World*. London: I.B. Tauris. pp. 43–54.

United Nations. (2007) *The UN Millennium Development Goals*. Available from http://www.un.org/millenniumgoals/ (accessed 30 May 2007).

United Nations Development Programme. (2002) *Handbook on Monitoring and Evaluating for Results*. New York: United Nations. Available from http://stone.undp.org/undpweb/eo/evalnet/docstore3/yellowbook/

Wälde, T. (1995) *A Requiem for the 'New International Economic Order' The Rise and Fall of Paradigms in International Economic Law*. Centre for Energy, Petroleum and Mineral Law and Policy, University of Dundee: Dundee, Discussion Paper 8. Available from http://www.dundee.ac.uk/cepmlp/journal/html/Vol1/article1-2.html (accessed 30 August 2006).

Waterston, A. (1979) *Development Planning: Lessons of Experience*. Baltimore: John Hopkins University Press for the World Bank.

Williamson, J. (1982) 'On the characterization of good economic policy: Is there a consensus?' *World Development*, 10 (9): 695–700.

Williamson, J. (1993) 'Democracy and the "Washington Consensus"', *World Development*, 21 (8): 1329–1336.

Williamson, J. (1994) 'In search of a manual for technopols', in J. Williamson (ed.), *The Political Economy of Policy Reform*. Washington: Institute of International Economics. pp. 23–47.

Wolfensohn, J.D. (1998) *The Other Crisis: 1998 Annual Meetings Address*. Washington: International Monetary Fund and the World Bank. Available from http://web.worldbank.org/WBSITE/EXTERNAL/NEWS/0,,contentMDK:20023629~menuPK:34472~pagePK:34370~piPK:34424~theSitePK:4607,00.html (accessed 9 October 2006).

Wollman H. (ed.) (2003) *Evaluation in Public-Sector Reform: Concepts and Practice in International Perspective*. Cheltenham: Edward Elgar.

Wood, A., Apthorpe, R. and Borton, J. (eds.) (2001) *Evaluating International Humanitarian Action: Reflections from Practitioners*. London: Zed Books.

World Bank. (1983) *World Development Report*. New York: Oxford University Press for the World Bank.

World Bank. (1998) *Public Expenditure Management Handbook. Poverty Reduction and Economic Management programme*. Washington: World Bank. Available from http://siteresources.worldbank.org/INTPEAM/Resources/part1.pdf (accessed 9 October 2006).

World Bank. (2006) *HIPC History*. Available from http://web.worldbank.org/WBSITE/EXTERNAL/TOPICS/EXTDEBTDEPT/0,,contentMDK:20263277~menuPK:528655~pagePK:64166689~piPK:64166646~theSitePK:469043,00.html (accessed 16 August 2006).

Yaffey, M., and Tribe, M. (1992) *Project Rehabilitation in Adverse Environments*. Aldershot: Avebury.

CHAPTER SEVEN

WHAT IS THE FUTURE FOR DEVELOPMENT STUDIES?

Will development research exist in the future? Should it? ... ... Development research should reinvent itself to address the increasing interconnectedness between North and South, local-global linkages, the pedagogy of the powerful, social change in the north and more genuine interdisciplinarity... ... Finally, we hope that over the next 40 years, development research will not just study processes of change, but also be an integral part of them. (Mehta et al., 2006: 5)

7.1. INTRODUCTION

In this book we have attempted to address two main questions in particular:

- What is DS?
- What constitutes a rigorous approach to research in DS?

In Section 7.2 of this concluding chapter we summarize what has been termed the 'foundations of knowledge' in DS. Section 7.3 consists of some closing reflections on the future of DS.

7.2. THE 'FOUNDATIONS OF KNOWLEDGE' IN DS

In each chapter of this book we asked a key question relating to the foundations of knowledge in DS. Our discussion has been based on a series of questions linked with Bevan's (2006: 7–12) foundations of knowledge framework. Each chapter has focused on a specific question:

- Chapter 1: 'What is development'? (And thus what is the scope of DS?)
- Chapter 2: 'What is the purpose of DS'?
- Chapter 3: 'What can we "know" in DS'?
- Chapter 4: 'What is the "big picture" in DS'? (Focusing on the role and nature of theory.)

- Chapter 5: 'What is "rigour" in DS'?
- Chapter 6: 'How are research and practice linked in DS'?

Box 7.1 elaborates these questions in more detail for each chapter briefly, providing a summary of the main issues with which we have been concerned.

7.3. CLOSING REFLECTIONS: THE FUTURE OF DS

Critics have argued that DS has been, at best, an irrelevance which has failed to meet its own aims to improve standards of living and, at worst, has been a neo-colonial or western imposition on 'the Other' by claiming to 'know' about 'the Other' and what is good for 'the Other'. By the end of the twentieth century, some were even predicting the total demise of DS due to the disappearance of the 'Third World' as a coherent category following the end of the Cold War. However, DS has thrived and has expanded its role in spite of, or perhaps because of, responses to these criticisms. Certainly, in terms of international policy interest, the volume of literature published, or in student numbers studying DS, the subject has not diminished.

In reply to the 'effectiveness' critique, a large part of the 'Third World' – notably East Asia and China – has seen some kind of positive transformation, albeit with contestation of the qualitative nature, extent and distribution of social progress. Whether DS can make any claims to be in part responsible is – of course – a highly contentious question. One might also note development 'success stories' (again with caveats) in countries such as India and Vietnam and 'improvements' in a range of international development indicators. Ofcourse, some countries have not experienced any great progress since the emergence of DS in the 1950s – a number of obvious examples are located in Sub-Saharan Africa.

When Apthorpe asked (1999: 544–5) 'is there a future for development studies?' there was a range of answers from the simple 'yes' or 'no' to more complex, 'yes, but...' or 'no, but...'. Mehta et al. (2006: 5) argue that DS should exist but needs to change:

> Our view is that development research can avoid the same fate of colonial studies and emerge as a way of learning about development and exclusion in both rich and poor countries, and lead the way in terms of forging new approaches in connecting global and local issues, policies, solutions and researchers. To do so we must start by forging equitable relationships between northern and southern researchers and institutes and decentralizing research processes. Finally, we hope that over the next 40 years, development research will not just study processes of change, but also be an integral part of them. (Mehta et al., 2006: 5)

In sum, we need to reflect on the role which the researcher and the practitioner in international DS plays in international development and on the links between knowledge, power and social change.

Box 7.1	The Foundations of Knowledge in Development Studies
1. The focus, domain, or problematic of study: what exactly are we interested in?	Chapter 1: What is 'development'? • All definitions of 'development' carry implicit value assumptions and imply policies/responses • The definition of 'Development' can be thought of as one or all three of the following: a process of structural societal change; a desired socio-economic outcome; and the result of a dominant discourse • The study of 'development' has focused on developing countries but many of the issues of structural change are relevant to all countries including industrialized countries
2. Values/standpoints/ideology: why are we interested?	Chapter 2: What is the purpose of DS? • DS has a clear commitment to addressing real-world issues • Continual reflection is needed when assessing 'development' and the circumstances of people in diverse socio-cultural settings • The underlying assumptions and positionality of the researcher need to be made explicit
3. Ontology and epistemology: what is the world assumed to be like? How can the world be known about?	Chapter 3: What can we 'know' in DS? • Because DS is cross-disciplinary the fact that different disciplines have quite different epistemologies or 'traditions' has to be allowed for • The essential issue is to pursue a rigorous approach to systematic research and study • Knowledge claims within DS involve levels of probability rather than certainty, and in most cases should avoid absolute 'closure'
4. Theories/conceptual frameworks and models: how can we explain and understand our object of study?	Chapter 4: What is the 'big picture' in DS' • There are disputes within and between intellectual disciplines about the nature of the theory which is most appropriate to the study of 'development' but there should be no dispute about the need for theory as part of a systematic approach to research and study • There are – broadly – two *types* of *theory* in DS. There are *grand theories of 'development'* – and *context-specific theories*. The first relates to overall views of development, and the second to detailed empirical work • Individual disciplines have pre-existing bodies of theory, and these can be adopted within cross-disciplinary DS research. Many DS researchers may wish to synthesize insights from theories adapted from constituent disciplines (i.e. 'package deals')

	• Awareness of the basis of theories, and of assumptions, is central to an understanding of how DS research is rigorous and of the extent to which bias is explicitly or implicitly present
5. Research strategies, methodologies, research instruments, modes of analysis and empirical conclusions: how can we establish what is 'really' happening? What (kinds of) conclusions can we draw from our research?	Chapter 5: What is 'rigour' in DS' • Mixing methods, and quantitative and qualitative approaches in particular, has become common in DS • In academic research broadly there has been increased attention to the quality of research and the issue of 'rigour' • Rigour is determined in the first instance by the extent to which the research process follows a set 'cycle' of activities • 'Traditional' criteria for rigour are reliability, replicability, generalizability and validity. Alternative criteria may be necessary in DS
6. Rhetoric and praxis: how are methods and techniques used and adapted within DS practice? How are DS research approaches relevant for DS practitioners?	Chapter 6: How are research and practice linked in DS? • It is possible to distinguish between two 'camps' of DS researchers and writers who can be represented as those concerned with discourse and with empiricism. There is limited overlap between the two camps • The need for policy- or practice-relevant results from research which is undertaken within a limited timeframe does not reduce the need for a rigorous and systematic approach • There is a critical need to contextualize policy- and practice-related research and study within a policy hierarchy and a policy cycle employing established methodologies and methods • DS research and writing has been innovatory in developing new and adapted methodologies and methods, some of which are transferable from the developing country contexts in which they first appeared • A distinction is necessary between policy objectives (e.g. better governance) and policy frameworks (e.g. conditionality), especially where subjective judgments and bias can readily intervene (e.g. analysis of the impact of structural adjustment programmes in developing countries)

NOTES

1 Factors such as better rainfall, lower prices for strategic imports (such as fuel oil) and higher productivity growth that had been anticipated in key areas of the economy could account for this order of magnitude of the fall in the rate of inflation.
2 The 'counterfactual' is what would have happened in the absence of the project – or of the policy. The counterfactual is 'speculative' on both ex ante and ex post bases because it is what might have happened. However, it is no more speculative than the ex ante targets for the objectives of project or policy interventions. This approach can, of course, be applied to the analysis of both public and private sector activities.

REFERENCES

Apthorpe, R. (1999) 'Development studies and policy studies: in the short run we are all dead', *Journal of International Development*, 11 (4): 535–546.

Bevan, P. (2006) *Researching Wellbeing Across the Disciplines: Some Key Intellectual Problems and Ways Forward*. Wellbeing in Developing Countries (WeD) Research Group Working Paper 25. Bath, UK: WeD.

Mehta, L., Haug, R. and Haddad, L. (2006) 'Reinventing development research', *Forum for Development Studies*, 33 (1): 1–6.

Author Index

Subject Index

Rigorous research, 112–117, 122–123
  definition, 2
Rigour, 71, 73
  and secondary data, 120 (box)
ROAMEF cycle, 138

Scaffold of Learning, 55 (box)
Science:
  and Positivism, 58
Science wars, 54, 60, 61
Shadow prices, 152–153
Situationality. See Positionality
Social Anthropology, 61, 66, 71, 72 (table)
  and Economics, 73 (box), 90
Sociology, 66, 71, 72 (table)
Software, 107, 124 n10
South Commission, 17
Stakeholders. See Participatory approach
Structural Adjustment Programmes (SAPs),
  135–136, 154 n1
  case study: methodology, 149–152
Structuralism, 84, 85, 95 n4
Subaltern, 48 n11
Sustainable Livelihoods Approach, 83,
  144–145, 145 (figure)
SWAP (Sector Wide Approach), 156 n9, 156 n10
Systematic research. See Rigorous research

Taiwan, 152
Tanganyika, 155 n4
Thatcherism, 134, 149
Theory:
  anatomy, 85, 86 (box)
  assumptions, 82, 83, 86–87, 88, 89 (box),
    89–90, 93, 93 (box), 94, 95
  basic concepts, 93 (box), 94
  consistency of, 93 (box), 94
  constructing frameworks, 92–94,
    93 (box), 95
  context-specific, 85, 94, 95 n6
  and cross-disciplinarity, 88–91
  current state, 86–87
  definition of, 83–87
  dependency, 84
  development concept, 84–85
  development strategy, 84–85
  development theory, 84–85
  dynamics, 85, 86 (box)
  general characteristics, 93 (box), 94
  grand theory, 85, 94, 95 n6
  histories, 85, 86 (box)
  and inference, 91–92
  language problems, 89–90, 95 n7
  Lewis model, 84, 85
  logic of enquiry, 91 (box)
  modernization, 84
  need for, 82–83
  neo-liberalism, 84

physiology, 85, 86 (box)
  requirements of, 88 (box)
Structuralism, 84, 85, 95 n4
Sustainable Livelihoods Approach, 83,
  144–145, 145 (figure)
  underlying assumptions, 94
Third World, 164
  definition, 16–17, 29 n7
  See also Developing countries
Transdisciplinarity, 67, 68
Transition countries, 18
Transnational corporations (TNCs), 149
Truman, Harry S., 14

Uncertainty principle, 61
United Kingdom, 134
  Green Book, 138
United Nations Conference on Trade
  and Development (UNCTAD), 16,
  18 (box), 119
United Nations Development Programme
  (UNDP), 13, 21, 23, 119, 141
  on developing countries, 18 (box)
  Human Development Report, 22, 120, 124 n19
United Nations Millennium Development
  Goals (MDGs), 13, 23–24, 24 (box), 25, 135
  data for, 125 n21
United Nations Research Institute on Social
  Development (UNRISD), 21
United Republic of Tanzania, 155 n4
United States Agency for International
  Development (USAID), 140, 156 n13
United States of America, 134, 136
Urbanisation, 124 n9

Vienna Circle, 60
Vietnam, 164

Washington Consensus, 149, 157 n25
Wellbeing in Developing Countries (WeD)
  Research Group, 30 n15
Western philosophers, 56–57 (table)
Wolfensohn, James, 155 n8
World Bank, 13, 23, 70, 77 n9, 119, 124 n15,
  124 n17, 134, 141, 155 n4, 155 n5, 156
  n18, 156 n20
  Comprehensive Development Framework
    (CDF), 135–136, 137, 149, 155 n8
  on developing countries, 18 (box)
  Participation in Practice, 144
  poverty data, 125 n22
  Poverty Reduction Strategy Papers (PRSPs),
    135, 154 n1, 156 n9, 156 n16, 157 n17
  Voices of the Poor study, 121 (box), 123 n4
  World Development Report, 120, 121 (box),
    124 n18, 124 n19, 155 n6

ZOPP, 140